Education, Equality and Social Cohesion

Education, Equality and Social Cohesion

A Comparative Analysis

Andy Green, John Preston
and
Jan Germen Janmaat

First published in 2006 by
PALGRAVE MACMILLAN
Houndmills, Basingstoke, Hampshire RG21 6XS and
175 Fifth Avenue, New York, N.Y. 10010
Companies and representatives throughout the world.

PALGRAVE MACMILLAN is the global academic imprint of the Palgrave Macmillan division of St. Martin's Press, LLC and of Palgrave Macmillan Ltd. Macmillan® is a registered trademark in the United States, United Kingdom and other countries. Palgrave is a registered trademark in the European Union and other countries.

ISBN-13: 978–1–4039–8797–6 hardback
ISBN-10: 1–4039–8797–1 hardback

This book is printed on paper suitable for recycling and made from fully managed and sustained forest sources.

A catalogue record for this book is available from the British Library.

Library of Congress Cataloging-in-Publication Data

Green, Andy, 1954–
    Education, equality and social cohesion : a comparative analysis / Andy Green, John Preston and Jan Germen Janmaat.
        p. cm.
    Includes bibliographical references and index.
    ISBN 1–4039–8797–1 (cloth)
        1. Education – Social aspects. 2. Educational equalization.
    3. Multicultural education. 4. Globalization. I. Preston, John, 1967–
    II. Janmaat, Jan Germen. III. Title.

LC191.G715 2006
371.2′6—dc22   2006042266

10 9 8 7 6 5 4 3 2 1
15 14 13 12 11 10 09 08 07 06

Printed and bound in Great Britain by
Antony Rowe Ltd, Chippenham and Eastbourne

Contents

List of Tables

List of Figures

Acknowledgements

Two of the chapters in this book are developed from previously published works and one started life as a conference paper. Chapter 1 is a revised version of Andy Green and John Preston (2001) 'Education and Social Cohesion: Re-Centering the Debate', *Peabody Journal of Education and Development*, 76(3 and 4). Chapter 3 is developed from a paper for a panel at the 2004 American Education Research Association conference and benefits from the advice of co-panellists Judith Torney-Purta and Jo-Ann Amadeo. Chapter 5 is developed from Andy Green and Susanne Wiborg (2004) 'Comprehensive Schooling and Educational Inequality: An International Perspective', in M. Benn and C. Chitty (eds), *A Tribute to Caroline Benn: Education and Democracy* (London: Continuum). Our thanks go to the editors and publishers of those volumes and particularly to Susanne Wiborg for allowing us to publish a revised version of our essay here. We also thank Tom May at QCA for compiling the data used in Figure 6.1.

Acknowledgements

Introduction: Education and the Rediscovery of Social Cohesion

How to promote and maintain social cohesion in the face of rapid globalization has become one of the key policy challenges of the new millennium (EC 2001; OECD 1997; UNESCO 1996). It is also, not coincidentally, a re-emergent theme in social theory. The renewed debate about how societies cooperate and what holds them together is, in part, a reaction to immediate and topical concerns. Politicians worry about social order and security in response to the current global threats from the internationalization of crime, civil conflict and terrorism. They also respond to the often deep anxieties amongst electorates about the more everyday issues to do with local crime, anti-social behaviour, racial intolerance, and community breakdown. For many, in the post-9/11 world, there is a mounting and pervasive sense that things are falling apart – that the centre cannot hold.

But concern over social cohesion is also part of a more fundamental questioning of what society means in a world transformed by globalization. It is now widely recognized that as new technologies create the possibilities for increasing inter-connectedness throughout the world – through travel, trade and communications – so too globalization engenders centrifugal forces which can dislocate traditional bonds, fragment societies and reinforce conflict and division. Increasing social pluralism and lifestyle diversity in the advanced states, in part the product of globalization, call into question older sources of social cohesion and produce new foci for identity and engagement. Traditional forms of political engagement – through parties, unions, and national elections – are in decline in many countries, as new and more diversified forms of identity politics and issue-based social movements are on the rise (Castells 1997). The reality – or, in some cases, the semblance – of homogeneous national identities, once thought so central to social cohesion,

1

is, it is said, undermined in the 'post-national' era by the proliferation of group and regional identities from below and by the development of supra-national political organization and of trans-national civil society from above (Beck 2000; OECD 1997; Touraine 2000). At the same time, increasing income inequality, both within and between states, gives rise to new global and domestic tensions and conflicts (Castells 1997).

With increasing evidence of xenophobia in Europe, and a resurgence worldwide of what some have, perhaps unwisely, called 'civilizational conflicts' (Huntington 1996), pessimists write of the rise of a 'new tribalism' (Horsman and Marshall 1994) whilst even the more sanguine ask 'Can We Live Together?' (Touraine 2000). Such trends arguably challenge both the integrity of institutional and social life and the sustainability of economic growth. As a recent OECD report has argued, social instability arises:

> in part because of a growing political disenchantment arising from the increasing income polarization, persistently high levels of unemployment, and widespread social exclusion that are manifesting themselves in varying ways across North America, Europe and the OECD Pacific. The diffusion of this malaise throughout society threatens to undermine both the drive towards economic flexibility and the policies that encourage strong competition, globalization and technological innovation. (OECD 1997, p. 3)

National governments increasingly look to education and training as a means to enhance social cohesion – or, in the words of one newspaper headline, as 'a social glue to fix the cracks in society' (Green and Preston 2001b). Many countries are devising new curriculum policies on education and national values or citizenship education (as recently in Japan, Singapore, the Netherlands and the UK), or seeking to use education policies to promote neigbourhood renewal or to enhance employabilty and social inclusion. International agencies have also sought to provide a lead, in some cases addressing the wider range of issues.

The Council of Europe has established an intergovernmental body, the European Committee for Social Cohesion, which seeks to promote policies which ensure employment opportunities for all, as well as the human and social entitlements which enable wider civic participation. European Union (EU) policy also attaches considerable importance to the enhancement of social cohesion throughout Europe. The Lisbon European Council in March 2000 set the EU a ten-year target to become 'the most competitive and dynamic knowledge-based economy in the world, capable of sustained economic growth *with more and better jobs and greater social cohesion'* (Lisbon European Council 2000; emphasis added). Increasing social cohesion within the EU is also identified by the Commission's *Memorandum on Lifelong Learning* as a major objective of education and training. As the *Memorandum* notes, in the complex social and political world in which today's Europeans live, it is important that education and training should both promote active citizenship and help individuals 'to live positively with cultural, ethnic and linguistic diversity' (EC 2001).

Policy responses to date, however, have often been partial, uncoordinated and poorly grounded in research evidence. Some governments, most notably in East Asia but also in some western European states like the Netherlands, have sought to reinforce national identity in schools in the hope that this will contribute to social harmony. But few have any clear vision about what national identity should mean in diverse modern societies and there is little evidence, as we will show later, that patriotic education actually adds to social cohesion, at least in contemporary western societies. Other governments have been attracted by the communitarian philosophies popular in North America and have sought to develop through education the citizenship skills which they hope will promote community and neighbourhood renewal. But they do this without centrally addressing the broader issues of values and identity which will determine how future generations deal with inter-community relations. Perhaps most frequently in Western Europe the emphasis has been on promoting social inclusion through education and training for employability and integration into the waged labour force. This addresses real problems of social exclusion through unemployment, but it leaves untouched many societal problems which bear on social cohesion, including low pay, inequality and cultural conflict. In each case the educational response is partial and uncoordinated, failing to make connections between reforms in education and necessary reforms in the related policy domains like welfare, labour market organization and political systems.

Most symptomatic of policy thinking in the West, and particularly in the UK and America, has been the widespread adoption of the new theories of social capital which see education as a crucial incubator of traits of individual trust, tolerance, and civic participation which are said to underpin the relations of reciprocity in well-functioning participative communities. It is partly on the basis of these theories, so popular amongst mainstream economists, that many governments have intensified their efforts to nurture civic skills in young people, through citizenship education curricula and the like. However, for all the insights that social capital theory has brought to the understanding of small groups, local communities and networks, it has little to say about how whole societies operate and what the conditions are for improving inter-community relations – surely the central concern for any kind of social cohesion. As we will argue in this book, social capital theory is at the root an individualistic notion, well suited to the concerns of neo-classical economists – from whom it arose and whose methodologically individualistic assumptions it shares – but poorly adapted to understanding the complexities of social cohesion in society at large.

This book takes a different approach. Its primary concern is with social cohesion at the societal level, rather than at the level of individuals and small groups and communities, and with how education can affect this and in what contexts. We therefore consider social cohesion outcomes in the widest sense – not just in terms of integration into the labour market, but also in terms of the wider societal attributes that may be involved in social cohesion, including structural social and economic issues of income inequality, low pay and social conflict and cultural manifestations in terms of trust, tolerance, political engagement and civil liberties. Our typical mode of analysis is at the level of whole societies and their systems and institutions, including not only education systems but also the welfare, political and labour market systems with which they interact.

Our findings from the cross-national statistical analysis are striking and form the basis of the core argument in this book. As the following chapters seek to show, education can have important effects on societal cohesion, but only within certain societal contexts and in conjunction with appropriate policies in other areas. Education can promote social cohesion but it is not so much how much education populations receive which matters, although levels of education may affect individual attitudes and propensities in some countries, as social capital theory argues. What matters most, however, and what best explains the variations between countries in how education impacts on society, is how education and skills are distributed and the values that children and adults learn in education.

Defining social cohesion

Social cohesion is a term widely used but rarely defined. To most people it probably signifies, at the minimum, a relatively harmonious society characterized by low rates of crime and high levels of civic co-operation and trust. Whether it should also mean a society of high tolerance towards others, including other cultures and religions, is not so clear to many people, including those who would see cultural homogeneity as a precondition for trust and co-operation (a proposition which we challenge later).

Whether, in addition, such a society needs to be relatively equal, in terms of incomes and opportunities, is also debated. Conservative philosophers would claim that societies may be well ordered despite being divided and hierarchical and they could certainly find historical examples to bear this out. Equally controversial is whether a cohesive society can ever be completely without social conflict and whether this would anyway be desirable. Arguably, to many, the preconditions for social cohesion, including equality and political rights, can only be won and maintained through conflict and struggles. Clearly there are many different ways of understanding what social cohesion means in real societies and different views as to how it is achieved.

Modern policy literature is generally no better at defining social cohesion and no more likely to share common interpretations of its meaning. In different contexts social cohesion may be used to emphasize: (1) shared norms and values; (2) a sense of shared identity or belonging to a common community; (3) a sense of continuity and stability; (4) a society with institutions for sharing risks and providing collective welfare; (5) equitable distribution of rights, opportunities, wealth and income; or (6) a strong civil society and active citizenry. Two recent policy papers on social cohesion utilize all of these terms, albeit in different – and somewhat confusing – combinations.

According to Jane Jensen (1998, p. 1): 'The term social cohesion is used to describe a process more than a condition or end state ... it is seen as involving a sense of commitment, and a desire or capacity to live together in harmony. For Jensen this does not necessarily involve widely shared values, since too much 'bonding' and value conformity can lead to stagnation and closed communities. But it does rely on the legitimacy of democratic institutions, on effective institutional mechanisms for intermediating conflict, and on active civic participation. For Judith Maxwell (1986, p. 3), on the other hand, 'social cohesion involves building shared values and communities of interpretation, reducing disparities in wealth and income, and generally enabling people to have a sense that they are engaged in a common enterprise, facing shared challenges, and that they are members of the same community'.

Reflecting these same differences in emphasis, Michalski, Miller and Stevens (1997) sketch for the OECD two alternative scenarios for social cohesion in the future. The 'individualistic' scenario foresees increasing societal flexibility through reduced government and regulation and an extension of individual rights and choices through the market. Cohesion here rests largely on shared material aspirations underpinned by economic growth and increasing personal opportunities. Alternatively, the 'solidaristic scenario' envisages widely shared values based on strong collective and public institutions.

Broadly speaking, these two different emphases in contemporary policy discussions replay the classic distinctions in social and political science between 'liberal' and 'social democratic' theories of social order. Within the liberal tradition of de Tocqueville and others, social cohesion is maintained primarily through an active civil society, with the role of the state limited to core functions of maintaining law and order, rights of property and basic political freedoms. Alternatively, the social democratic tradition places more emphasis on equality and on the enabling role of the state and public institutions in providing the basis for social cohesion.

Social cohesion is a concept with a long and complex history in social thought, arguably moving through various cycles of use and disuse (Gough and Olofsson 1999). All societies have been concerned with problems of social order and their philosophers have written extensively about them, from Aristotle in Antiquity down to Hobbes in the seventeenth century. However, it was during the nineteenth century that an explicitly sociological approach to the problem developed which examined the social forces, institutions and values which hold – or fail to hold – society together. In fact, it might be said that social order and social cohesion represented the defining problematics of the new discipline of sociology developed by Comte, Saint-Simon, Durkheim, Spencer, Weber and Tönnies in nineteenth-century Europe. The founding fathers of the new 'science of society' (or 'secular religion' as detractors were likely to call it) concerned themselves with social cohesion because they were aware that they lived in an era of rapid transition when traditional bonds and ties were eroding and where the centrifugal forces of industrialization and democracy could rip apart all previous social connections. As Marx and Engels, contemplating the whirlwind of capitalism, famously wrote: 'All fixed, fast-frozen relations, with their train of venerable and ancient prejudices and opinion, are swept away, all new formed ones are antiquated before they can ossify. All that's solid melts into air … ' (Marx and Engels 1968, p. 38) We are currently living in a similarly transformative age and ask similar questions.

The answers provided by the nineteenth-century social thinkers to the problem of social cohesion were varied, as they are today. All noted that industrialization and the division of labour were transforming social and spacial relations. Societies once based on proximate face-to-face community (what Durkheim termed 'mechanical solidarity') were moving towards some new form of order with more diverse and distributed social connections. To Durkheim this meant the erosion of the 'collective conscience' and the close-binding values of traditional society and their replacement by new forms of 'organic solidarity' based on the mutual interdependencies created by the functional division of labour. To Tönnies (2001) it meant the shift from society based on community (*Gemeinschaft*) to society based on contract (*Gesellschaft*). Such changes were seen to be inevitable, but they did not guarantee that social cohesion and order would prevail.

To some, like Herbert Spencer, the English liberal and social Darwinist, unfettered market relations were enough to hold society together. For Alexis de Tocqueville, writing as a French liberal on democracy in Jacksonian America (1955), the key to stable democracy and social harmony lay in the vibrancy of associational life. However, for most continental European thinkers of the Age, no such benevolent 'hidden hand' existed in the market, and civil association alone was not enough. For Comte and Tönnies it was ultimately only the state that could hold society together. Durkheim criticized both Comte's insistence on moral consensus and Comte's and Tönnies reliance on the state. There had to be other forces, beyond market and state, which maintained cohesion, although he recognized that the state had to act as a 'moral force' in promoting core values and meritocracy. In times of rapid transition, and particularly when technological change outran society's moral capacities for adaptation, pathological or 'anomic' social disorders arose which required new remedies. Primary amongst Durkheim's candidates for this were the new intermediary associations of civil society that stood between the state and the market – most notably professional associations (Lukes 1973). Education also had a key role to play, and Durkheim became a key advocate of the Third Republic's characteristic educational policy of promoting social solidarity through schooling. Society, he wrote, requires a degree of homogeneity: 'Education perpetuates and reinforces this homogeneity by fixing in the child, from the beginning, the essential similarities that collective life demands' (1998, p. 51).

Durkheim wrote as a liberal socialist republican in late nineteenth-century France (Lukes 1973), but his writings left a complex legacy informing both Left and Right theories of social order and social cohesion. In the American liberal tradition, a particular strand of Durkheim's thought was appropriated by the school of structural functionalist sociology developed by Parsons and Merton (Parsons 1991). This stressed the role of the division of labour and functional interdependence in complex modern societies as a source of self-reproducing order. However, it failed adequately to address the processes of change. Whereas Durkheim was keenly aware of social contradictions as a source of historical transformation, and of inequality as a source of social division, Parsonian theory assumed value consensus and the unproblematic reproduction of social relations (Holton and Turner 1986, p. 205).

Other, mostly continental European, appropriations of Durkheim, on the other hand, have had different emphases. The French *Annales* school of historical writing, originally inspired by Durkheim and the anthropologist Marcel Mauss, saw contradiction and conflict at the heart of social change. European social democracy, which also owed a substantial debt to Durkheim, took a different path, placing more stress on the role of state and organized intermediary civic associations as the basis of cohesion in modern societies. Indeed, it is hard to separate the idea of the modern welfare state and 'social partnership' from such continental conceptions of social cohesion.

Both traditions have stressed in their different ways the importance of education to social cohesion. In Parsonian theory, schools have the vital role of ensuring the efficient allocation of skills in the labour market as well as socializing children into the key normative values of society, not least by promoting loyalty to a meritocratic belief system which is taken to be the main ideological cement of society. Social democracy, and particularly the Nordic variety, has, on the other hand, placed more stress on the role of education in promoting equality and in fostering social solidarity though common experience and learning (Boucher 1982).

According to Gough and Olofsson (1999), the trajectory of theories of social cohesion in the social sciences follows a common pattern of orthodoxy, followed by fragmentation and then re-discovery. The political upheavals of 1968 provided new challenges, ending the period of functionalist orthodoxy in social science and leading to a new fragmentation of social theory into multiple currents based on post-modernist and Foucauldian concerns with identity and subjectivity. The 'micro-sociological' continued to dominate social theory during the 1990s with the Foucauldian stress on the micro-politics of power in the literature on 'governmentality' and on the internalization of government and governance in the discourses and practices of individuals. In general the post-modernist rejection of metanarratives in social thought, and the Foucauldian emphasis on micro-politics, were not propitious for the types of macro-sociological investigation which have typically characterized analyses of social cohesion.

However, there was still important work on macro issues in social cohesion, not least by David Lockwood (1992) who criticized both functionalist, value-consensus theories of cohesion for neglecting considerations of power, and conflict theories for underestimating the role of institutions in accommodating and mediating social conflict. Lockwood continued to analyse macro-social aspects of social cohesion, distinguishing between two dimensions which he referred to as 'social integration' and 'system integration'. Social integration focused 'upon the orderly or conflictual relationships between *actors*' whereas system integration concerned the 'orderly or conflictual relationships between the *parts* of a social system' (Lockwood 1992, p. 400 quoted in Mortensen 1999).

In recent years there has, arguably, been a renewed theoretical and policy interest in the macro issues to do with globalization, markets, inequality and social cohesion, not least as some of the more socially dysfunctional consequences of market-led globalization have increasingly come to light. Gough and Olofsson (1999, p. 3) argue that social cohesion has thus re-emerged as a concept but as a 'more diverse and complex issue'. If they are correct – and this book tries to encourage the trend – this is certainly to be welcomed, since few would doubt that the question is amongst the most important facing societies in the coming decades.

This book seeks to analyse the role of education in promoting societal cohesion and thus lies squarely within the tradition of comparative macro-societal analysis which we have roughly sketched above. Its primary concerns are with understanding how education systems, in conjunction with other societal systems of welfare and labour market regulation, impact on various aspects of cohesion at the level of whole societies. It is also centrally concerned with questions of educational distribution and how inequality may affect social cohesion. By adopting this approach we are inevitably partisan as regards the different traditions of theorising about social cohesion.

Our concerns with equality and with the role of the state and public institutions in underpinning social cohesion place the analyses here clearly within the frame of social democratic theorizing about education and social cohesion. At the same time, the concern with value formation and the role of collective identities in the promotion of societal cohesion draws from the other strand of the Durkheimian and social democratic tradition which is concerned with the moral foundations of social solidarity, although we would hope without falling into the traps of Parsonian value consensus theory. The two strands, of course, lie in some tension with each other. Concern with social inequality inevitably leads to considerations about the social processes and movements, often conflictual, that may alter the parameters of power and lead to greater social equality. Concern with social cohesion often implies a search for social consensus which may not be possible in conditions of unequal power. This too often leads to an ahistorical functionalism which ignores the necessary struggles that have historically mitigated class, ethnic and other inequalities and which preceded the development of the social and welfare apparatuses which made possible greater degrees of social cohesion.

The essays here focus largely on the contemporary relationships which seem to connect education, equality and social cohesion. They do not seek to illuminate the historical processes by which these came to be. In so doing they tell only a part of the story and may seem excessively functionalist to some readers on that account. In defence we can only say that it has not been an object of the book to make a historical analysis of social movements which have led to cohesive societies, as far as these exist, but that does not mean that we assume that social cohesion can drop out of the sky ready made. For most people, in most societies, social cohesion is probably a desirable state, so long as it is based on equality, or at least relative equality, of access to goods, opportunities and power. But such situations have rarely been achieved, historically, without social conflicts and struggle. Such is the paradox of social cohesion.

A note on methods

Much of the existing work on education and social attitudes – by economists, political scientists and social psychologists – focuses on individuals in specific countries, using individual-level data. This book departs from this approach to a large extent. This is because its focus is on societal relationships and system-level effects where national contexts are deemed highly important to understanding relationships. The study is therefore based primarily on cross-national comparative analysis. It uses cross-national statistical analysis where possible and, where not, as in chapters 5 and 6, it employs logical comparative methods (Ragin 1981) based on the analysis of qualitative data and descriptive rather than analytical use of quantitative data. A cross-national comparative approach – both quantitative and logical/qualitative – seems to us the best, and indeed often the only, way to investigate the societal relationships which are of the concern in this book. There is too little variation between systems (of welfare or education, for instance) within countries, in most cases, for it to be possible to conduct comparative analysis within one country. In addition, many of our variables (skills distribution, income distribution, strike rates and so on) are integral properties of the collective which are meaningless at the individual level where they can only appear as statistical constants (Wilkinson 1996).

There may, of course, be objections, especially from a methodologically individualist perspective, to this type of cross-national analysis. These may relate particularly to the so-called 'ecological fallacy' (Pearce 2000) where conclusions about the relationships between variables at the individual level are inferred from analysis of the relationships observed at the national level using national or aggregate data. We have generally sought to avoid this problem by restricting our analysis largely to society-level relationships. Where relationships observed in the cross-national data do seem to conflict with relationships others have found at the individual level, as is the case, for instance, in the relationships between 'trust ' and 'association', we seek to explore the discrepancies, usually by analysing the additional contextual factors that come into play when you analyse across societies. Chapter 4, using both individual and national-level analyses, specifically explores the differences in the relationships found in the analyses at the individual and national levels, thus emphasizing the importance of both the national and regional contexts in explaining the patterns of relationships. In most cases, we find that where correlations can be found between traits of individuals which are not evident in variations of their aggregates between countries, this is because other national factors have entered into the equation in the latter case, which overwhelm, or intermediate, the relationships at the individual level.

We consider that the methods adopted here not only avoid those 'fallacies' described by methodological individualists, but also go beyond some of the limitations set by their methodologies. The ecological fallacy is, after all, often wrongly understood as being exclusively about fallacious individual-level deductions from national-level data correlations. In fact, it can work in different directions and the problem is better described as one of 'cross-level fallacies' in general (Smelser 1976), where analytical inferences are made at a level which is different from the level at which the data are observed. Disciplines such as psychology are often prone to the 'individualistic fallacy' (Pearce 2000), the reverse of the one traditionally described, where relationships holding within a sample of individuals in a particular time and place are universalized and assumed to be apparent in the variations between whole societies. An example would be the frequent assumption, which we explore in chapter 3, that because more educated individuals tend to be more tolerant in some developed modern societies, more educated societies are always more tolerant – which is, historically, clearly not true.

Our comparative approaches vary, inevitably, according to the data available for the different variables of interest at different points in the analysis. Where we have quantitative data for a sufficiently wide range of countries we employ statistical analysis of country-level data to test our hypotheses. For the most part these analyses use purely cross-sectional data, since time series data for our key variables are often not available. This, of course, limits our ability to ascribe causality to the relationships observed. However, in chapter 2 we conduct a time series analysis of data which are available for different time points, and this provides more robust evidence of causality in the relationships which we find.

In these country-level analyses we use genuinely national data where it is available (as with rates of strikes, levels of national income and public spending, distributions of skills and incomes, and so on). Where necessary we also use nationally aggregated individual-level data (as with levels of trust and tolerance and test scores), but here we are careful to triangulate, where possible, with other national-level data to test the appropriateness of the aggregates as proxies for collective properties. In most cases this can work quite effectively.

Trust, for instance, is usually measured at the individual level by asking respondents how far they trust other people. However, it is clearly a relational phenomenon since people only trust others they deem to be trustworthy. That the individual data on trusting actually reflects this relational syndrome is supported by the – rather remarkable – fact that the aggregates for countries based on these data generally co-vary with other measures of 'national trustworthiness', such as the famous *Readers Digest* 'dropped wallets' test (how many are returned?) and other surveys which ask individuals about their perceptions of the trustworthiness of peoples from other countries (Inglehart 1990; Knack and Keefer 1997). Of course, with complex phenomena such as these, no quantitative indicator is going to be fully adequate, which is why the work here also relies heavily on logical comparative analysis which uses more qualitative data on system characteristics.

In chapter 4, which is able to draw on multi-level data, we conduct a comparative analysis both at the national level and at the individual level, in the latter case comparing the strength of relations between individual-level variables in different countries. In the final chapter, we attempt to identify regional models of lifelong learning and social cohesion, but here in a purely aggregative fashion, so that the national level remains the main unit of analysis. We do not analyse supra-national regions as genuine collectivities, although this could, of course, be done through analysis of the geopolitics of some regional units such as the European Union (EU). Our premise here is rather that cultural and historical affinities have created commonalities between countries' education and social regimes in certain regions.

The structure of the book

The chapters is this book, three of them substantially revised versions of earlier publications, have been organized to provide a logical progression through the different aspects of our subject, bearing in mind our initial hypothesis that education affects social cohesion both through socialization and through the distribution of skills. The first four chapters examine the relations between educational outcomes and various aspects of social cohesion. The first two are concerned with how education influences social outcomes through the distribution of educational achievement, and the second two with its impacts through socialisation and values and identity formation. Chapter 5 then returns to the question of inequality in education and examines the characteristics of education systems that generate more or less equal educational outcomes. Chapter 6 brings together both parts of the investigation by analysing the relationships between the different national and regional models of lifelong learning and the various regimes of social cohesion and economic competitiveness with which they are associated.

Chapter 1 lays out the theoretical basis of the argument, showing the limitations of individual-level analysis of education and social outcomes and proposing an alternative societal model of educational effects on social cohesion. The first part examines the evidence from Putnam and others that more educated individuals are likely to be more trusting in others and in institutions, to join more associations, to be more politically engaged and to show higher levels of tolerance. While acknowledging the power of the evidence for a number of countries, the chapter argues that such individual-level statistical associations tell us little about the relation between education and cohesion at the level of society and nothing about the educational mechanisms that might effect this in particular contexts. Social capital theorists like Putnam argue that individual propensities towards trust, association, tolerance and political engagement form a coherent set of characteristics which are encouraged by education and which act to strengthen social capital at the local level. However, social capital at the level of the community does not necessarily translate up into cohesion at the societal level since intra-community bonding does not necessarily lead to inter-community harmony. Many societies shown to have rich deposits of social capital in local communities, like Northern Ireland and the USA, are not socially cohesive. Social capital and social cohesion are not the same thing and how education affects each may be different. The chapter argues that relationships between education and social cohesion cannot be adequately analysed at the individual level because such analyses ignore the effects of powerful contextual influences, such as the nature of the state and its re-distributive and welfare systems, which are not visible at the individual level.

In its second part the chapter uses this comparative societal approach to develop a 'distributional' model of education effects on social cohesion. The hypothesis is that education impacts on social cohesion in two ways: first, as traditionally argued, through socializing young people into certain values which are conducive to co-operative social life, and second, more controversially, through the way in which it distributes knowledge and skills throughout adult populations. The second of these hypotheses is provisionally tested using aggregated cross-sectional international data from the International Adult Literacy Survey (IALS) on skills distribution and from the World Values Survey (WVS) and Interpol on various indicators of social cohesion. The statistical analysis for 15 countries shows that aggregated measures of association, tolerance and trust do not co-vary across countries – casting doubt on the validity at the national level of the social capital argument that associational membership increases levels of trust and tolerance. However, a number of measures do co-vary, including: trust in people, trust in institutions, civic co-operation and, inversely, violent crime. These are combined as a single factor representing social cohesion and correlated with measures of inequality from the skills data and income inequality using the gini coefficient measure.

The results are striking. There are strong correlations cross-nationally between educational inequality and income equality, as other studies have shown, and between income equality and social cohesion, as might be expected. However, most suggestive are the associations between education and social cohesion. Average levels of skills show no relationship with measures for social cohesion. Education equality, however, relates strongly to the combined measure for social cohesion. The more education-equal countries, like the Nordic states in the sample, are generally those with highest measured levels of social cohesion. The less education-equal countries, like many of the English-speaking countries, rank lower.

In chapter 2, we build on this initial cross-sectional analysis by using time series data. We use more sophisticated statistical modelling techniques to examine the relationship between educational inequality and a number of measures of social cohesion (including civil rights, political rights, unrest and crimes against the person). Educational inequality is associated with each of these measures of social cohesion, even controlling for income inequality and real income per head. In the cases of civil rights, political rights and unrest there is a nonlinear relationship between educational inequality and these measures with a 'critical' level of educational inequality beyond which these features of social cohesion deteriorate substantially. There is, additionally, a positive association between educational inequality and crimes against the person (murder, homicide and rape). Looking at levels of educational inequality in existing education systems we find that there is a strong correspondence between education systems with weak comprehensivization and strong marketization and selection which is associated with higher levels of educational inequality and lower levels of social cohesion.

In chapters 3 and 4 we shift our attention from adult skills and inequality to focus on schools and the formation of values and identities.

In chapter 3, we examine the literatures on the relationships between tolerance and social cohesion and between education and tolerance. Tolerance emerges as a complex and multifaceted concept with no clear or fixed relationships in theory to other aspects of social cohesion. National measures for tolerance show no co-variations with other measures of social cohesion, so that some countries, like the Nordic countries, with high levels of social cohesion on other measures, have relatively low scores for certain types of tolerance. The mechanisms by which education impacts on tolerance are also seen to be complex and highly context-bound. While theoretical models suggest plausible ways through which educational inequality may impact on tolerance in society, little statistical evidence for this can be found. There is evidence, for various countries, that levels of education affect individual propensities towards tolerant or intolerant attitudes, either through the development of cognitive skills or through value formation. But here again the relationships vary substantially between countries and for different social groups.

This debate concerning values in schools and social cohesion is continued in chapter 4. We examine first the relationships between ethno-linguistic fractionalization (a measure of ethnic and linguistic diversity) and social cohesion. We find that the liberal nationalist argument about ethnic homogeneity and social cohesion does not stand up to our empirical investigation. There is no evidence in our data that countries with greater degrees of ethnic homogeneity are more trusting. This puts into question the widely held assumption that it is the social homogeneity of countries such as Japan and the Nordic states which is largely responsible for their apparently high levels of social cohesion. In terms of associations between patriotic school curricula and social outcomes we find mixed results. Although in countries with patriotic school curricula institutional trust is greater, there is no evidence that it leads to greater political participation and it has negative effects on tolerance in some regions. Again the relationships between education and social attitudes appear highly context bound.

Chapters 5 and 6 are concerned with education systems and their impact on educational inequality and social cohesion. In chapter 5, we examine the role of schooling in the production of educational inequalities. Comprehensive schooling is seen to be centrally important in mitigating against educational inequality as supported by recent data from the International Adult Literacy Survey (IALS) and the Programme for International Student Assessment (PISA). Using this and other contextual data, we find clear regional/cultural groupings in terms of schooling and inequality. For example, the (primarily) English-speaking countries, with the exception of Ireland and Canada, display high levels of educational inequality with relatively marketized education systems that increasingly promote selection. Alternatively, the East Asian and Nordic countries have more comprehensive education systems and mixed-ability classes and generally achieve much more equal outcomes in education.

The final chapter discusses the different 'regimes' of economic competitiveness and social cohesion to be found in different regions of the developed world, distinguishing their component parts and examining the interactions between the various contexts which shape them, including labour market systems, welfare regimes, notions of statehood and lifelong learning systems. Broadly, three types of high skills 'knowledge economy', supported by different systems of lifelong learning, can be observed in the western world.

The liberal 'Anglo-Saxon' model, with economic competitiveness based on flexible labour markets, high employment rates, long working hours and high skills elites, promotes 'social inclusion' through economic participation, but also constrains welfare spending and generates inequalities which both undermine social cohesion. The 'social market' model, in core European countries such as Germany and France, achieves high rates of labour productivity through high technological investment and widely diffused workforce skills, but competitiveness is reduced by shorter working hours and lower employment rates. More labour market regulation contributes towards worker solidarity through increasing wage equality but, at the same time, creates barriers to employment for the low skilled which undermines overall societal cohesion. The social democratic model of the Nordic countries achieves higher levels of economic competitiveness by combining high labour productivity, also based on widely diffused skills, with high rates of employment, facilitated by extensive adult learning. Specific forms of labour market regulation (including centralized union bargaining and Active Labour Market policy) successfully promote both income equality and high employment rates which, along with universalist welfare policies, are highly conducive to social cohesion. In this sense the model comes closest to the European Lisbon Objectives of the competitive and socially cohesive knowledge society. However, here social democratic welfarism appears unusually dependent on solidaristic national identities which are relatively intolerant of ethnic and cultural diversity and which define the limits of social cohesion in Europe's most cohesive states.

The chapter argues that in each of these types of knowledge economy lifelong learning systems play different supporting roles where the limits of their contributions to social cohesion are set by the prevailing contexts. In the liberal model education contributes to social cohesion through enhancing employability, but is constrained from playing a larger role through high levels of inequality and through individualistic resistance to socializing children into solidaristic values systems which would enhance more co-operative behaviour. By contrast, in the social democratic model education actively advances social cohesion both by promoting employability and equality and through identity formation, but through the latter in such a way as to reinforce the existing limits of cultural pluralism and ethnic tolerance.

In conclusion, the book returns to some of the policy issues which were set out in the first chapter. In particular, we discuss the efficacy of current strategies for promoting social cohesion through education. The emphasis on skills for employability in the UK is seen to promote a form of 'social inclusion' through employment which is positive but partial since it fails to address the sharp divisions that arise with increasing income inequality amongst those in work. The introduction of Citizenship Education stresses the acquisition of skills for democratic engagement which may enhance social capital and community, but fails centrally to address the issues of values formation and educational equality which, on this book's analysis, are the key to promoting cohesion at the societal level. Social democratic policies in Nordic countries which emphasize equality, cooperative behaviour in school and the development of solidaristic national values are considered as powerful agents of social cohesion. However, they are also fragile and limited, not least since the forms of national identity promoted are ill-adapted to increasingly multicultural populations.

In conclusion, the book calls for educational policies which enhance equality, encourage co-operative values and promote forms of identity which are both solidaristic and culturally inclusive. This is not mere rhetoric. In the pages which follow we provide theoretical and empirical justification that comprehensive systems of education are not just desirable, but essential for social cohesion.

1
Education and Social Cohesion: Re-Centring the Debate

Education is a powerful generator of social capital. According to recent research on the USA, Italy and the UK (e.g. Emler and Frazer 1999; Hall 1999; Nie *et al.* 1996; Putman 1995b, 2000), more educated individuals tend to join more voluntary associations, show greater interest in politics and take part in more political activities. They are also more likely to express trust in others (social trust) and in institutions (institutional trust), and are more inclined to 'civic co-operation' – or at least to profess that they do not condone 'uncivil' behaviour. Education is clearly not the only factor that predisposes people towards joining, engaging and trusting, but it is a powerful predictor, at the individual level, even when controlling for other variables such as wealth, income, age and gender. To Robert Putnam (1995a, p. 667), current doyen of social capital theorists, 'Human and social capital are clearly related, for education has a very powerful effect on trust and associational membership, as well as many other forms of social and political participation'.

Precisely how education contributes towards civic engagement and social capital, and under what conditions, is not yet well understood. We know comparatively little about the mechanisms through which learning influences different kinds of individual social behaviour, the contexts within which such effects occur, and how and why they change over time in different countries. Social capital theorists who have specifically addressed questions about learning, notably James Coleman (1998), have mostly treated education as an outcome of social capital rather than as a cause. Those, like Putnam, who do take it as an independent variable have not generally gone beyond describing statistical associations between levels of education and social capital outcomes. Outside of the social capital debate, there have been some social psychologists and political scientists (e.g. Emler and Frazer 1999; Nie *et al.* 1996), who have sought to provide causal explanations as to how these effects occur. However, their analyses remain largely at the level of the individual.

What none of this work has begun to do is to provide the theoretical and empirical links between education and social cohesion at the macro societal level. In fact, arguably, none of the traditions above have a conceptual apparatus designed to address this question. Writings on education and civic participation see education as providing individual resources of skills and knowledge which can facilitate certain individual social behaviours, but they tend to address societal effects through individual aggregation rather than analysis of societal institutions and cultures. Extrapolating from individual effects to societal effects may require more than simply grossing-up of individual outcomes, since individual effects may be relative or 'positional', as Nie suggests with his theory of education effects on political engagement through competition for limited network-central positions in society (Nie *et al.* 1996). Social capital theory, despite using the language of individual resources and the deliberate analogy with human capital, claims to treat the 'norms, networks and trust' that constitute its central concern as properties of social relations as well as individual attributes (Coleman 1988). But the theory was first extensively developed by Coleman to apply to local communities, and has arguably been subsequently most successfully applied at that level, rather than at the level of whole societies (Woolcock 2000).

The assumption common amongst social capital theorists that countries with communities rich in social capital will also usually be more cohesive as societies is largely unexplored in the literature and highly debatable, since in reality this all depends on the norms and values of particular constituent communities and whether the different communities are at war or at peace with one another. Some countries cited in the research as having rich deposits of community social capital, such as contemporary Northern Ireland (Schuller, Baron and Field 2000) and 1950s America (Putnam 2000), would hardly be considered models of social cohesion on any of the traditional measures of the latter.

Clearly, it does not automatically follow that because education raises levels of community participation amongst individuals, it will also increase societal cohesion. Nor does it follow that the mechanisms through which learning generates community participation and social capital are the same as those by which it may help to promote societal cohesion. Yet these are rapidly becoming key assumptions of policy makers in America and the UK, who see lifelong learning as promoting social cohesion through the benefits which increased individual resources and competences bring to community renewal and social inclusion.

Social capital theory made rapid inroads into Anglo-American social science and policy making in the 1990s, largely displacing – or simply conflating – earlier, more 'European' discourses of social cohesion and social solidarity. However, for all its advances in the understanding of community networks, and despite the success of the theory in bringing the 'social' back into dominant neo-liberal discourses of politics and economics (Schuller, Baron and Field 2000), there may also be dangers in forgetting the insights of some of the earlier traditions which treated cohesion as an explicitly societal phenomena. Social capital and social cohesion are not necessarily the same thing.

In this chapter we seek to put the analysis of education and social cohesion back in the centre of the picture. We do this firstly through a critical review of some of the existing literature on education and social capital which points to the limitations of individual-level analysis of what are fundamentally societal issues. Secondly, we outline some alternative models for understanding how education impacts on social cohesion in different societies, drawing on an analysis of some of the aggregated cross-national data on skills, income distribution and social cohesion. The argument suggests some causal mechanisms for the social impacts of education which are quite different from those which normally underpin arguments about human and social capital.

The historical origins of the debate about education and social cohesion

How education impacts – at the societal level – on social cohesion and social solidarity is hardly a new question. Historically, it has been a primary concern not only of various social movements and state policies, both of the Left and the Right, but also of mainstream social theory, from Emile Durkheim down to Robert Merton and Talcott Parsons. In the introduction to this book we gave a short history of the concept of social cohesion; here we discuss how the concept has been intimately connected with education.

As a theoretical and political concept, social cohesion has clearly taken diverse forms, from the authoritarian and nationalistic to the liberal, communitarian and social democratic versions that have tended to prevail in western states during the past half-century. The role of education in promoting social cohesion has also been construed in a multitude of ways by different historical groups, political ideologies, and state regimes. Crudely put, in nineteenth-century Western Europe dominant social/political groups, whether of liberal or conservative orientations, tended to see education as a force for social order, whilst subordinate classes – and more particularly radical labour movements and revolutionary groups – tended to celebrate its potential for collective improvement through forging class consciousness and political solidarity (Simon 1981). In the twentieth century education has been mobilized in equally diverse ways in support of class or ethnic solidarism, nationalism, and democratic citizenship in its various forms.

When mass public education first appeared in northern Europe and America during the era of state-building in the late eighteenth and early nineteenth century, it was seen primarily, at least by the dominant social groups, as a means of building integrated national polities with cohesive national identities. The national education system first emerged precisely as an instrument of state formation, providing an effective means for training state functionaries, promoting loyalty and social order amongst the masses, disseminating dominant national ideologies and languages, and accustomizing populations to the new regulative regimes of the nascent modern bureaucracies (Boli 1989; Green 1990, 1997; Kaestle 1983; Weber 1979). Later, say from the mid-nineteenth century, education become important for providing the skills and knowledge needed for the 'second', science-based, industrial revolution (Hobsbawm 1969) and the civic attitudes deemed essential for maintaining stability as franchises and democratic rights were extended. As the social historians Ramirez and Boli (1987) write, 'European states became engaged in authorizing, funding and managing mass schooling as part of an endeavour to construct a unified national polity.'

Contemporary advocates of mass education, from the 'old world' of aristocratic Europe to the 'new world' of America, almost invariably justified the massive and unprecedented exercise of state intervention as a necessary and critical part of nation-building. Noah Webster, Federalist educational campaigner and author of numerous popular dictionaries and spelling books in the American Early Republic, argued that education was a necessity for developing the American 'national character' which, in a land of immigrants and new institutions, was 'not yet formed'; Andrew Lunt, a vocal Democrat supporter of public education in the later Jacksonian period, proclaimed that education was the 'very bulwark of the republic' and the 'pillars' on which American democracy was supported (quoted in Kaestle 1983). Northern continental Europe was equally, though often initially less democratically, concerned with education as nation-building. Baron Dubin, writing in Prussia in 1826, claimed that: 'Practically all modern nations are now awake to the fact that education is the most potent means of development of the essentials of nationality' (quoted in Fuller and Robinson 1992, p. 52).

From a later and more democratic vantage point, and less specifically concerned with issues of national identity, Emile Durkheim provided the first systematic theorization of the historical role and social function of mass education precisely in terms of social integration: 'Society,' he wrote, 'can only exist if there exists among its members a sufficient degree of homogeneity. Education perpetuates and reinforces this homogeneity by fixing in the child, from the beginning, the essential similarities that collective life demands' (Durkheim 1992, p. 51).

Durkheim wrote as a liberal socialist republican in late nineteenth-century France (Lukes 1973), but his theories left a complex legacy informing both Left and Right notions of education and social order. Social democratic traditions in continental Europe continued through the next century to stress the importance of schooling for social solidarity and democratic citizenship, most notably in the Nordic countries (Boucher 1982). Various strands in twentieth-century conservative thought, and particularly the tradition of 'romantic' conservatism which Raymond Williams traced from Burke and Coleridge down through Ruskin, T.H. Green and Michael Oakeshott (Williams 1958), have also emphasized the importance of education to social cohesion, in this case with the emphasis on maintaining the 'organic community' with its stable social hierarchies and more narrowly conceived notions of national values. The educational campaigner and philosopher of aesthetics, Roger Scruton, most notably adopted this position in his diatribes against multicultural education at the time of the 1988 Education Reform Act in the UK (Hillgate Group 1987). At least one major strand in twentieth-century western sociology – the tradition of Parsonian functionalism – continued to focus on education and the transmission of the normative values.

In the post-Second World War period, newly independent states, particularly those in East Asia, continued to regard education as an important vehicle of nation-building (Inkeles and Sirowy 1983; Green 1999; Gopinathan 1994; Hill and Fee 1995). However, generally speaking, in the advanced western states, this aspect of schooling became gradually less emphasized. This was partly, at first, because of the sharpened postwar awareness of the dangers of nationalist appropriations of education, and then later because of the difficulty of finding adequate ways of conceptualizing national identity in the more culturally pluralist societies of the global age (Castells 1997; Hildebrand and Sting 1995). At the same time, education became increasingly associated with the goals of economic development. Skills formation came rapidly to overshadow citizen formation as the primary goal of public education in most developed states (Green 1997). The rise of human capital theory in the 1960s provided academic justification for the more economically instrumentalist views of education which had already gained prominence amongst western policy makers, particularly in English-speaking countries. Even as the discourse of lifelong learning became ubiquitous in the 1990s, its main rationale remained, at least in the more neo-liberal states, the goal of economic competitiveness (Coffield 2000).

The tide now appears to be turning, to a degree at least. The European Commission, with its model of 'social Europe' and a *raison d'être* of integration, has always maintained a concern with social solidarity and the ways in which this may be promoted by education. The recent Lifelong Learning Memorandum (EC 2000) arguably pushes this further onto centre stage. Various countries have been reviewing their citizenship education policies (Australia, France, the UK, and – more or less continually – in the East Asian states) (Osler and Starkey 2001). The New Labour Government in the UK has also shown an increasing preoccupation with problems of social exclusion and concomitantly with the social – or wider, non-economic – benefits of learning (Green and Preston 2001a). These policy shifts can no doubt be traced to growing concerns, throughout the advanced economies, about the socially fragmentary effects of globalization, and the symptoms of community breakdown and social disorder that seem to accompany rising consumerism, individualization and the cultural and religious conflicts that arise in reaction to globalisation (Beck 2000; Green 1997; Touraine 2000).

Education and social integration have thus re-emerged on the policy agenda, this time in new clothes. The dominant policy discourse, at least in the Anglo-Saxon countries, is no longer about social cohesion and social solidarity, and the impacts of education on these, but rather on community renewal and the impact of education on 'social inclusion' via the labour market. The dominant theoretical discourse has changed as well. Theories of social integration have been superseded in current theory by the burgeoning new discourse of social capital. In both cases – in terms of policy and theory – there has been a significant shift from the macro societal perspective on social cohesion (whether of the Left or Right) to the more micro – individual and community level – analysis. The role of education in shaping 'social' outcomes is re-established, but the social is now conceived in a different – more individualized – way.

The rise of social capital theory

Social capital theory is heir to a long American tradition of liberal, democratic localist thinking which dates back at least to de Tocqueville's 1836 essay on *Democracy in America* (de Tocqueville 1966; Foley and Edwards 1998; Showronek 1982; Skocpol 1996). This remarkable text, for all its deafening silences on class and racial divisions, provided an extraordinarily prescient commentary on social customs and civic society in the New World, celebrating the vibrant associational life of the Jacksonian North as a democratic alternative to the étatism of contemporary continental Europe. It left behind a potent legacy of anti-state civic ideology in American political culture that is now being re-appropriated, ironically – and significantly – at precisely the point when many fear that associational life there is in serious decline. Its return has been by a circuitous route.

The notion of social capital was first extensively elaborated in Pierre Bourdieu's theoretical work (Bourdieu and Passeron 1979; Bourdieu 1980, 1986), as one of a cluster of concepts, including human capital and cultural capital, which sought to disentangle the various resources and processes which underpin the acquisition and transmission of power and status in modern capitalist societies. Bourdieu's subtle formulations, though at times conceptually blurred and fuzzy, were carefully contextualized both socially and historically. However, they have been all but forgotten in recent developments of the field within Anglo-Saxon economic and sociological thought, where the dominant approach has been the more decontextualized universalism of methodological individualism. Two strands have been most prevalent in the rise of the social capital research industry.

The first is the tradition inaugurated by James Coleman in his influential 1988 essay 'Social Capital in the Creation of Human Capital' which sought to illustrate how customary and apparently non-rational social behaviours could be understood as attempts to overcome economic externalities and market failures. Drawing on his previous work on social exchange theory, and working alongside Gary Becker at the University of Chicago (while the latter was simultaneously applying human capital logic to new areas of non-market behaviour), Coleman sought to extend rational choice theory further into the social domain by analysing the role that trust and social reciprocity played in resolving problems of collective action. Coleman was careful to limit his analysis to specific, bounded, local communities rather than to whole societies, arguing that social capital was primarily a 'public good' and a relational property of people in particular communities, rather than a portable or 'fungible' individual asset (Brown and Lauder 2000).

Following Coleman, economists took up the idea and applied it to a growing range of social contexts and issues, including mortality (Kennedy *et al.* 1998), political participation (DiPasquale and Gleaser 1999), economic growth (Knack and Keefer 1997), and judicial efficiency (LaPorta *et al.* 1997), among others. In one account at least (Fine 2001; Fine and Green 2000), this development can be seen as part of the evolution of the economics profession as it seeks to overcome the acknowledged limitations of its own traditional paradigm based on rational agents, utility maximization and equilibrating markets, largely divorced from their historical, cultural and institutional contexts. The latest wave of neo-classical economics, and particularly the 'information-theoretical' approach associated with Joseph Stiglitz's former work at the World Bank, attempts to overcome some of these limitations by understanding non-market-conforming behaviours in terms of rational responses to information asymmetries and deficits. A number of economists and sociologists at the World Bank subsequently begun to use the notion of social capital in analyses of anything from housing markets to crime, health and growth rates. Their work is disseminated to the outside academic community via a popular website (http://worldbank.org/poverty/scapital) which is dedicated to social capital debate.

Social capital thus came to be seen by these economists (and the sociologists working with them) as an immensely flexible conceptual tool which could be used explain a wide array of social phenomena – previously ignored or assumed away by economists – in a way which could be made consistent with market economic logic. In the process, and by virtue of a single concept, whole tracts of the social geography were re-appropriated for economics without reference to any of the theoretical maps developed by generations of sociologists. Michael Woolcock, animator of the social capital website at the World Bank, noted the positive and negative sides of this: 'several critics,' he writes, 'not without justification, have voiced their concern that collapsing an entire discipline [sociology] into a single variable [social capital] ... is a travesty, but there are others that are pleased that mainstream sociological ideas are finally being given their due at the highest levels' (cited in Fine 2001, p. 167).

The second strand of recent social capital theory is primarily associated with the work of the political scientist, Robert Putnam, who moved from his early work on civic association and local government in Italy (Putnam 1993) – where social capital appears as an essentially post hoc theory in the coda to the book – to a full-scale study of the trends in social capital in the USA (Putnam 2000). Putnam's work has been immensely influential, partly because of his exhaustive compilation of data on various social capital measures and partly because his liberal communitarian message about the power of civic association is highly palatable to market-oriented governments and commentators seeking politically acceptable solutions to global problems of social fragmentation. His analysis and policy message are both, however, based on a paradox.

In *Making Democracy Work* (1993), he argued that the superior performance of local government in the northern regions of Italy was due to the higher reserves of social capital accumulated there over thousands of years. These were seen, following Coleman, as essentially the by-product of other historical developments and cultural movements. In *Bowling Alone: The Collapse and Revival of American Community* (2000), his more recent study of social capital in the USA, he seeks to show both that social capital suffered a precipitous decline in a mere thirty years after the late 1960s, and that it is ripe for renewal.

The contention that social capital accumulates historically at a snail's pace but can be dissipated very rapidly is somewhat curious from a historical point of view, and would certainly have surprised Putnam's intellectual forebear, de Tocqueville, whose greatest work, *The Old Regime and the French Revolution* (1955), was devoted to showing how even revolution failed to expunge the legacies of the Ancién Regime in France, in fact building on centralized statism that was its hallmark. As historians frequently remind us, whilst institutions can be suddenly and radically transformed, at least on the surface, cultures change very slowly. Equally contradictory is Putnam's optimism about the possibilities of a socially willed reprise of social capital in America, given the earlier adherence to Coleman's notion of social capital accumulating almost involuntarily as a by-product of other processes. The antinomies of Putnam's title and theme about collapse and revival appear both naïve and politically expedient in the final essay on the possibilities of communitarian revival. Cassandra and Pangloss both, Putnam can apparently appeal to a wide policy audience, but he has found more critics amongst his academic readers.

Putnam's paradoxes

Putnam defines social capital as the 'features of social life – networks, norms and trust – that enable participants to act together more effectively to pursue shared objectives' (Putnam 1995a). These objectives are not always laudable, and Putnam has increasingly acknowledged the 'dark side' of social capital (Schuller, Baron and Field 2000), but for the most part he treats the concept normatively as a positive basis for enlightened community and active democracy. In the positive civil society scenario, a number of characteristic attitudes and behaviours, including association, volunteering, donation, political engagement, trust and tolerance, are seen to work together in a virtuous spiral to produce desirable collective outcomes. 'Other things being equal,' Putnam writes (2000, p. 137) 'people who trust their fellow citizens volunteer more often, contribute more readily to charity, participate more often in politics and community organizations, serve more readily in juries, give blood more frequently, comply more fully with their tax obligations, are more tolerant of minority views, and display many other forms of civic virtue.' How these behaviours are connected is not always clear, and Putnam acknowledges that causality for individuals can run in different directions, but his claim is that the evidence (which he doesn't cite) weighs on the side of joining forming the basis for trust, rather than the reverse. For Putnam (2000), as for de Tocqueville, what counts most is the vibrancy of associational life – 'the social networks' from which arise 'the norms of reciprocity and trustworthiness'.

Education has a powerful effect on social capital, being the strongest predictor of individual associational membership, trust and political participation (Putnam 2000, p. 667). According to Putnam, the US data show that the last two years of college attendance make twice as much difference to trust and group membership as the first two years of high school, irrespective of gender, race and generation. Highly educated people, says Putnam, 'are much more likely to be joiners and trusters, partly because they are better off economically, but mostly because of the skills, resources, and inclinations that were imparted to them at home and in school' (Putnam 2000, p. 667).

Despite rising levels of education, however, social capital in America is in decline, according to Putnam's analysis in *Bowling Alone*. On all his measures of membership, trust, political engagement and voting, there has been a steady erosion since the late 1960s which applies across genders, ethnic and social groups and educational levels. These declines, according to Putnam, cannot be explained by urbanization, mobility, time pressures or the changing roles of women. They are primarily generational effects reflecting the passing of the socially engaged New Deal generation and its replacement by generations of so-called 'boomers' and 'Xers' who have more privatized lifestyles and spend more time watching TV. America, the quintessential land of association, has, in the course of two generations, become disassociated.

At the level of the individual, Putnam's analysis of social capital has much to commend it. He has compiled a huge mass of data based on a wide array of indicators which shows, fairly conclusively, at least for contemporary America, that there is a relation between individuals trusting, joining and becoming politically engaged, and that education relates to all of these, either directly or indirectly. He has also charted the trends over a substantial period, showing that the behaviour of the American public is indeed changing in significant ways. Several critics have contested his analysis of declining levels of association, but if you accept his (largely fixed) choice of indicators, the evidence is clear and comprehensive. However, for all this, and despite his claims to be providing an account of social change in America, he has said very little about American society as such, how it hangs together or fails to hang together, and how education impacts on social cohesion at this societal level. A number of obvious problems stand out and illustrate the weakness of Putnam's approach in providing explanations at the societal level using tools more appropriate for the analysis of individual and community behaviour.

First, if association is the key to social capital – and by extension social cohesion – as Putnam maintains, why is it that the USA, which ranks highest on levels of membership amongst a wide range of countries in repeated World Values Surveys (Inglehart 1990), is so palpably lacking in social cohesion on any of the more conventional measures like crime and inter-ethnic conflict? Secondly, why, if education is such a strong determinant of individual joining and trusting, is social capital declining so fast in America when education levels are still rising, and most with the younger generations who are precisely the most educated? Thirdly, if the decline is due to factors other than education, which on Putnam's account it must be, how do these impinge at societal and individual levels? Putnam finds it difficult to answer these kinds of questions with conviction because his argument, which is pitched at the level of individual behaviour, lacks the cultural, institutional and political dimensions that are critical to understanding societal change.

Putnam argues that associational membership is the key to social capital and social cohesion. But what evidence do we have for this? We know that in contemporary America individuals who join more also tend to trust more and to be more politically engaged than those who do not. We also know that in various other contemporary societies the correlation holds at the individual level (Brehm and Rahn 1997; Hall 1999; Stolle and Rochen 1998). However, if you extend the analysis to a larger set of countries, as Newton and Norris (2000) have done using pooled data on 17 countries in the World Values Survey, the association at the individual level becomes extremely weak, and no correlation at all can be found at the societal level (see also Knack and Keefer 1997; Norris 2001). America has an exceptionally high level of membership relative to other countries but exceptionally low levels of voting and only moderate levels of trust (Inglehart 1990).

Putnam's contention, which is at the heart of social capital theory, that these various characteristics 'form a coherent syndrome' (2000, p. 137) may apply at the level of the individual in some countries but the proposition does not hold for all. As Stolle and Rochen (1998) show in relation to Sweden, Germany and the USA, context, including the role of the state, may have an important bearing on how these characteristics interact. Consequently, there may also be no relation at all between joining and trusting at the societal level. It may be the case that individuals who join more also trust and engage more politically in some contexts, but there may be independent factors that determine the levels of each of these separately at the societal level which are far more powerful than the associations at the individual level. This may mean that some countries have both high levels of trust and moderate levels of joining relative to other countries, as seems to be the case for instance in some Nordic states, whilst others, like the USA, have relatively high levels of joining and lower levels of trust (Inglehart 1990). If these core social capital characteristics do not co-vary across countries it suggests that they have little meaning as a single factor at the societal level.

The primacy accorded to association in Putnam's account of social capital is contentious in other ways. His main concern is how much people associate and join, and his analysis of this is largely quantitative. However, quantitative approaches can miss the key issue for social cohesion. What do people join for and how does it enhance social integration? Putnam acknowledges that there are different kinds of association and that those that encourage 'bridging' between groups and associations and with individual outsiders are more important to social capital than those which merely encourage in-group bonding. This is an important point. As Mark Granovetter (1978) has shown, weak but extensive ties may have more beneficial social effects than the strong ties of dense, but relatively closed networks. Societies with excessively close and closed family ties may tend towards the 'amoral familism' described by Banfield (1958) which may be neither trusting nor innovative in societal terms. Equally, as Mancur Olson famously argued (1971) for some of the victorious allied powers after the Second World War by contrast with their defeated but reconstructed rivals, states with long established and powerful interest groups – and thus high levels of association – may become prone to sclerosis and slow growth.

The importance of these qualitative distinctions in forms of association are acknowledged in principle by Putman. However, in his own analysis he is unable to distinguish effectively between organizations which involve bridging and those which involve bonding, so that his conclusions regarding overall trends in association are based on gross aggregates rather than on any qualitative analysis of the way people associate. This proves to be a fatal weakness in his account and renders his analysis superficial as a commentary on social cohesion.

In terms of institutional and societal behaviour, there is no necessary relationship between associational membership and social trust. It depends entirely on the types of organizations involved and their objectives. Active and long-term membership of some types of organization may incubate trust through reiterated social interactions as predicted in game theory (Fukuyama 1999; Granovetter 1978; Axelrod 1986); this may be a generalized trust if the organizations are relatively 'encompassing' and heterogeneous, and if they are pursuing collective public goals which go beyond the narrow interests of small groups of people. Under certain historical circumstances, major political parties or coalitions of parties might fit this description, constructing what one tradition describes as national popular ideologies or hegemonic social relations (Gramsci 2001). Trade unions may also at times play this role, especially where they are large general or industrial unions representing disparate occupations at different levels, as opposed to craft unions and professional associations representing narrower interests. Likeswise, major churches and religions, where they are broadly ecumenical (members of evangelist churches in the USA trust less than the average, whereas members of the broad mainstream Churches trust more – see Putnam 2000).

On the other hand, membership of exclusivist organizations with self-interested goals may encourage trust amongst their members but positively erode trust in society at large (Newton 1999). Extremist or racist organizations, for instance, may well produce high levels of internal bonding but be guaranteed, at the same time, to generate distrust from their members to people outside and towards their members from people outside. Timothy McVeigh and his co-conspirators in the Oklahoma bombing were all members of bowling clubs, which provides a salutary and somewhat ironic commentary on Putnam's thesis (Fine 2001).

The crux of the matter in terms of social cohesion is whether associations foster in their members trust in the generality of people rather than simply in other members, and whether this increment to the pool of public trust is not counterbalanced by any diminution in trust amongst those outside generated by the existence of the same organization. Putnam's analysis is simply unable to evaluate this, which weakens his argument about the overall trends in American society. His case is that the gross levels of membership in the US are declining and that this must be bad for trust and ultimately for democracy. Others have argued just as plausibly that levels of association are actually quite stable in the USA, but that people are joining different types of organization whose membership levels Putnam does not measure, and which may be less conducive to social cohesion (Fukuyama 1999). On Putnam's own evidence (and that of Warde *et al.* for the UK: 2001), the types of membership that are declining fastest are precisely those involving the large, encompassing, multi-interest associations, such as the party and union. Membership growth tends to be in single-function or single-issue organizations, like sports clubs and self-help and environmental groups, or within lobby-type organizations, which, by definition, are serving narrow interests. What matters for social cohesion is the type and aims of association rather than the quantity.

In a recent study of social cohesion and fragmentation in modern societies (Fukuyama 1999) Francis Fukuyama considers the changing nature of associational life and the apparent paradox, in America, of the coexistence of relatively high levels of association and growing levels of distrust and social fragmentation. The answer, he says, 'has to do with moral miniaturization: while people continue to participate in group life, the groups themselves are less authoritative and produce a smaller radius of trust. As a whole, then, there are fewer common values shared by societies and more competition amongst groups' (p. 49). Whether or not one shares Fukuyama's socially conservative analysis of the causes of societal fragmentation, he has certainly pointed to a dilemma at the heart of social capital theory and one which underlines the importance of societal explanations of social cohesion.

Putnam's analysis remains ultimately at the level of the quantifying of individual behaviour. From his perspective he is unable to provide meaningful measures of cohesion in society at large, let alone to provide meaningful explanations of changes over time. Where there should be analysis of cultural and ideological shifts, of changes in economic and social structures, and of new institutional arrangements, there are simply extrapolations made from individual associations. True to his liberal, individualist tradition, he overlooks the importance of role of the state and institutions in providing the structural basis for social cohesion

(Skocpol 1996), remaining largely silent on the effects on social relations of two decades of neo-liberal government, with rising consumerism and individualism and the gradual dismantling of the welfare apparatus. Despite his own empirical demonstrations of the clear cross-regional correlations between social capital and income equality, he fails to explore the connections in America between declining social capital and rising inequality and social conflict. In Putnam's hands, social capital provides a distinctly romantic view of society devoid of power, politics and conflict (Edwards and Foley 1998; Skocpol 1996).

What both strands of social capital thinking have in common, and the reason why they can relate so readily to mainstream paradigms in neo-classical economics, is that, despite ostensibly dealing with questions of collective action and community, they are equally wedded to a liberal, individualist view of society. Social capital economists ultimately still adhere to a methodological individualism that seeks to explain all social phenomena in terms of individual preferences, rational calculation and utility functions, assuming universal – and hence a-social and a-historical – principles of utilitarian human behaviour. As Fine and Green (2000) note, history only enters into mainstream economics as 'path dependence', 'random shocks' and 'unexplained initial conditions', while society is absorbed as exogenous givens limiting but not constituting elected individual preferences. Putnam and his followers, whilst making passing reference to culture and institutions, also fundamentally locate and operationalize their analyses at the level of individual behaviour, despite acknowledging the relational nature of social capital. Neither is able to address the broader questions of social cohesion and the effects of education on it.

A societal approach to social cohesion

An alternative approach to social cohesion is to view it from a societal perspective. This assumes that cohesion in society at large involves not only bonding and trust within particular groups and communities but also between them; and that this entails some common sense of citizenship and values. Inevitably, therefore, it is concerned with questions of power and resource distribution, conflict and conflict resolution and the state forms, institutions, ideologies and cultures that shape these in any given country. Although regional differences within countries will be important, many of the factors that most determine societal cohesion in a given country will be structural and national in nature and will require analysis at the societal level. These are often best analysed through comparative qualitative methods (Ragin 1981) which give purchase on the effects of different national-level factors. Where quantitative approaches are used, they will generally involve cross-national comparisons that use countries as the units of analysis because many of the national contextual or 'ecological' factors will be invisible to individual level.

Econometricians are often sceptical of cross-national statistical analysis. The limitations of datasets often mean that there are too few units of analysis (countries) to run reliable statistical regressions (Ragin 1981). Also, cross-national correlations will sometimes produce results which conflict with the results of individual-level statistical analysis and which will be dismissed as 'ecological fallacies' (Wilkinson 1996). To methodological individualism, phenomena which can't be explained statistically as the result of the accumulation of individual actions do not exist. However, this simply ignores the fact that many societal phenomena are indefinable and hence unmeasurable at that level – as is notably the case with income inequality. Alternatively, they remain unobserved because they exist as constants. What this means, essentially, is that these contextual factors cannot be used statistically to explain variations between individuals and therefore cannot be entered into the models. However, this should not necessarily imply that they are not major determinants of individual behaviour, nor that they are not highly significant in providing the contexts in which other variables, which can be observed, work. Statistical analysis may be satisfied when it can use individual-level variables to understand 10 per cent of the variance in individual behaviour in a given national population. However, much larger variations in behaviour between individuals in populations across different countries may remain quite inexplicable.

A cross-national societal approach to social cohesion is likely to differ from an individual-level human capital or rational choice perspective in other important ways. It will start from the assumption that all relations are context-bound, that is to say specific to historical times and places and the structures and environments that pertain to them (Foley and Edwards 1998). In terms of the social effects of education this would imply an a priori scepticism towards any propositions about universal relationships based on time- and place-specific data, such as the often-cited association, for instance, between education and tolerance. From a comparative and historical point of view such ideas are very easily refuted. It would also imply taking institutional and cultural factors seriously. Modern economics, at least in the form of the new institutional economics, has begun to take institutional structures into account as, of course, classical political economy always did before the marginalist movement narrowed economists' concerns. However, cultural factors are still massively underestimated in modern economics and rational choice sociology, appearing, if at all, only as individual preference, which, of course, is precisely what culture is not. Lifestyle and culture are not synonymous.

Comparative, cross-national analysis, on the other hand, is almost bound to attend to the importance of cultures since there is overwhelming evidence that countries do in fact differ substantially, regularly and enduringly on a whole variety of cultural measures, not least to our concerns, in terms of aggregate levels of trust, association, political engagement and tolerance. As Ronald Inglehart tersely concludes from his exhaustive study of data for 25 countries in the World Values Survey (1990), 'The peoples of different societies are characterized by enduring differences in basic attitudes, values and skills: In other words they have different cultures' (1990, p. 3). These cultures are not monolithic and nor are they immutable. However, in given times and places they act as important determinants of social and political behaviour which cannot be left out of account.

To provide an obvious example: more educated people in most contemporary western societies tend to be more tolerant, other things being equal, than less educated people, as countless research studies have shown (see Nie *et al.* 1996). However, this does not mean more educated societies, past or present, are always more tolerant, nor, even, that educated people are more tolerant in all societies. Nazism arose in Weimar Germany, one of the most highly educated countries on earth at the time. This may mean that education did not have any positive effects on tolerance in Germany then. German Protestants, after all, were on average more educated than Catholics, but they were also more likely to vote for the National Socialists, who received support from all social classes. Alternatively, it may simply mean that any positive education effects were overshadowed by other factors. The analysis of data on education and social attitudes across a range of countries in the World Values Survey shows only very weak correlations between average national levels of education and social capital, suggesting that the associations demonstrated at the individual level in various countries are outweighed in cross-country comparisons by other national factors, as we show below.

Education and social cohesion: a cross-national societal perspective

In what follows we use a comparative, cross-national approach to develop and perform preliminary tests on an alternative model for the effects of education on social cohesion at the societal level. At this stage, this serves primarily illustrative and exploratory purposes. We do not progress in this chapter to the point of providing any institutional and cultural explanations for the posited relations, but the hypotheses are based on the foregoing theoretical analysis and are constructed in such a way that they are amenable to this kind of qualitative causal explanation. We extend this analysis in chapter 2 to analyse relationships over time in educational inequality and a number of social cohesion variables.

   We start by identifying a set of variables that co-vary at the national level and which analysis of the literature suggests may form a plausible combined indicator of national level social cohesion. We then propose and test a model for the effects of education on social cohesion at the national level, using aggregated data for a sample of countries from various existing cross-sectional datasets.[1] In order to explore most fully our hypothesis we use two datasets. The 'main' dataset is a cross-sectional set of 15 economically advanced democracies for which we have data on social cohesion aggregates, skills and income distributions. Except where indicated otherwise in the text, our analysis refers to this dataset. However, in order to explore further the robustness of the hypothesis related to social cohesion measures we use additionally an expanded dataset of 38 developed and developing countries that could be categorized as 'market economies'. The data on these countries are rather more limited – we have information on two social cohesion measures (trust and civic participation) and on income distribution. In the final section we discuss the efficacy of this model and its relation to other models.

   Our model hypothesizes that education affects national levels of cohesion not only through socialization, but also through the indirect effects that the distribution of educational outcomes has through income distribution. Put simply, countries with education systems producing more equal outcomes in terms of skills and qualifications are likely to have more equal distribution of income and this in turn promotes social cohesion. The model is theoretically plausible because there is already considerable evidence (Nickell and Layard 1998; OECD 2001; Checchi 2001) for a range of developed countries that skills distribution and income distribution correlate highly at the national level, and that cross-nationally income distribution is powerful predictor of social outcomes such as crime (McMahon 1999) and health (Wilkinson 1996).

Measuring social cohesion

Our analysis starts from the proposition that social cohesion can only be measured at the societal level with indicators which are appropriate to that level and with sets of indicators which do actually co-vary and cluster at the national level. Social capital theory uses measures of association, trust, civic co-operation and political engagement to represent social capital at the individual/community level. However, as the discussion above suggested, these do not form a coherent syndrome at the national level. Some countries with comparatively high levels of association have moderate to low levels of trust (USA) and others with lower levels of association (Denmark and other Nordics) have high levels of trust (see Inglehart 1990). Furthermore, on the basis of analysis of trends, there are some countries (USA) where trust and association appear to be declining in tandem (if you follow Putnam at least) and others where they are moving in different directions (for instance in the UK – see Hall 1999). Analysis by Knack and Keefer (1997) of data on 29 market countries in the World Values Survey (WVS) showed that there was no correlation between aggregate levels of trust and association across countries after controlling for education and income. Other studies have confirmed this (Norris 2001; Newton and Norris 2000).

Our own analysis of a slightly different sample of 15 developed countries in the WVS (without controls) confirms that there is no correlation across countries between three of the social capital measures. These measures, the countries used and data sources are described in Appendix 1 at the end of this volume. We use measures for general trust and trust in democracy (GENERAL TRUST and TRUST IN DEMO-CRACY), for civic co-operation in terms of attitudes to cheating on taxes and public transport (TAX CHEATING and TRANSPORT CHEATING), a civic participation measure (MEMBERSHIPS), a tolerance indicator (TOLERANCE) and measures of violent crime and a perception of risk of assault in the local community safety (CRIME and COMMUNITY SAFETY). Note that these crime and community safety variables are coded so that a reduction in crime or risk would be thought to be socially beneficial.

As Table 1.1 shows,[2] there is no significant relationship[3] between general trust (GENERAL TRUST), associational memberships (MEMBERSHIPS) and opposition to cheating on public transport fares (TRANSPORT CHEATING) at an aggregate level. Figure 1.1 shows, in the form of a scatterplot, the lack of a clear relationship between group memberships (MEMBERSHIPS) and general trust (GENERAL TRUST) at the national level – elements which are often taken to be central to the 'coherent syndrome' of social capital. This lack of a relationship between civic participation and general trust was also found in our expanded dataset of 38 market economies. As shown in Figure 1.2, a scatterplot indicates little correlation between general trust and civic participation as

Table 1.1 Correlations between social cohesion aggregates

	General trust	Memberships	Trust in democracy	Tax cheating	Transport cheating	Crime	Tolerance	Community safety
General trust	1							
Memberships	.003	1						
	.990							
Trust in democracy	.563*	-.226	1					
	.029	.417						
Tax cheating	.077	.592*	-.312	1				
	.786	.020	.257					
Transport cheating	.195	.071	.223	.554*	1			
	.486	.801	.425	.032				
Crime	-.146	.407	-.177	.430	-.087	1		
	.603	.132	.528	.110	.757			
Tolerance	.095	.351	-.262	.121	-.526*	.250	1	
	.737	.200	.345	.667	.044	.370		
Community safety	-.724**	.013	-.372	.026	.075	.012	-.266	1
	.005	.965	.210	.932	.808	.970	.380	

Note: * Correlation is significant at the 0.05 level (2-tailed).
** Correlation is significant at the 0.01 level (2-tailed).

39

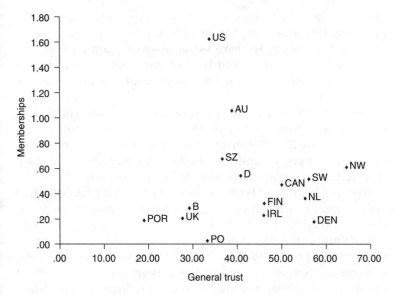

Figure 1.1 A 'coherent syndrome'? Civic participation and general trust

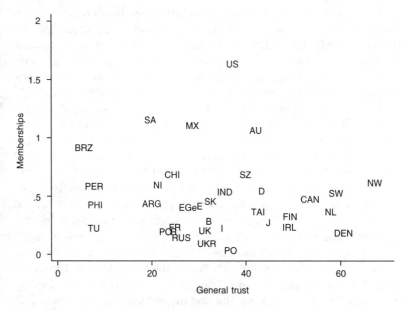

Figure 1.2 Civic participation and trust in an expanded dataset

confirmed by statistical tests (r = −.069, p = .628). In the diagram, the abbreviation for each country is centred on the data point. Note that to facilitate interpretation, we have excluded some countries from this diagram (Bulgaria, Hungary, Austria and Iceland as they overlay other country names) but details of figures for all countries can be found in the data appendix.

However, as Table 1.1 shows, there are significant correlations between general trust (GENERAL TRUST) and trust in government (TRUST IN DEMOCRACY)[4] in the main dataset (r = .563, p = .029). There are also strongly significant relationships between general trust and a feeling of local safety (COMMUNITY SAFETY) (r = −.724, p = .005) (p < 0.001) and between norms of civic co-operation such as never cheating on taxes (TAX CHEATING) and never cheating on public transport (TRANSPORT CHEATING) (r = .592, p = .020) (p < 0.001). These do not significantly correlate in our analysis with trust and membership, but in Knack and Keefer's (1997) analysis of the same data, which uses an aggregated factor based on answers to a larger number of questions about honesty and civic co-operation, there is a correlation between trust and civic co-operation values. Civic co-operation might therefore be included as a co-variant of trust, although we have not done so in this analysis.

Table 1.1 also reveals a significant negative correlation between tolerance (TOLERANCE) and never cheating on public transport (TRANSPORT CHEATING) which might indicate that there is a perverse relationship between these liberal attitudes at a national level (r = −.526, p = .044). Those countries with a higher proportion of the population trusting people in general are also significantly more likely to have a high proportion of the population who are prepared to cheat with their public transport fares. Interestingly, we also find a positive and significant relationship between civic participation (MEMBERSHIPS) and only one measure of civic co-operation, namely a belief that it is never right to cheat on taxes (TAX CHEATING) (r = .592, p = .020).

Taking trust (general and institutional), civic co-operation and crime as indicators of national-level social cohesion arguably makes good sense. Crime is a traditional negative indicator that would be readily recognized as valid by policy makers and people in general in many cultures. One could hardly imagine it being said that high levels of violent crime were a marker of social cohesion at the societal level, although it might be argued that they are compatible with certain kinds of group solidarity. In our analysis, we find that individuals at least consider that they are less at risk of crime in more trusting communities, although this does not necessarily correlate with observed crime rates (although there is some debate in the literature as to whether recorded or perceived crime is a better indicator of actual crime rates: Van Kesteren, Mayhew and Nieuwbeerta 2000). Civic co-operation is also intuitively connected to social cohesion, at least in principle. People may sometimes massage their tax returns, break speed limits and jump the lights at crossings, but they will generally admit that these are not socially responsible things to do, and lament their increasing prevalence. Social and institutional trust seem to go together since trusting in institutions involves trusting in people (although there may be societies where ordinary people trust each other but not officials in institutions). Social trust has also proved to be a reasonably robust measure in various studies and, according to Norris (2001), is the main driver of the often-cited links between social capital and growth and democratic stability.

Repeated WVS surveys show substantial and durable differences between countries on average levels of trust (Inglehart 1990). The WVS 'Trust' question ('Generally speaking, would you say that most people can be trusted, or that you can't be too careful in dealing with people?') has been criticized on the grounds that it is impossible to know whether those answering it are expressing their trust in close friends and family or the wider society of individuals. However, a number of factors suggest that it is general trust that is being measured. As Knack and Keefer (1997) show, trust values across countries in the WVS correlate closely with the results of the *Readers' Digest* 'dropped wallet' test for a range of countries. They also correspond closely with the stable results of repeated Euobaromter surveys asking individuals whether people from other specified countries are trustworthy (Ingelhart 1990).[5] Furthermore, the very low proportion of those expressing trust in some countries in WVS (10 per cent in Brazil) also suggests that the question is not measuring narrow radius trust.

It is quite possible that cross-country variations in positive responses to the trust question are measuring simultaneously differences in both trusting and trustworthiness, but this hardly matters since trust is understood as a component of social cohesion precisely as a relational, dynamic and institutionally dependent phenomena. Trust breeds trust; distrust, distrust. Trustworthy people are likely to generate trust among others with whom they are in contact, and untrustworthy people the opposite. Societies where honesty and reliability are underpinned by social norms and institutional codes are more likely to be trusting societies because people are more likely to experience reasons to be trusting. Trust is thus measured as an individual attribute, but its aggregated value points to societal features. As Alan Fox (1997, p. 67) puts it: trust and distrust 'are embedded in the rules, roles, and relations which men impose on, or seek to get accepted, by others'.

Correlation between education and social cohesion measures

In order to test the correlations across countries between education and our measures of social cohesion we need some valid national measures of education. Years of schooling measures used in WVS, our main dataset, are rejected, because length of schooling is a poor indicator of quality of learning and skills acquired. We therefore use the data on literacy in the International Adult Literacy survey (IALS). This survey has been criticized by some (Blum, Goldstein, and Guérein-Pace 2001) for cultural bias, but at least it has the merit of attempting to provide direct measures of skill, rather than proxies such as schooling years or qualifications. One may assume that the skills that it is measuring are related to both the quantity and quality of the education received.

As Table 1.2 shows, there are no significant correlations ($p < 0.05$) across countries in the main dataset between aggregates for education levels (SECONDARY LITERACY – the mean level of upper-secondary attainment in literacy) and measures for social cohesion (MEMBERSHIPS; TRUST IN DEMOCRACY; GENERAL TRUST; TAX CHEATING; TRANS-PORT CHEATING; CRIME; COMMUNITY SAFETY and TOLERANCE). This should be no surprise given what we have said already about the likelihood that national cultural and institutional factors greatly outweigh gross education effects on social cohesion. We therefore look next at the impact of educational inequality on social cohesion, on the basis that comparative historical and theoretical literature suggests that social cohesion is highly sensitive to distributional effects.

Table 1.2   Upper secondary attainment and social cohesion aggregates

	Correlation	Sig.
General trust	.354	.196
Memberships	−.120	.670
Trust in democracy	.244	.381
Tax cheating	−.376	.167
Transport cheating	−.487	.066
Crime	−.055	.845
Tolerance	.491	.063
Community safety	−.505	.078

Educational inequality and social cohesion

We have used results from all cycles of the International Adult Literacy Survey (IALS) in order to ascertain the distribution of educational outcomes, in terms of literacy skills, across a number of countries also included in the World Values Survey (WVS). Using a similar methodology to Nickell and Layard (1998, p. 67) we calculated a test score ratio based on the differences between the average literacy levels of those who attended the minimal compulsory education for that country and those who continued their education after the upper secondary level. Following the method used by the OECD (2000) when assessing the social consequences of inequalities in literacy, we used the prose measure of literacy rather than the quantitative measure of literacy employed by Nickell and Layard (1998, p. 67). There may be questions about the suitability of these measures, or a combined measure as a proxy for skill distribution in the labour market, and this is an issue for further debate.

Table 1.3 shows the mean prose scores for those whose educational level is less than upper secondary, for those who have attained upper secondary education and for those who have attained some tertiary education. The test score ratio (SKILL INEQUALITY) is the ratio of the score of those attaining tertiary education to those attaining lower than upper secondary education. Hence it is the ratio between the level of

Table 1.3 Literacy and skill inequality

Country	Lower secondary literacy	Secondary literacy	Tertiary literacy	Skill inequality
Australia	250.60	280.00	310.40	1.24
Belgium	242.50	281.00	312.30	1.29
Britain	247.90	281.90	309.50	1.25
Canada	233.40	283.80	314.80	1.35
Denmark	252.80	278.10	298.50	1.18
Finland	261.60	295.90	316.90	1.21
Ireland	238.80	288.20	308.30	1.29
Netherlands	257.50	297.00	312.10	1.21
Norway	254.50	284.40	315.10	1.24
Poland	210.50	252.70	277.30	1.32
Portugal	206.60	291.50	304.80	1.48
Sweden	275.40	302.30	329.10	1.19
Switzerland	228.10	274.10	298.30	1.31
USA	207.10	270.70	308.40	1.49
Germany	265.60	283.80	310.10	1.17

Table 1.4   Skill inequality and social cohesion

	Correlation	Sig.
General trust	−.592*	.020
Memberships	.333	.225
Trust in democracy	−.283	.307
Tax cheating	.265	.340
Transport cheating	.171	.543
Crime	.398	.142
Tolerance	−.060	.831
Community safety	.404	.171

Note: * Correlation is significant at the 0.05 level (2-tailed).

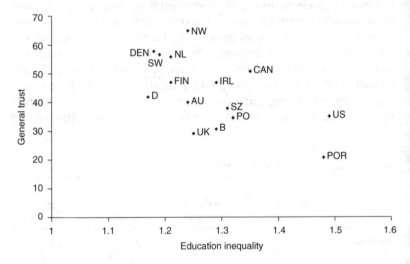

Figure 1.3   Education inequality and general trust

attainment of those who have experienced post-compulsory education and those who have attained the lowest level of secondary education.

The results show that measures of inequality in skills outcomes are rather higher in English-speaking countries such as the UK, the USA and Canada than in some northern continental and Nordic countries such as Germany and Sweden. The relative positions of countries here confirm some of the findings on skills spreads by Brown, Mickelright and Waldmann (2000), based on analysis of IEA data for test scores at 14, and Brown, Green and Lauder (2001) based on adult distributions of qualifications.

If we then correlate national measures of skills distribution against national measures of social cohesion (Table 1.4) we find that there is a significant ($p < 0.05$) correlation ($r = -.592$, $p = .020$) between educational inequality (SKILL INEQUALITY) and one commonly used measure of social capital, the general level of trust (GENERAL TRUST). Hence, the higher the level of educational inequality, the lower the level of general trust. This relationship is shown in Figure 1.3.

However, membership (MEMBERSHIPS), Putnam's key measure of social capital, does not correlate positively with educational equality. In fact in this case the effect of the education variable, which is below the 0.5 per cent significance level, appears if anything to be reversed, so that number of memberships, for instance, show a positive correlation with educational inequality ($r = .333$, although not significant at the 5 per cent level). This finding, though interesting in itself, need not trouble our thesis since association is not taken to be a measure of national level social cohesion.

Education and income inequality

If educational equality correlates with social cohesion, at least in terms of general trust, across countries, how does this association work? Our model hypothesized that education impacts on social cohesion both directly through socialization effects and indirectly through effects of skills distributions on income distributions. We are unable to test for the socialization effects since we have no measures for 'effective' socialization outcomes. In any case average levels of education in our correlation do not show any association with social cohesion outcomes. We can, however, test the effects of educational distributions on income distributions and we do this using a method adapted from Nickell and Layard (1988).

In measuring the degree to which skill differentials correspond to income inequality, Nickell and Layard (1998) employ earnings ratios, the ratio of incomes between individuals of differing educational levels. In this chapter, we employ gini coefficients which are a more general measure of earnings inequality for the whole population. Gini coefficients employed are provided in Table 1.5.

Figure 1.4 shows the relationship between educational inequality, measured by the test score ratio SKILL INEQUALITY, and income inequality in each of the 15 countries in our sample. As can be seen, there is an association between distributions of literacy skills and income inequality in these 15 economies. Economies with a high degree of skill disparity also have high degrees of income inequality, and vice versa. There is a clear relationship between the test score ratio (SKILL INEQUALITY) and the gini coefficient. This relationship is statistically significant ($p < 0.01$) with a positive and large correlation coefficient ($r = .650$, $p = .009$).

Table 1.5 Gini coefficients (mid-1990s)

Country	Gini
Australia	35.20
Belgium	25.00
Britain	36.10
Canada	31.50
Denmark	24.70
Finland	25.60
Ireland	35.90
Netherlands	32.60
Norway	25.80
Poland	32.90
Portugal	35.60
Sweden	25.00
Switzerland	33.10
USA	40.80
Germany	30.00

Source: World Bank (2001).

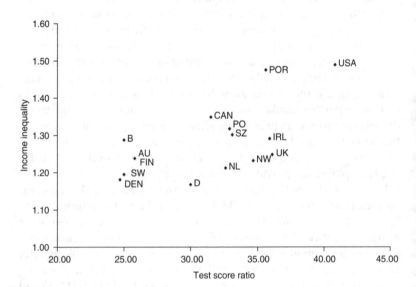

Figure 1.4 Educational inequality and income inequality

Income inequality and social cohesion

The next stage in the model requires that we test whether or not there is an association between income inequality and social cohesion. Putnam (1993; 2000, pp. 360–1) found that income inequality and aggregate social capital correlated across regions in both Italy and the USA, although he made little analytical use of this empirical finding, consigning its mention to a footnote in *Making Democracy Work*. We seek here to find whether this applies at the national level and with which measures of social capital. In order to do this we employed the 1990 and 1995 sweeps of the World Values Survey to calculate measures of general trust and association. Following Knack and Keefer (1997) our measure of trust was based on the percentage of individuals in each country who answered 'yes' to the question whether people in general can be trusted. The association measure employed was the average number of memberships of various associations for each country. These associations included church, religious, art, music and educational organizations, unions, political parties, environmental organizations, charitable organizations and other voluntary organizations.

Table 1.6 provides the results of the analysis of correlations between income inequality and our social cohesion aggregates. For the 15 countries in the main dataset we failed to find a significant relationship between income inequality and associational membership. However, a significant positive relationship between income inequality and violent crime (CRIME) ($r = .640$, $p = .010$) and the perceived risk (COMMUNITY SAFETY) of assult in the community ($r = .636$, $p = .020$) was identified in addition to a significant negative relationship between income

Table 1.6 Income distribution and social cohesion

	Correlation	Sig.
General trust	−.547*	.035
Memberships	.414	.125
Trust in democracy	−.305	.269
Tax cheating	.403	.136
Transport cheating	−.009	.975
Crime	.640*	.010
Tolerance	.636*	.020
Community safety	.240	.389

Note: * Correlation is significant at the 0.05 level (2-tailed).

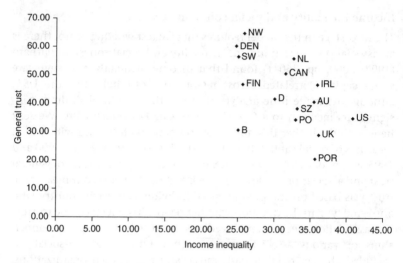

Figure 1.5   Income inequality and general trust

inequality and general trust (r = −.547, p = .035). Scatterplots show descriptively the relationship between income inequality, crime (Figure 1.6) and general trust (Figure 1.5).

In order to explore further the relationship between income inequality and associational membership, we expanded our range of countries to include the 'market economies' used by Knack and Keefer. We find a weak but significantly positive relationship between income inequality and association, with average group memberships highest in those countries that have the highest degree of income inequalities (Figure 1.7). (Note that we have excluded Canada, Belgium, Portugal and Ireland from this diagram to aid interpretation.) As Figure 1.7 shows, this relationship may be unduly influenced by a number of outlying countries, particularly middle income countries (MICs) and less developed countries (LDCs) with high levels of income inequality and high levels of civic participation. However, even if we remove these countries (Mexico, Brazil, Chile and Nigeria) from our sample, and also the USA, which is another outlier, a weak positive, but significant, relationship between income inequality and associational membership remains (r = .514, p = 0.02). What we may be seeing here is the effect of associational activity undertaken to offset social grievances.

Using the expanded dataset, we also find that the negative relationship between income inequality and general trust is maintained – that is, countries with more unequal distributions of income are also those in which there is less agreement that people in general can be trusted from

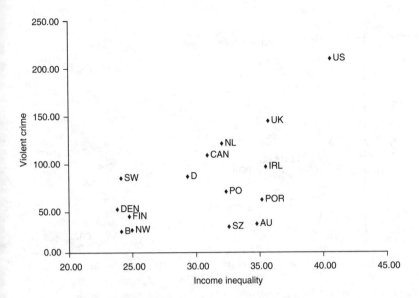

Figure 1.6 Income inequality and crime

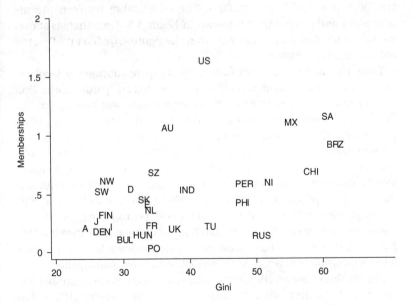

Figure 1.7 Income inequality and civic participation in an expanded dataset

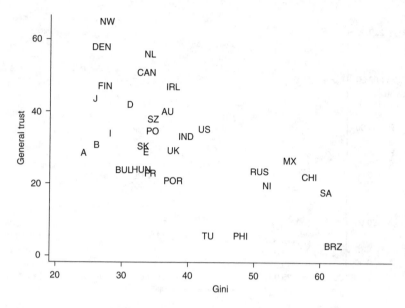

Figure 1.8 Income inequality and general trust in an expanded dataset

the WVS ($r = -.655$, $p = <0.001$). The relationship between income inequality and general trust is shown in Figure 1.8. Note that, as above, we have excluded some countries from the figure (Sweden and Peru) to aid visual interpretation.

Table 1.7 takes the analysis further by applying controls for GNP per capita, hence the correlation coefficients presented are 'partial' correlation coefficients. The measure of GNP per capita used was taken from the Purchasing Power Parity Index employed by the World Bank (1996, pp. 188–9). After introducing controls, the partial correlation coefficients between income inequality and general trust (GENERAL TRUST) ($r = -.526$, $p = .037$) remain significant. As before, we find that inequality decreases general trust but increases violent crime (CRIME) ($r = .660$, $r = .010$) and increases perceptions of risk of crime (COMMUNITY SAFETY) ($r = .628$, $p = .029$). We also find that controlling for GNP per capita makes the association between income inequality and civic participation significant ($r = .595$, $p = .025$). Hence, even in our reduced sample, it is possible to locate a positive relationship between income inequality and civic participation.

The findings here on the effects of income inequality on national levels of trust confirm other findings by Knack and Keefer (1997) that income equality (with, in their case, value consensus as proxied by

measures of ethnic homogeneity) provides the best statistical explanation of cross-national patterns of variation. The findings on the effects
of income inequality on violent crime also parallel the findings of crim-
inologists on violent crime across countries (Braithwaite and
Braithwaite 1980; McMahon 1999; Messner 1982). Braithwaite and
Braithwaite (1980) showed a statistically significant correlation between
greater inequality of earnings and higher homicide rates. Messner
(1982) found that the extent of income inequality accounted for 35 per
cent of the differences in homicide rates among the 39 countries for
which he had data. Taken together, these results suggest that income
inequality is an important factor in social cohesion. Our results here on
the positive relation between inequality and association (of any type)
also add support to our argument that association works in a different
way from other social capital measures at the national level and should
not be considered as a measure of social cohesion.

Our analysis here suggests that there is a cross-national statistical relationship between educational equality and trust, one of the key measures
of social cohesion, as has also been confirmed by Duthilleul and Ritzen
(2002) in their study based on PISA test data for 15 years olds (as opposed
to our test data for adult skills) which built on two of the authors' original
formulations (Green and Preston, 2001). The analysis above of the significant effects of educational inequality on income inequality, and of
income inequality on various measures of social cohesion, would also
seem to suggest that the effects of educational equality on social cohesion
work through income equality, and may impact on aspects of social
cohesion other than those captured by the trust measure. However, this is

Table 1.7 Income inequality and social cohesion
(with controls for GNP/capita)

	Correlation	*Sig.*
General trust	−.562*	.037
Memberships	.595*	.025
Trust in democracy	−.032	.293
Tax cheating	.430	.125
Transport cheating	−.004	.989
Crime	.660*	.010
Tolerance	.270	.350
Community safety	.628*	.029

Note: * Correlation is significant at the 0.05 level (2-tailed).

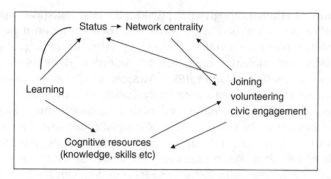

Figure 1.9   Learning effects on social capital
Source: Adapted from Nie *et al.* (1996).

not to discount the possibility that educational equality has an effect on social cohesion independent of income inequality. In fact in a previous study (Green, Preston and Sabates, 2003) we found, using multivariate analysis, a clear linear relationship between educational equality and a compound index for social cohesion which was not mediated by income.

Some conclusions

The analysis above leads to a number of tentative conclusions regarding the effects of education on social cohesion at the national level.

First, the measurement of social cohesion at the national level requires different combinations of indicators from those normally used in social capital analysis. While association, trust, tolerance, civic co-operation and political engagement may form a coherent cluster of variables at the individual level in certain countries, they do not co-vary sufficiently at the national level to be considered measures of a single underlying phenomena. In particular, associational membership would seem to work quite differently from other variables at the national level and appears to be a poor correlate of national social cohesion. We would suggest, as indicated earlier, that this is because associational membership involves so many different types of social relations that have quite different effects in terms of social integration. Used purely quantitatively, membership has very little meaning in terms of cohesion at community or national levels. Whatever the salience of de Tocqueville's original (qualitative) argument about the importance of the vibrant of community association for a strong civil society, quantitative approaches to this, which are unable to distinguish between narrow and self-interested association and more encompassing and consensus-building forms of association, are of little use in looking at modes of social integration in the modern world.

Secondly, there would appear to be a set of variables which do co-vary at the national level and which may form one basis for measurement of social cohesion. These include social and institutional trust from the original social capital measures, and also perception of crime crime, which is a more conventional measure of social cohesion. Civic co-operation may also be associated, although our own analysis here has not sought to confirm Knack and Keefer's findings on this point. We would suggest that other conventional measures of societal cohesion and conflict – such as tolerance, national pride, rates of industrial conflict and incidents of inter-ethnic violence – need further testing and theoretical discussion before being included as positive or negative measures of social cohesion.

Thirdly, there appears to be no significant correlation at the national level between aggregate levels of skill (in literacy) and social cohesion, using our measures. This confirms our earlier argument that education effects may well be greatly outweighed by more powerful institutional and cultural factors at the national level. However, this does not mean that the role of education is insignificant. Education may have an important effect through way in which it socializes young people, which is invisible in our crude measures of educational outcomes. As we show here, it would certainly appear to have a significant indirect effect through its impact on equality.

Fourthly, inequality of educational outcomes is closely connected to income inequality which has a powerful effect on many of the measures of social cohesion, although we cannot be clear yet about which way all the causal arrows run.

It is quite probable that income equality impacts on educational equality through equalizing access to education. It is also likely that social cohesion and solidaristic cultures and political ideologies promote both income equality and educational equality through equalizing aspirations and supporting certain types of policy interventions. Minimum wages and other forms of labour market regulation that make wage agreements binding and inclusive for entire sectors may well, for instance, enhance income equality (Blau and Kahn 1996; Nickell and Layard 1988). Measures to equalize resources for and admissions to schools may make educational outcomes more equal, as may shared aspirations about the value of schooling, as has been argued in the case of the – at least until recently – highly egalitarian Japanese education system (Green 1999). These relationships remain to be investigated analytically, but our analysis here of correlations at least suggests that there is an issue to be explored.

Existing models of education effects on social capital and civic participation (Bynner and Ashford 1994; Nie *et al.* 1996; Emler and Frazer 1999) suggest that education impacts on association and political engagement directly by conferring useful cognitive resources and

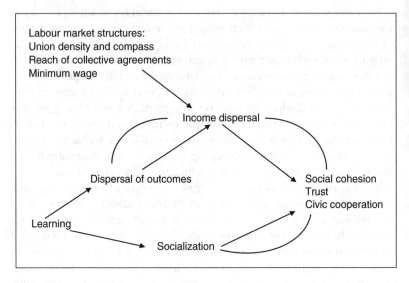

Figure 1.10 Learning effects on social cohesion

indirectly by giving access to jobs which confer network centrality (as shown in Figure 1.9). Our model here in no way contradicts this, but rather seeks to explain educational impacts on a different kind of outcome – that is: social cohesion. In this model skills and qualifications are still important, but it is mainly the way they are distributed which affects social cohesion. In addition to this we posit, but do not explore, the possibility that different forms of school socialization may have differential impacts on social cohesion at the national level. The full hypothesized model is shown in Figure 1.10.

In the following chapters we investigate, using other data, some of the claims made by this model and find support for both the dispersal of outcomes and socialization channels. If proved valid, this model of educational effects on social cohesion has significant policy implications.

Current citizenship education policies in England (and some other English-speaking countries) focus strongly on the development of social competences (Kerr 1999; Osler and Starkey 2000). This may well be beneficial for association and political engagement, but may have rather less impact on trust, civic cooperation and social cohesion generally. To address these issues through education more attention would have to be placed on the development of shared or co-operative values and on the attenuation inequalities in educational outcomes.

2
Educational Inequality and Social Cohesion: An Over-Time Analysis

Introduction: the importance of time

In the previous chapter we examined the relationship between educational inequality and social cohesion in a cross-sectional analysis. That is, we took a single time period and examined the correlations between educational inequality, income inequality and several measures of social cohesion. Although we found some evidence that educational inequality correlates with measures of social cohesion in this time period, ideally we would want to know whether these relationships hold over extended periods of time. This will allow us a more robust test of whether there are causal relationships at work. In this chapter we move beyond this single snapshot of relationships by modelling changes in educational and income inequality and a number of social cohesion outcomes over time. In practice, we take a series of snapshots for a number of countries and combine them together to give the illusion of time, rather like the individual cells in a film when run together give the illusion of movement. The repeated cross-sections which we take (for 1960, for 1965 and so on) for the same countries over time give us a cross-sectional time series dataset which can then be analysed to examine whether the indicative evidence for the mid-1990s in chapter 1 was coincidental, or whether there might be a relationship which holds for a group of countries throughout a number of decades.

This type of analysis, using cross-sectional time series data, is extremely important when considering social cohesion. Unlike social capital which, empirically, seems to be prone to large fluctuations over short periods, social cohesion would theoretically best be seen over long historical time. Although social capital links and bonds can be dissipated within a decade (the 1960s according to Putnam 2000), societal-level trust and the institutions which support it may take longer to be established and maintained. In this analysis, the length of time which we are considering (1960–1990 at the longest) might be thought to be insufficiently long. Part of Skocopol's (1996) critique of social capital theory is that its focus on the present (and on co-operation, rather than conflict) is insufficient but inevitable since the theory is not equipped to tackle truly transformative periods of social change which involve revolution, social upheaval and social crisis. Whilst in sympathy with this position, we would argue that even within the relatively short time period analysed here, there are various substantive economic and social changes – including the breakdown of the Keynesian consensus, the rise of mass unemployment and the reduction of both state socialism and the welfare state. Whether educational systems still have some influence on the social outcomes of societies across these times of great upheaval is of considerable importance. This period of significant change in both education systems (comprehensivization, expansion of mass higher education followed by marketization) and social outcomes, therefore, represents an ideal terrain for testing whether there is a relation between educational outcomes and social cohesion.

Theoretically, there are a number of reasons for thinking that there might be over-time relationships between educational inequality and social cohesion. One indirect mechanism is through income inequality. Inequalities in the distribution of skills and qualifications over time become inequalities in the distribution of income. Individuals leave the educational system (although they might re-enter at a later date) with a certain level of qualification. According to human capital theory, (in as much as qualifications are an indicator of people's current and future productivity) skills and qualifications determine wages. The wider the distribution of qualifications, the wider the range of wages (all other things being equal). Over time, the picture becomes more complicated as the skill and qualification distributions of those more recently qualified interact with the skill and qualification distributions of the population as a whole. This might mean that qualifications which might have previously have led to labour market success (such as a degree) might now offer a less favourable labour market position. As a result, growing credentialism may have increasingly negative consequences for social cohesion as certain groups attempt to maintain their educational position through social closure (Ball 2003). When considered over time, there is therefore a complex and circular relation between education inequality and social cohesion through the nexus of income inequality.

Similarly, the impact of educational inequalities and social cohesion through psychosocial and sociological mechanisms are equally complex when considered over time. For example, psychological stress arising through inequality of income (Wilkinson 1996) may be exacerbated by inequalities in education, particularly when the structure of the education system changes between generations. Ethological approaches would emphasize the effect of status hierarchies in social interaction and their potential societal stressor. Hierarchical distinctions and anxieties concerning social position may be exacerbated over generations – not only between current and recent graduates, for example, but also between those from new and established universities. Social interactions also become more complex as increasing diversity of educational outcome produces divergent norms and values (Gradstein and Justman 2001). Aside from micro perspectives on educational inequality and lack of cohesion, education is increasingly becoming less efficacious as a mechanism of social mobility (at least in the UK) and inequalities in education may enhance competition between classes for limited resources, not only in labour markets but also in civic and political arenas. As the work of Robert Nie and his co-authors (1996) shows, disparities in educational qualifications over time means that those at the top of the qualification distribution are increasingly active in political life, whereas those at the bottom are increasingly disaffected and marginalized. Following their analysis, it is not that the functioning of democracy is challenged by increasing educational inequality, but democracies can become increasingly unrepresentative of the large groups who are not active in the political process.

In this chapter we analyse education and social cohesion using cross-sectional time series data for a number of countries, focusing primarily on two groups of social outcomes. First is a set of outcomes related to the political culture of the country. We examine the degree to which countries protect what liberal theorists call 'negative liberties' – that is civil and political liberties. Curtailments of such liberties are taken to be expressions of state intentions to reduce the ability of individuals and groups to articulate, mobilize and organize. With this in mind, we also consider the number of incidents of 'unrest' in countries over time in terms of strikes, demonstrations and riots. Secondly, we consider a set of outcomes related to various types of crime, stressing crimes against the person (murder, homicide and rape). We would consider countries where liberties are in decline and where unrest and crime are increasing to have reduced levels of social cohesion. This statement is perhaps more contentious than it first appears and there may be counter-examples.

For example, liberties are not always indicative of social cohesion. Freedom of speech, or unhindered freedom to own private property, may be concurrent with 'hate' speech or uncontrolled intrusion of private ownership into public life. Unrest might be considered a sign of a healthy democracy, or an unhealthy one on the cusp of positive social change. It is important not to lose a sense of historical context in this kind of analysis; the type of cohesion which is implicitly being valued here is in terms of a liberal society with democratic institutions and low levels of social unrest. Some may judge such societies to be exploitative and coercive or sclerotic, as mentioned in chapter 1, and we return to the problematic of characterizing different types of social cohesion in the final chapter. For the present, we are interested in whether educational inequality plays a role in social cohesion, as characterized by these measures.

Surprisingly, for most social cohesion outcomes in this chapter we find that there is a significant (although not necessarily linear) relationship between educational inequality and the social cohesion outcome investigated over time. For civil liberties, political liberties, unrest and a number of different categories of crime we find clear over-time correlations with educational inequality. We identify these relationships even when we control for other important variables which have been found to be associated with these outcomes – such as income inequality and GDP per capita. Although we cannot use this data to identify mechanisms through which educational inequality might influence social cohesion, we are confident that educational inequality is associated with social cohesion independently of an initially convincing third variable explanation (income inequality). In the conclusion to this chapter, we discuss the implications of these findings for education systems and equalities. We argue that there is not necessarily a simple, linear association between educational inequality and social cohesion. Increases in educational inequality do not necessarily result in less social cohesion. In fact, at low levels of educational inequality, an increase in educational inequality could be associated with increased social cohesion. Although the mechanisms underlying this relationship are not clear, one possibility might be that expansion of higher levels of the educational system are initially associated both with higher educational inequality and with the establishment of institutions and structures which might be initially necessary to reduce social conflict.

Methodology

Our hypothesis in this chapter is that educational inequality is associated with social cohesion outcomes over long periods of time. In order to investigate this hypothesis we operationalize quantitative outcomes at the country level for educational inequality, outcome variables and control variables and construct a specialized dataset with cross-sectional time series data. For each case (the country) there are data on the variables under investigation over several discrete time intervals (in this case every five years). For civil liberties, political liberties and unrest we have data on these variables for the periods 1960–1990 and for crime we have data on variables for the years 1960–1975.

For our measure of educational inequality in this chapter we used the dataset developed by Thomas, Wang and Fan (2000) for the World Bank. Their dataset measures educational inequality for 85 countries over the period 1960–1990 reported at five-yearly periods (that is for 1960, 1965 … 1990). Their measure of educational inequality, the education gini (*edgini* – variable names are given in italics in this chapter), is based upon the proportions of the population achieving any of seven levels of education (partial primary, complete primary, partial secondary, complete secondary, partial tertiary, complete tertiary) and is analogous to the conventional measure of inequality of income, the gini coefficient (*gini*). Although the Thomas, Wang and Fan dataset measures qualifications rather than skill inequality it is constructed using a robust method and has been utilized in recent econometric research on inequality (see, for example, Checchi 2000). The minimum possible level of *edgini* is 0 (perfect educational equality) and the maximum is 1 (perfect educational inequality). Although educational inequality is the variable of substantive interest we additionally controlled for other variables found to be associated with social cohesion outcomes: namely income inequality and real income. We also control for real GDP per capita in US$ (*gdp*). In the case of the political outcomes (civil rights, political rights and unrest) we control for both income inequality and real GDP. In the case of crime we controlled for only income inequality as the dataset is insufficiently large to support a number of controls.

For our political variables we used the ACLP dataset of political stability variables (Przeworski, Alvarez, Cheibub and Limongi 2000) which was originally intended as a resource for political scientists and as an evidence base on the benefits of democracy. We focussed on three variables: political liberty (*pollib*), civil liberty (*civlib*) and 'unrest' (*unrest*).

Political liberty (*pollib*) is ranked on a seven-point scale through an index derived by 'Freedom House'. We reversed this scale so that higher scores indicate greater political liberty. In our new scale, 1 indicates regimes where political rights are non-existent and there is severe oppression. 6 represents regimes where there is political corruption, violence and political discrimination against minorities. Regimes ranked 7 have free and fair elections and there is self-government or genuine participation for minority groups.

Civil liberty (*civlib*) was also ranked by 'Freedom House' on a seven-point scale which we have reversed. Regimes ranked 1 on this scale are regimes where there is no freedom and no developed civil society. Regimes ranked 6 have deficiencies in a few civil liberties, but are still relatively free. Regimes ranked 7 have freedom of expression, assembly, education and religion.

Unrest (*unrest*) is an aggregated scale of riots, strikes and peaceful demonstrations which Przeworski, Alvarez, Cheibub and Limongi (2000, pp. 192–3) argue proxies for a variable which is variously denoted as 'mobilization' in the literature on the transition to democracy and 'unrest' in the literature on political stability. We aggregate these events in order to form a meaningful scale variable.

Riots are defined as the number of demonstrations or clashes of more than 100 citizens involving the use of physical force. Strikes are the number of strikes of 1,000 or more industrial or service workers that involved more than one employer and were aimed at national-government policies or authority. Peaceful demonstrations were defined as any peaceful public gathering of at least 100 people for the primary purpose of voicing their opposition to government policies or authority, excluding demonstrations of a distinctly anti-foreign nature. As Przeworski, Alvarez, Cheibub and Limongi (2000, pp. 192–3) raise the issue of substantive differences in these variables (particularly unrest) between developed and developing countries, we restrict our analysis of countries in the dataset to Europe, North American and other OECD countries.

For crime, we used the Archer and Gartner (AG) 'Violence in Crime in Cross-National Perspective 1900–1974' dataset which includes reconstructed data on murder, rape, robbery, theft and assault. We calculated per capita measures of crime using the population measure also included in this dataset. The AG dataset was then merged in order to combine the crime measures with measures of income inequality, educational inequality and real GDP per. capita. Due to the limited information in this dataset, we calculated values for 1960, 1965, 1970 and 1975 on the basis of the average of data available for the preceding years and used a sample of all available countries.

Through merging datasets, we created two new datasets. As some countries were members of one dataset and not another this obviously reduced the number of countries available for analysis. One dataset was on political variables, educational inequality, income inequality and real GDP per capita for twenty countries over the period 1960–1990. The other dataset was on crime, educational inequality and income inequality for twenty five countries over the period 1960–1975. These two datasets are provided in appendix one. We assumed that the outcome variables were continuous and employed cross-sectional time series regression models (fixed effects) to test the relationship between each outcome and the independent variables in the case of our political variables and a pooled linear regression in the case of crime. In order to capture possible non-linearity we employ squared and inverse terms for educational inequality, the gini coefficient and real GDP per capita for civil liberties, political liberties and unrest (following Checchi 2001). However, in the case of the crime variables we were not able to include additional terms to show nonlinearity due to the small number of observations in the dataset. In the analysis (below) we report unstandardized regression coefficients, t-statistics and indicators of significance at 1 per cent (**) and 5 per cent (*) for each independent variable.

Educational inequality, liberty and unrest

In contemporary writing on education and political outcomes, much of the emphasis is on individual, micro, measures of engagement, interest or attitude (Emler and Frazer 1999). The impacts of education on macro-political processes are less frequently considered, other than indirectly through ideology. Perhaps this is due to a different emphasis in this political science literature, or to a 'historicist' approach to educational theorizing. Although there is a literature on the aggregate impact of education and income inequality on rights and liberty, for example, there is no empirical work on the impact of educational inequality on civil and political rights. Furthermore, in much of the writing on education and social cohesion, rights are believed to have evolved early in the process of state formation with education playing a role in socialization and dissemination. As stated above, although on a historical scale there do not appear to have been massive changes in rights and unrest in recent history, by using increasingly graduated measures of these variables we find some evidence of a relationship.

Table 2.1 shows the correlations between variables, with an * indicating those variables with a correlation coefficient where $p < 0.05$. It is these highly significant relationships which we report on here. As can be seen in the table, there is a positive correlation (0.44) between educational inequality (*edgini*) and income inequality (*gini*) as we might expect. In support of the hypothesis that there is a negative relationship between educational inequality and social cohesion we also observe that

Table 2.1 Correlations between variables in political dataset

	edgini	gini	gdp	civlib	pollib	unrest
edgini	1					
gini	0.44**	1				
gdp	−0.49**	−0.10	1			
civlib	−0.31**	0.21	0.79**	1		
pollib	−0.17	0.31*	0.77**	0.94**	1	
unrest	0.19*	0.18	−0.17	−0.17	−0.16	1

Notes: * significant at 5%; ** significant at 1%.

there is a negative correlation between educational inequality and civil liberties (−0.31) and a positive relationship between educational inequality and unrest (0.19). Surprisingly, we observe a positive relationship between income inequality (*gini*) and political liberty (*pollib*) with a correlation (with no controls) of 0.31. Less surprisingly, there is also a positive relationship between national income (GDP per capita) and both political and civil liberties (0.77 and 0.79 respectively). Finally, there is a very strong positive relationship between civil and political liberties (0.94).

Table 2.2 shows the relationship between the civil liberties indicator and independent variables. As can be seen, there are positive relationships between civil liberties and the linear educational inequality term ($t = 2.34$) and the squared educational inequality (*edgini2*) term ($t = 2.29$). There is a negative relationship between civil liberties and the inverse educational inequality (*edginiinv*) term ($t = 2.86$). The net result of these terms taken together on civil liberties is shown in Figure 2.1. The scale on the y-axis (*civ*) shows the impact of educational inequality on civil liberties predicted by the model. Note that the model predictions will not necessarily fit within the expected values of civil liberties (1–7) as linear regression presumes a fully continuous variable (0–infinity) while we have used the standardized values of civil liberties. However, the shape of the regression is of interest. As can be seen, there is generally a negative relationship between educational inequality and civil liberties. After an initial decline as educational inequality rises from zero, the relationship stabilizes (and increases until *edgini* is of the value 0.22) until educational inequality reaches 0.42 after which point it drops quickly.

There is additionally an income inequality impact on civil liberties with all income inequality terms (*gini*, *gini2* and *giniinv*) significantly ($t > 1.96$) impacting on this variable. There are no significant impacts of

Table 2.2 Civil liberties: regression results

	Civlib
Edgini	109.596
	(2.34)*
edgini2	−109.885
	(2.29)*
edginiinv	3.230
	(2.86)**
Gini	−5.422
	(2.81)**
gini2	0.057
	(3.00)**
Giniinv	−1,617.433
	(2.33)*
Gdp	0.001
	(1.16)
gdp2	−0.000
	(1.61)
Gdpinv	3,273.571
	(0.07)
Constant	131.796
	(2.19)*
Observations	56
Number of id	18
R-squared	0.45

Absolute value of t statistics in parentheses

Notes: * significant at 5%; ** significant at 1%.

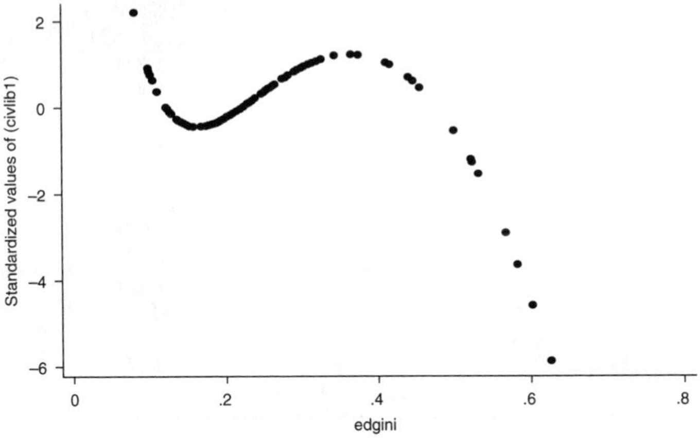

Figure 2.1 Educational inequality and civil liberties

GDP on civil liberties which are significant at the level of $p < 0.05$. As these results show, even when controlling for national income (per capita) there is a negative relationship between civil liberties and educational inequality.

Unsurprisingly, given the close correlation between civil and political liberties (0.91) there is a similar relationship between political liberties and the inequality variables. As can be seen in Table 2.3, there are significant relationships at the 5 per cent level between political liberty and the squared and inverse educational inequality variable. Additionally, at the 10 per cent level of significance there is a relationship between the linear educational inequality term (*edgini*) and political liberty. Taking each of these effects into consideration produces the relationship demonstrated in Figure 2.2 which uses a standardized scale of political liberty.

Table 2.3   Political liberties: regression results

	Pollib
Edgini	141.662
	(1.89)
edgini2	−160.462
	(2.08)*
Edginiinv	3.772
	(2.08)*
Gini	−6.386
	(2.07)*
gini2	0.066
	(2.16)*
Giniinv	−2,048.331
	(1.84)
Gdp	0.001
	(1.76)
gdp2	−0.000
	(1.90)
Gdpinv	71,189.985
	(0.99)
Constant	146.804
	(1.52)
Observations	56
Number of id	18
R-squared	0.37
Absolute value of t statistics in parentheses	

Notes: * significant at 5%; ** significant at 1%.

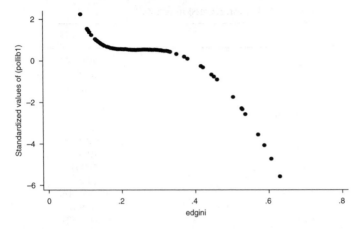

Figure 2.2 Educational inequality and political liberty

Again, the net effect of these variables operating together gives a non-linear relationship between political liberty and educational inequality. In this case, political liberty declines with increasing educational inequality until a local minimum of 0.24 is reached. Following this, political liberty increases until educational inequality reaches 0.34, at which point it declines again.

Unrest, an aggregate variable indicating riots, strikes and demonstrations, shows highly significant associations with educational inequality. As can be seen in Table 2.4, educational inequality is the most important variable in explaining unrest, with a significance level of $p < 0.01$. Again, there is a nonlinear relationship between educational inequality and unrest with a local minimum at 0.45 (see Figure 2.3 which shows the relationship between educational inequality and a standardized unrest variable). Beyond this level of educational inequality, unrest increases quickly. Other variables in the model are not significant at the $p < 0.05$ level, although there is a relationship between *gdpinv* (inverse of GDP) and unrest which is significant at the 10 per cent level ($t = 1.69$).

Educational inequality and crime

Various forms of crime against the person, such as homicide, may be thought to be symptomatic of low levels of social cohesion. Crimes against property, such as theft, are more problematically related to social cohesion as these crimes are often associated with periods of economic prosperity. Somewhat paradoxically, for example, theft has been found to

Table 2.4 Unrest: regression results

	Unrest
Edgini	−726.344
	(3.58)**
edgini2	802.474
	(3.69)**
edginiinv	−14.170
	(2.85)**
Gini	−2.199
	(0.32)
gini2	0.001
	(0.02)
Giniinv	−2,550.165
	(0.93)
Gdp	−0.002
	(1.49)
gdp2	0.000
	(1.33)
Gdpinv	−115,243.833
	(1.69)
Constant	368.652
	(1.63)
Observations	73
Number of id	18
R-squared	0.38
Absolute value of t statistics in parentheses	

Notes: * significant at 5%; ** significant at 1%.

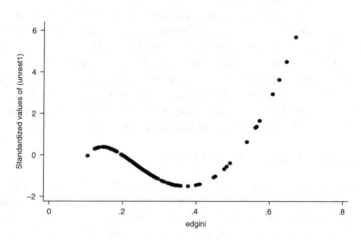

Figure 2.3 Educational inequality and unrest

fall in times of unemployment or recession. With general falls in prosperity there is less opportunity to benefit from stealing. Therefore we consider three types of crime against the person – murder, homicide and rape – which might be associated with inequalities. We calculate a measure of crime adjusted for the population of each country. In the case of murder, and particularly homicide, making cross-national comparisons is reasonable, however there must be a note of caution in relation to constructing comparative data on rape. Archer and Gartner (1984, p. 51) report that their statistics on this crime may be the least reliable of their data.

As shown in Table 2.5, crimes against the person are correlated at the 5 per cent level. There are correlations between homicide and rape (0.86), homicide and murder (0.79) and rape and murder (0.83). There are also positive and significant correlations (at the 5 per cent level) between educational inequality and crimes against the person (0.29 for murder and homicide and 0.31 for rape). There is also a significant correlation between homicide and income inequality (*gini*).

Table 2.6 provides the results of three pooled regression analyses of crimes against the person and measures of inequality. What is surprising

Table 2.5 Correlations between variables in crime dataset

	edgini	*gini*	*murder*	*homicide*	*rape*
edgini	1.00				
gini	0.17	1.00			
murder	0.29*	−0.00	1.00		
homicide	0.29*	0.29*	0.79**	1.00	
rape	0.31*	0.12	0.83**	0.86**	1.00

Notes: * significant at 5%; ** significant at 1%.

Table 2.6 Crime: regression results

	murderpc	*homicdpc*	*rapepc*
edgini	0.16	0.14	0.17
	(2.08)*	(1.82)^	(2.08)*
gini	−0.01	0.00	0.00
	(−0.40)	(1.83)^	(0.53)
Constant	0.00	−0.13	−0.05
	(0.01)	(−1.82)^	(−0.81)
Observations	47	47	47
R-squared	0.04	0.15	0.10
Absolute value of t statistics in parentheses			

Notes: ^ significant at 10%; * significant at 5%; ** significant at 1%.

is that even when we control for income inequality, we find a significant relationship between educational inequality and these measures. The associations are small, but significant. In the cases of murder and rape they are significant at the 5 per cent level and in the case of homicide they are significant at the 10 per cent level.

Discussion

As the results show, there are clear over-time relationships between educational inequality and social cohesion. Although in terms of crime we do not know the exact functional form of the relationship (only that more educational inequality is associated with increased crime), in terms of political outcomes (political rights, civil rights and unrest) there appears to be a 'tipping point' at an educational gini coefficient of 0.34–0.45 beyond which indicators worsen dramatically. Before this point there is actually an increase in political and civil rights and a fall in unrest. The reasons for this may be due to the relationship between levels of educational qualifications and educational inequality. Some educational inequality may be necessary in the initial expansion of educational qualifications and social systems may be able to 'accommodate' limited educational inequality without worsening social cohesion. However, beyond a certain level of educational inequality rights worsen and unrest increases.

In terms of the European and OECD countries in the TWF dataset this means that those in Table 2.7 are at, or close to, the point beyond which further educational inequalities will result in a decline in social cohesion. One may attempt to generalize from these countries the types of system characteristics which may result in educational inequality and (potentially) lack of social cohesion. In Table 2.8 we have extracted those countries with gini coefficients of less than 0.34 in all years in dataset 1. As can be seen, many of the countries named – particularly Japan, and the Nordic states – have comprehensive education and extensive welfare systems. In chapters 4 and 6 we return to these issues of system effects.

The analysis in this chapter develops that in chapter 1 by moving from an examination of purely cross-sectional relationships to an analysis of the effects of educational inequality on social cohesion over time. The results show that there are strong grounds for arguing that there is a relationship between educational inequality and political outcomes but that this relationship is nonlinear. It is primarily those countries at

Table 2.7 Selected European and OECD countries with *edgini* > 0.35 in 1990

Country	edgini 1990
France	0.35
Spain	0.36
West Germany	0.37
Portugal	0.43
Yugoslavia	0.47

Table 2.8 Selected European and OECD countries with *edgini* < 0.35 in 1990

Country	edgini 1990
Canada	0.16
Australia	0.21
Japan	0.25
Netherlands	0.25
Switzerland	0.26
Denmark	0.26
Finland	0.27

the upper end of the educational inequality spectrum which should be most concerned about worsening political outcomes. We also found associations between educational inequality and crimes against the person. That educational inequality is shown to be associated with high crime and poor political outcomes over time independently of income inequality is an extraordinary result. The implications are that it is not only equality of income, but also equality of educational outcome, which may be important in influencing aggregate social outcomes.

We have capitalized on a number of existing datasets in this analysis, but a few caveats need to be made. First, unlike in the previous chapter, we use a measure of educational achievement based on levels of education completed. Since levels of education completed do not necessarily indicate a given standard of achievement in many countries, this is arguably a cruder measure than those based on direct tests of skills or on formal qualifications or diplomas attained. However, there is not currently an adequate time series dataset for either of the latter measures. Secondly, there are a number of missing values, particularly with regard to the crime data, which would require the use of additional datasets to rectify. Thirdly, we may need to introduce more sophisticated econometric models in order to analyse the nature of time lags. Finally, the UK was not included in this analysis as an 'educational gini' coefficient for this country does not yet exist using the TWF methodology.

Despite these limitations in the data, however, the analysis in this chapter would seem to suggest that there may be important lessons to be learnt regarding the impact of worsening educational inequality on social cohesion in the developed countries and that further research needs to be conducted on this.

3
Education, Tolerance and Social Cohesion

Introduction

In the two previous chapters, we examined the effects of inequality in the distribution of skill and education across adult populations. We found that at a national level there are cross-sectional and over-time associations between educational inequality and a range of social cohesion outcomes. Perhaps surprisingly, educational (and not just income) inequality is important in terms of social cohesion. In this chapter we shift our concern to what many would consider to be another key element of social cohesion – tolerance. Here the relationship between education, equality and social cohesion is not as straightforward as might be expected.

Our argument in this chapter is largely based upon the literature on education, educational inequality and tolerance considered cross-nationally, with some empirical data analysis. We first consider the relationship between education and tolerance in Putnam's theory of social capital. We emphasize that although at face value the relationships might appear straightforward (that education leads to greater tolerance that in turn is associated with a more cohesive society), tolerance appears to be a highly complex phenomenon. Moving from social capital to theories of social cohesion, we argue that there is an ambivalent relationship between tolerance and social cohesion. In fact, tolerance has not traditionally been a central component of theories of social cohesion. Using some empirical data we show that tolerance is not closely connected to other components of social cohesion.

Putnam (2000) finds that levels of education and tolerance for individuals are related. More highly educated individuals in the US tend to have more tolerant attitudes. Similar assumptions have been made in studies of other countries (Emler and Fraser 1999; Haegel 1999; Winkler 1999). However, using cross-country analysis of aggregate measures for tolerance and education we find no correlations between tolerance and either levels of education or distributions of skills. That education levels do not correlate here with levels of tolerance may be because other contextual factors (such as societal levels of racism) at the country level overwhelm any associations. The lack of any observed relation between educational inequality and tolerance at the country level may be because education affects tolerance through value formation which is not captured in the measures of distributions of skills in literacy which we use.

Cross-national evidence on education and racial tolerance shows that the specific manifestations of 'educated tolerance' (or 'uneducated intolerance') are highly country- and context-specific. For example, Winkler (1999) and Haegel (1999) find that in Germany and France, respectively, there are substantial effects of education on tolerance and, in France, that the (supposedly universal) association between racism and authoritarianism is more apparent in 'educated' than 'uneducated' racists. Peri (1999), on the other hand, finds that for Italy there is only a weak effect from education and that the relation between intolerance and authoritarianism is also rather small. Relationships between education and tolerance vary not only synchronically across countries but also diachronically over time. Societal tolerance is highly situational and may change markedly over relatively short historical periods. After the events of 9/11, for instance, Islamophobia alone amongst other indicators of intolerance rose sharply in the US.

What is tolerance?

Tolerance is a multi-dimensional concept which may cover a wide range of related and unrelated attitudes. Tolerance may be understood, for instance, as acceptance of intra-group lifestyle differences (permissiveness) or it may be understood as openness towards other cultures (as in 'ethnic' or 'cultural' tolerance). These propensities may not necessarily coincide. Equally there may be relativistic 'libertarian' conceptions of tolerance as acceptance of all values, no matter how 'abhorrent' to the social mainstream, which are quite different from 'liberal' notions that accept value differences but only where they do not transgress certain core values. Libertarian attitudes may involve a general permissiveness towards 'deviant' majority group behaviour but not necessarily include attitudes conducive to ethnic or racial tolerance. Research evidence suggests that at the individual level in certain social contexts education is associated both with more 'permissive' attitudes and greater acceptance of other cultures (Putnam 2000). However, effects at the societal/ national level may be more complicated.

Tolerance may be seen to represent a 'thin' type of sociability. It is minimal in that it suggests a respect for others that does not necessarily imply high levels of social interaction or social solidarity. This 'thinness' is not necessarily a weakness in that it may be conducive to a type of cohesion based on mutual coexistence in liberal societies: where individuals and communities pursue their own cultural and individual interests with little mutual interaction but also without excessive friction. But tolerance does not necessarily imply any understanding of structural and institutional inequalities and of unequal power relations, let alone any desire to rectify these. As normally used, the term tolerance implies a certain laissez-faire attitude of 'live and let live' but not necessarily any desire for interaction or to pursue a common purpose. It has no necessary relation to more profound forms of solidarity, being conspicuoulsy absent for instance, from the notions of solidarity inscribed in 'liberté, égalité, fraternité' trinity of French Revolutionary and Rebublican thought.

In fact, the concept of tolerance is a rather a late arrival in theories of social cohesion, arising from liberal conceptions of individual, and, more recently, group rights (Kymlicka 1995). Additionally, in automatically imposing an in-group/out-group identification tolerance towards 'out-groups' is historically and socially located. As the work of Roediger (1991) and others (Ignatiev 1995) have shown, concepts of ethnicity and race are socially constructed and contested and change over time. Understanding societal changes in prevailing forms of tolerance is difficult given changes in our understanding of the 'other' (whether that be white, non-white, immigrant, straight or gay) over time.

Individuals experience a range of tolerances which may be understood as a highly contextual set of related and unrelated attitudes covering a wide range of situations. This distinction between different types of tolerance has been noted in comparative studies. Halman (1994) reports on the results of Eurbarometer surveys across EU member states which seek to gauge attitudes towards 'foreigners'. In the 1988 survey, 37 per cent of those surveyed thought that there were too many people of a foreign nationality living in their country whilst 33 per cent thought there were too many of another race, and 29 per cent too many of another religion. There were substantial differences in responses across countries, but a correspondence between responses relating to foreign nationals and other races. Most likely to believe there were too many foreign nationals in their country were respondents from (in descending order) Belgium, the UK, France, West Germany and Denmark.[1] Least likely (in ascending order) were those from Ireland, Spain, Portugal and the Netherlands. Most likely to believe that there were too many from other races were respondents from (in descending order) West Germany, the UK, France and Belgium and least likely from (in ascending order) Ireland, Portugal, Spain and the Netherlands. The Danish respondents were most likely to be concerned about the numbers from other religions and cultures, but least likely to be concerned about the numbers from different social classes. In the 1988 data there is a close correspondence between the proportion in each country believing that there are too many 'foreigners' and the proportion saying that their lives were disturbed by their presence, although it was the other 'races' which were perceived as most disturbing to quality of life rather than the foreign nationals.

The 1993 survey showed considerable changes in levels of intolerance in a number of countries, with declines in West Germany but an overall increase in most countries. Most marked were the increases in Denmark where the proportions finding the presence of foreigners 'disturbing' rose in respect of other nationals (from 10 to 21 per cent), other races (from 13 to 20 per cent) and other religions (from 15 to 19 per cent). By 1993 the Danish respondents were far more likely than those in other countries to be disturbed by those of another religion (39 per cent as against 19 per cent in the next highest country – Belgium) and most likely overall to be bothered by people of different nationalities, races or religions. However, the European Values Survey (EVS) – which asks respondents whether they dislike having different categories of people as neighbours – shows Danes to be the most tolerant as regards such groups as 'drinkers', 'drug addicts' and 'political extremists', suggesting that it is quite possible to combine intra-group 'permissiveness' with closure towards foreign cultures. The EVS data for 1981 and 1990 show increases in levels of tolerance in the UK, West Germany, the Netherlands and Ireland, and decreases in Belgium, Denmark, France and Italy.

These data suggest interesting regional variations in attitudes, with southern Europe coming off apparently better in relation to tolerance than northern Europe, but does not tell us as much as might be expected about how far different national groups are, as it were, 'inherently' or culturally prone to intolerance. Levels of discomfort with foreigners appear to be quite 'situational' as they correspond closely to actual levels of immigration and to perceptions of difficulties arising from the presence of immigrants. They also change rapidly from one period to another (presumably in response to actual circumstantial events – like unification in Germany, which initially at least seems to have had a positive effect – or to political climate shifts). They may therefore tell us very little, for instance, about whether one national population will respond more intolerantly than another to the presence of a given proportion of 'foreigners' and under otherwise similar circumstances. It should also be noted that although the proportions feeling discomforted by foreigners have risen across EU countries, the vast majority still say that they are not disturbed by their presence. In so much as intolerance appears to have risen, and during a period of rising levels of education, we may conclude from this analysis that it is wise to be cautious about assuming any direct effect of average education levels on aggregate levels of tolerance. If there are such effects they may be overwhelmed by other, more powerful contextual effects.

Social capital, community cohesion and tolerance

Recent theories of what might be called 'micro-cohesion' (the cohesion of small groups or communities) – particularly theories of social capital and community cohesion – make explicit links between education, micro-cohesion and tolerance. In social capital theory, participation in local associations (which is correlated with educational attainment) produces localized and – eventually – generalized trust which is in turn correlated with higher levels of tolerance. Although tolerance is not automatically created by the generation of social capital it can be considered to be one of the positive externalities, or over-spills of social capital formation. In *Bowling Alone* (2000), Putnam provides a number of empirical illustrations of the relationship between social capital and higher levels of tolerance (Putnam 2000, pp. 354–6). However, even given Putnam's positive spin on social capital, he provides a number of important caveats to the assumption that mutuality in small groups will eventually lead to tolerance.

First, and somewhat disingenuously given the overall tenor of *Bowling Alone*, Putnam distances himself from a 'kumbaya' interpretation of social capital theory. Participation in civic associations does not automatically lead to social solidarity between groups. Indeed, in a number of cases the creation of social capital within in-groups, as for instance in racist organizations, is recognized to be anathema to tolerance. As Putnam (2000, p. 355) points out, bridging social capital (between groups) is important to the generation of wider societal tolerance. Given systemic racial inequality, one may also add that the formation of linking social capital (between individuals with different hierarchical positions) might also be important in this respect. Unlike the formation of bonding social capital (which is synonymous with associational membership in Putnam's analysis), the formation of bridging and linking social capitals is much less well articulated. The relationship between social capital and tolerance in Putnam's theory is therefore tenuous. Associational membership is suggestive of the generation of trust, but tolerance requires a set of alternative conditions that are poorly specified in the theory.

Additionally, although education may be conductive to associational membership a number of recent studies suggest that there may be limits as to its ability to increase societal tolerance. Firstly, individuals may base their educational participations around the exclusion of other groups. This may apply to attendance at school (Ball 2003), but even in adult education individuals might orientate their participation in order to foster social exclusion (Preston 2004). Additionally, although the social-psychological evidence points to a direct association between greater levels of education and increased tolerance in the general population in some countries, for specific entrenched groups education may be less effective. A recent study in the UK using the NCDS (National Child Development Study – a representative cohort study of individuals born in 1958) showed that individuals who scored extremely highly on scales for racism and authoritarianism did not significantly change their views following participation in adult education (Preston and Feinstein 2004).

Therefore, even in Putnam's theory of social capital the presence of group solidarity does not necessarily indicate that tolerance will result. Furthermore, it is indeterminate as to whether tolerance will be a positive outcome of social capital formation. In fact, social capital formation can often be seen to work against tolerance without the existence of further bridging and linking networks between groups.

Social cohesion and tolerance: close relations?

Whereas Putnam suggests that social capital and tolerance are connected in modern societies, historically theories of social cohesion have generally been less concerned with the question of tolerance. This is partly due to the particular historical provenance of such theories. As argued in the introduction, the concept of social cohesion originates in nineteenth-century sociology and political economy at a time when the over-riding concern was with how to maintain social order and how to build integrated polities in the new nation-states undergoing the fragmenting effects of industrialization and social transformation. Tolerance was not generally high on the list of political priorities in such societies and, indeed, the process of state building often implied a determined suppression of particularistic identities in the quest for social integration – as, for instance, in the French revolutionary and postrevolutionary opposition to the use of local dialects and languages in France (Weber 1979). The Jacobin, Saint-Just, for instance, famously declared in his attack on old idioms and particularisms in Year 11 of the French Revolution that 'Federalism and superstition speak in bas-breton; the emigrés and hatred of the Republic speak in German' (Green 1999, p. 162) and this attitude of suspicion toward the local and different was not uncommon in the following half-century in many countries in the early stages of nation-building.

The concern to achieve social integration in the face of the disruptive and fragmenting effects of industrialization and the new division of labour often rendered localism and 'diversity' problematic for many nineteenth-century thinkers. Seminal theorists such as Marx, Weber, Spencer and Durkheim each had different perspectives on what social cohesion meant and how it could be achieved, but none of them laid any particular stress in their theories on the importance of tolerance for cultural and religious diversity to the building of social solidarity, whether the latter was seen in terms of state or class. Marx's internationalism was clearly more deep-seated, but for most social theorists social cohesion was understood in terms of a putatively unitary and homogenous nation-state, without consideration given to questions of cultural diversity. Durkheim was notable for his support of Dreyfus, the falsely accused Jewish army officer, during the notorious Dreyfus Affair in France, but for all his altruistic opposition to manifestations of racism in French political life, his theories of social solidarity and common values had little to say about cultural diversity. The same is true for Talcott Parsons, the heir to a particular line in Durkheimian thought, who saw social integration as taking place through '... *the system of norms*, taking shape in a civic and political culture within the framework of *stable institutions and a modern state*' (Gough and Olofsson 1999, p. 2; emphasis added). The coexistence of separate cultural institutions or value sets was not an integral part of Parsonian theory.

It is only in later writings that we find mention of *intolerance* as representing a central aspect of social cohesion. Much of this is linked to the post-1968 focus on identity politics and cultural diversity which loomed large in post-modern and post-colonial writings and, in particular, those which examined the construction of the 'Other' in social discourses

(Hall and du Guy 1996; Said 1978). These and other writings have certainly placed questions of racism, xenophobia, difference and diversity more at the centre of political debates about social inclusion and social cohesion. However, theorists of social cohesion have still found it difficult to integrate these issues into their theoretical frameworks and major theorists of social cohesion still leave out questions of tolerance and diversity altogether. Indeed, in a recent survey on social cohesion in the UK, Lockwood (1999) does not consider tolerance as an indicator.

There are clearly a number of reasons for this absence. One, as indicated, is that classical theories of social cohesion have largely ignored the question. Another is that social cohesion theory arguably has an inbuilt tendency towards a structural functionalism that overemphasizes issues of value consensus and structural integration often to the point where considerations of diversity, conflict and change are ignored or simply categorized as dysfunctional, as in the writings of Mortenson (1999). A third reason may also be found in the apparent fact that 'tolerance' is indeed a rather different social property from those characteristics of 'trust' and 'civic co-operation' which are generally taken to be principal measures of social cohesion.

This theoretical failure to integrate notions of diversity, conflict and tolerance into social cohesion theory is not one which we can rectify here, but it should be noted that it has highly disabling consequences for our understanding of what social cohesion means under modern social conditions and how it can be achieved. Most notably, it leads to weaknesses in both synchronic and diachronic forms of explanations since, on the one hand, it leaves a theoretical lacuna around the questions of inter-community relations, which are at the heart of any understanding of social cohesion and, on the other, it blocks an understanding of the processes by which cohesive societies develop, since these precisely involve an understanding of how societal conflicts, whether they relate to class, ethnicity, religion or culture, are instrumental in creating the conditions for enhanced societal cohesion. On the most cursory historical examination it is clear that societal cohesion is never a fully achieved state but rather a continual process of becoming and un-becoming; a dialectical process where greater social cohesion emerges, exceptionally, at certain points, from its opposite: social division and conflict.

Our purpose here is not to theorize these relations, however, but simply to point out that the 'tolerance' – and related conceptions of 'difference' and the 'Other' – does not fit neatly into the cosy syndrome of 'positive' characteristics associated with social capital. On the contrary, when considered in a societal perspective, tolerance can often be seen to be in tension with other aspects of social cohesion, so that in fact the nature of the relationships between tolerance and other social cohesion attributes may well be the key to defining the different forms of social cohesion that can be found in real societies. Clearly one can have countries which are relatively culturally homogenous, as is often argued in the case of the Nordic countries, where a degree of social cohesion is achieved in spite of a level of intolerance to minority cultures and where that intolerance sets the limits of social cohesion. On the other hand, there are countries which have been more culturally heterogeneous historically and which are better able to tolerate diversity, as is sometimes claimed for Spain, but where greater inequalities and lower levels of trust set the limits to social cohesion. Clearly we need to think in terms of different forms of social cohesion, constituted by different configurations of social relations, institutions and dominant attitudes and beliefs.

Education inequality, tolerance and social cohesion

Given that much current policy discussion about social cohesion, at least in continental Europe, focuses on questions of income and welfare distribution, we may have expected to find a relationship between educational inequality and tolerance. Educational inequality leads to markedly different labour market (not to mention civic) outcomes and may be expected to lead to lower levels of tolerance, particularly if, as Gowricharn (2002) suggests for Nordic countries, this puts pressure on the welfare systems. However, we did not find such a relationship.

As we have shown in chapters 1 and 2 there is a close relationship between educational inequality and many measures of social cohesion such as trust and crime. We were therefore surprised to find that there were not the same relationships between educational equality and forms of tolerance. In chapter 1 we found that there was a low correlation between the measure of educational inequality used and the measure for tolerance ($-.06$, not significant even at the 10 per cent level). We tried subsequent modelling exercises using changes in tolerance from the ISSP and measures of educational inequality from the TWF dataset (see chapter 2) and again found no significant associations, even at the 10 per cent level of significance. There are two possible reasons why there is no significant relationship between educational inequality and tolerance as compared to other variables. First, it might be that tolerance is not part of a cluster of 'social cohesion' elements. Secondly, the mechanisms by which education influences tolerance may be different from

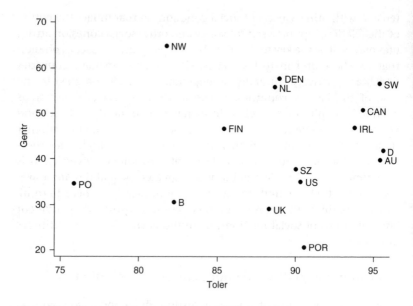

Figure 3.1   Tolerance and general trust in WVS

Note: Pearson correlation: 0.1, not significant.

those whereby it influences social cohesion. In other words, elements of education other than educational inequality are more important.

As discussed above, the relationship between tolerance and other components of social cohesion may be questioned. Therefore, the mechanism by which we have suggested that educational inequality impacts upon social cohesion may not be found in the case of tolerance. Using the dataset of 15 countries described in chapter 1 we found that there was no correlation between tolerance and general trust and a negative relationship between tolerance and civic co-operation.

Figure 3.1 shows the relationship between tolerance and general trust for a selection of countries in the 1996 World Values Survey (WVS). As can be seen, there is no positive or negative association between tolerance and general trust. Particular countries and country groupings are of interest in terms of the relationship between tolerance and trust. For example, Canada and Sweden show here high levels of trust and tolerance but Norway (NW) is a Nordic country with remarkably high levels of trust but, in comparison with other countries, low levels of tolerance. Conversely, the UK has higher levels of tolerance but low levels of general trust, like the USA.

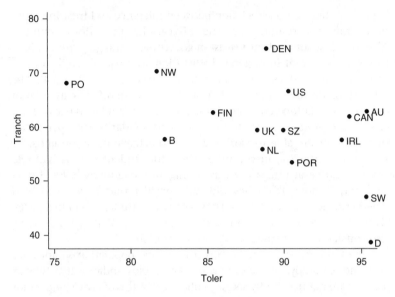

Figure 3.2 Tolerance and civic co-operation in WVS

Note: Pearson correlation: −0.56, significant at 5% level.

Figure 3.2 indicates that the relationship between tolerance and other indicators of social cohesion may actually be perverse. Comparing tolerance with a measure of what is called civic co-operation (the percentage of people who believe that it is never justified to cheat on public transport) shows that the higher the level of tolerance, the lower the level of civic co-operation (Pearson correlation −0.56, significant at the 5 per cent level). Countries with low levels of tolerance (Poland, PO and Norway, NW) have relatively high levels of civic co-operation whereas countries which score high on tolerance (such as Sweden, SW and Portugal, POR) have lower levels of civic co-operation. With a cross-sectional dataset such as this (from the 1996 WVS) it is not possible to speculate regarding causality. However, what is evident is that tolerant societies are not automatically those with high forms of civic co-operation.

However, we conducted a similar exercise using data from the IEA Civic Education Survey of 14-year-olds across countries (more details of this survey and its items are given in the next chapter). As can be seen in

Figure 3.3 there is no association between tolerance and trust in institutions from the responses of the 14-year-olds in various countries. Although institutional trust (trust in government and government institutions) is different from general trust (literally trust of people 'in general'), tolerance does not appear to be associated with 'trust'. One interesting finding from the IEA study was a significant association (Pearson correlation 0.58, significant at the 5 per cent level) between tolerance and student perceptions of student solidarity (the perception that students are able to work together to achieve common ends). As shown in Figure 3.4, in countries where the student sample had relatively negative attitudes towards immigrants (Germany, GER; Latvia, LAT; and Estonia, EST) they did not consider that they could work together to achieve joint aims. However, where students had higher levels of tolerance towards immigrants (Cyprus, CYP; Portugal, POR) they also considered that student solidarity was high.

These findings, from the WVS, with a whole population sample, and from the IEA study, with a sample of 14-year-olds, indicate that tolerant societies are not necessarily socially cohesive in terms of civic co-operation or trust. Our findings are indicative, rather than causal, but there seems

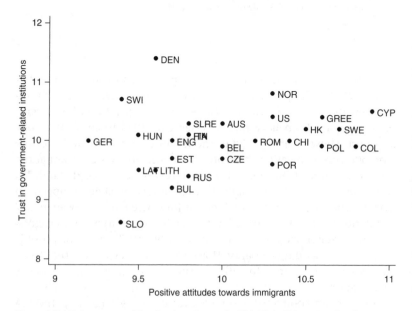

Figure 3.3   Tolerance and institutional trust in IEA Civic Education Study

Note: Pearson correlation: 0.24, not significant.

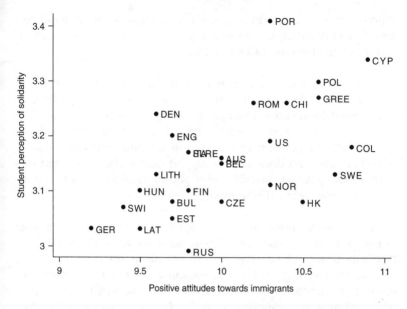

Figure 3.4 Tolerance and student solidarity in IEA Civic Education Study

Note: Pearson correlation: 0.58, significant at the 5% level.

to be little reason from these illustrations to suppose that tolerance can be simply equated with other measures of social cohesion at a national level. One interesting, and possibly contradictory, finding is the relationship between tolerance and student solidarity in the IEA. Here there is some evidence that there is a relationship between tolerance and a form of 'community cohesion' (in terms of the 'student community' of each country). As this is a survey of 14-year-olds, it is difficult to make inferences that this is indicative of, or would eventually become, social cohesion as envisaged at the level of the nation. However, this might indicate that there is some evidence for social capital, or community cohesion perspectives, that relate tolerance and 'micro-cohesion' in certain settings.

Education and tolerance: possible mechanisms

In an exhaustive review of the literature on the relationship between education and political outcomes, Emler and Frazer (1999) contend that the evidence does point towards higher levels of education being associated with greater levels of tolerance for many countries. The extent of generalization in these findings must be acknowledged, though, and considered historically there are glaring counter-examples. As Abramson and Inglehart (1994, p. 800) remind us:

> ... the assertion that education has some inherent tendency to instill democratic values does not stand up in historical perspective. In Germany during the Weimar era, for example, the National Socialists won student elections in eight universities, at a time when the Nazis won only 18 per cent of the vote in national elections ... Today, higher education does tend to support democratic values, but this relationship reflects specific historical conditions and is not an automatic consequence of education.

Contrary 'specific historical conditions' have also been evident in more recent examples of relatively well-educated societies, like Serbia and Northern Ireland, which have not been notable for tolerance. Clearly, at the societal level, high skill or qualification *levels* are not necessarily sufficient to guarantee a tolerant society. In some societies the content of education may be as important as the levels of qualification achieved or the ways in which these qualifications are distributed. As we shall see in chapter 4, a strongly nationalistic and patriotic curriculum has very mixed associations with social cohesion outcomes and might be particularly detrimental to tolerance in some contexts. However, even if there are powerful situational determinants of tolerance there might still be a role for education in increasing certain types of tolerance.

In a wide-ranging review of research for several European countries, Hagendoorn and Nekuee (1999) collected evidence concerning education and racial tolerance based largely on micro-data. According to Hagendoorn (1999), there are two main causal mechanisms by which education may lead to increased racial tolerance. First, education leads to increased cognitive skills involving enhanced abilities to categorize, understand causal relationships and perceive states of the world. Hence individuals will be increasingly able to understand that potentially racist statements, for example blaming migrants for unemployment, are based on faulty reasoning. Secondly, individuals might adopt racially tolerant values as part of socialization through schooling. There is much research evidence for a number of contemporary societies, according to Hagendoorn, that years and levels of schooling have a large impact upon the stating of racist views, although there is little evidence to suggest that particular interventions or types of curriculum lead to a reduction in racism (Hagendoorn 1999, p. 5). In addition, there is evidence that courses which stress individuals' critical capacities seem to have a greater effect than other courses (Hagendoorn 1999, p. 6).

Given the quantity of research evidence supporting this second mechanism, Hagendoorn (1999) admits that there remain a number of paradoxes in the education–racism literature. For example, despite rising education levels in the US and many education interventions aimed at increasing racial tolerance there is evidence that US youth are as racist as they were after the Second World War. Hagendoorn explains that rising levels of education may simply moderate the expression of racism. Although educated individuals may not wish to state racist views in public (or in a survey), they may be racist in their private lives and in informally supporting discriminatory practices. Pettigrew and Meertens (1995) refer to this as a difference between blatant and subtle forms of racism amongst those of different social classes and educational levels. From a longitudinal survey of evidence from the Netherlands, Verbeck and Scheepers (1999) show that those with intermediate education are not likely to be blatantly racist but are more likely to be subtly racist than those with lower levels of education.

There are a number of differences across societies in the influence of education on tolerance and supposedly related attitudes. In some countries (such as Italy) the influence of education on tolerant values has been found to be small and indirect (Peri 1999) whereas in others (France, Germany) large effects have been identified (Haegel 1999; Winkler 1999). Moreover, the relationship between racial intolerance and other personality characteristics (namely authoritarianism) differs from country to country. Peri (1999) finds that in Italy the influence of education on tolerance is indirect, operating through channels of conformism, traditional values and professional employment. In a French study, Haegel (1999) examines the influence of education on both authoritarian values and racial tolerance. She finds a positive association of education with tolerance, although the effects are weaker for those with vocational qualifications. Interestingly, there are different levels of ideological consistency depending on the individual's level of education. For those individuals with low levels of education, there is little relationship between authoritarianism and racial tolerance despite the fact that those in this position are likely to feel insecure about the future. Although individuals with higher levels of academic education are more likely to be tolerant, those who are racially intolerant are highly likely to hold authoritarian attitudes.

As Haegel (1999) shows, individuals with different levels of education may exhibit different clusters of values. She relates this to the French education system and the 'coercive flip-side' of the French model of assimilation, which downplays ethnic differences in the classroom (Haegel 1999, p. 34). Similarly, for Germany, Winkler (1999) shows that there are different pathways for racism between individuals with different levels of education, although he arrives at different conclusions from Haegel concerning the relevance of authoritarianism. Through structural equation modelling, Winkler (1999, p. 126) demonstrates that there are different pathways explaining racism for highly and less highly educated people. He suggests that sociocultural insecurity, comprising right-wing views, national pride and authoritarianism, is a powerful predictor of racism for those with lower levels of education, whereas for those with higher levels of education authoritarianism is not significantly related to racism. Winkler's 1999 study additionally provides some support for sociocultural insecurity being a particular predictor of racism for those with lower levels of education. There is a difference in the role which authoritarianism plays in the formation of racism amongst those with low levels of education in the two countries.

In terms of the cognitive mechanisms by which education influences racism, De Witte (1999) distinguishes between various forms of racism. He refers to these different categories as general racism (negative attitudes towards migrants), biological racism (a belief in the hereditary superiority of one's own race) and cultural and economic racism (a belief that the cultural habits of migrants differ and that they expose nationals to resource competition). It is this last form that De Witte refers to as 'everyday racism' as it is the least ideologically formed and the most prevalent form. Although 'everyday racism' has shown little change in Belgium over time, it is at a higher level than in other European countries. De Witte (1999) contends that cognitive capacity is a strong mechanism in the reduction of everyday racism. He argues that research for Belgium (Gavaert 1993) and for the Netherlands (Raajmakers 1993) has shown that those following vocational courses are more likely to exhibit everyday racism and that this may be due to the greater attention paid to cognitive skills in Belgian academic education, although it might also be argued that this is a class effect, since those following vocational courses are likely to come from less affluent social groups and thus are more likely to perceive competition over scarce resources. However, De Witte (1999, p. 68) does not necessarily reject the socialization function of education and believes that there is a difference in the emphasis placed on values in the academic track (De Witte 1999, p. 69). Again, the mechanisms through which education influences tolerance are contextualized by the specific features of a national education system.

In the debate concerning the influence of education on tolerance, there may be little to choose between whether education influences values or cognitive skills. Values are obviously important, as are national characteristics and the nature of the education system in each country. So too is the role of the curriculum in building individual resources. It may be helpful, then, to see values and cognitive resources as jointly part of a process of formation of racial tolerance. Sniderman and Gould (1999) see the process of racial tolerance as the interaction of values acquired through socialization, values invoked at the moment of choice, and cognitive sophistication. Education has an influence not only on long-term value formation, but also on the exercise of values at the moment of choosing whether to express a racist opinion or action. In addition, reasoning is involved in both the long-term formation and short-term exercising of values. However, as Halman (1994) shows, rising absolute education levels have not led to an increase in racial tolerance. Education does not remove the individual from society – individual values are embedded in a social and national context.

Conclusion: tolerance, inequality and beyond

We have shown in this chapter that tolerance is a complex and multi-faceted variable and that there are no straightforward relationships at the national level between tolerance and other aspects of social cohesion, despite the associations found by social capital theorists at the individual level. Classical social cohesion theory does not posit any specific relationships between tolerance and social cohesion and cross-country statistical analysis can show few significant correlations between tolerance measures and other measures of social cohesion. Tolerance would appear to be something of a 'rogue' variable in social cohesion and, as our illustrations show, not necessarily connected with wider social trust or civic co-operation.

In terms of the effects of education on tolerance, the relationships observed across countries would seem to be equally complex and context-bound. Even though there may be similar educational mechanisms which lead to increases in some forms of tolerance cross-nationally, the ways in which these mechanisms operate within national contexts are quite specific. There is no universal relationship between levels of education in society and levels of tolerance which operates independently of wider social contexts. At the same time, there is little hard empirical evidence at present that educational inequality affects tolerance. However, we should certainly not completely foreclose this debate on account of the current lack of statistical evidence since there remain quite strong theoretical arguments which suggest that relationships may exist.

Future research, for instance, may well find it useful to consider the material as well as attitudinal pathways through which education may influence tolerance in society. One possible approach is through what sociologists of ethnic relations have referred to as 'realistic conflict theory' which dates back originally to the work of the black American Marxist Oliver Cromwell Cox in the 1940s (Cox 1970). Although sometimes rightly criticized as class reductionist, realistic conflict theory, in its more sophisticated forms, does provide a theoretical framework for examining educational impacts on racism and intolerance in terms of structural inequalities (such as educational inequalities) rather than in terms of individual moral deficits.

Verbeck and Scheepers (1999) offer a recent elaboration of the theory. They argue that 'A central assumption of realistic conflict theory is that socioeconomic competition for scarce resources between groups such as ethnic groups leads to the formation of negative attitudes of the other groups. The competition may be concrete such as in housing or labour, or abstract such as in culture, power and status' (Verbeck and Scheepers 1999, p. 179). According to realistic conflict theory, individuals from lower social classes and with lower levels of education are more likely to face real or perceived conflicts over resources. Within this perspective, education systems could be seen to influence the formation of tolerant and intolerant attitudes in two ways. First, educational systems that produce more unequal educational outcomes are likely to produce societies which are materially more unequal and where there is the kind of particularly intense competition amongst certain groups for scarce resources which may breed intolerant attitudes. Secondly, more unequal education systems will produce groups of less educated individuals whose relative lack of 'cognitive resources' and of 'protective' values may lead them to be more prone to making the false attributions of blame over resource scarcity which realistic conflict theory suggests may serve to foment racist attitudes.

The theory clearly has its limitations. Historically, racism has often developed amongst the most affluent and powerful groups in society who had limited reason to feel competition over scarce resources with immigrant or ethnic minority groups. They may, of course, have been in exploitative relations of power with members of these groups, in their positions as slave owners, colonial administrators, or low-paying employers, which it may have been expedient to rationalize through racist ideologies (Roediger 1991), but such explanations would hardly seem to be sufficiently encompassing to account for racism amongst more affluent social strata as a whole. Similarly, realistic conflict theory has difficulties explaining the range of attitudes at the other end of the social class spectrum, where sections of the 'native' working class in many societies, while in potential material conflict with immigrants and minorities, have not developed hostile or racist views. Within education in contemporary England, for instance, working-class students frequently resist, rather than accept, racist doctrines (Gillborn 1995).

These limitations lead us to be critical of 'left realist' perspectives that focus on resource conflicts without considering the complex processes of differential value formation and political socialization amongst different sections of each social class and how these affect social responses in different societal contexts, whether these be at work or in the housing market or in different welfare arenas. Nevertheless, it is quite possible to conceive of a less deterministic version of realistic con-flict theory, allowing more saliency to processes of representation and identity formation, which could contribute to the understanding of how racist and intolerant attitudes and behaviours develop. Within such a framework it is then possible to see how educational inequality may have impacts on 'tolerance'. This could be both through its effects on resource distribution and the intensity of conflict over resources, and in terms of the distribution of cognitive resources and values which will shape how individuals and groups interpret such situations, and whether they do this in ways that engender racism and intolerance.

4
Ethno-Linguistic Diversity, Civic Attitudes and Citizenship Education

This chapter focuses on the cognitive and affective aspects of social cohesion; that is on the opinions, attitudes and identities of people regarding the society they live in. It seeks to explore whether these attitudes are linked to the degree of ethno-cultural diversity of a country, and how they relate to various elements of citizenship education.

The point of departure for the first part of this question is the rather provocative argument regarding identity and democracy developed by Tamir (1993), Miller (1995) and Canovan (1996). These theorists, often referred to as liberal nationalists, contend that liberal democracy functions best within the framework of a nation-state. In their view, a system of common democratic values and institutions is always grounded in a distinct national culture and is not easily established and maintained across diverse cultures. Canovan (1996), for instance, criticizes political thinkers writing about liberalism, social justice and democratic theory for failing to see that they tacitly assume the existence of a homogeneous nation-state. Miller (1995), perhaps the most vocal advocate of liberal nationalism, argues that a unified national culture is a precondition for one of the main principles of liberal democracy – social justice (that is, welfare policies aimed at a certain redistribution of resources). Social justice policies require substantial sacrifices from the taxpaying citizenry. People, he argues, are only prepared to make these sacrifices if they consider the unknown beneficiaries as part of 'us', as persons willing to reciprocate the donors once they are in need of state support. This far-reaching trust in the beneficiaries can only happen in situations where donors and recipients share a common national identity, Miller claims. In his view, other social identities are not able to provide the same level of deep, trust-generating bonds.

Huntington (2004) also stresses the importance of a single national culture for democratic government. In *Who Are We?: America's National*

Identity and the Challenges It Faces he argues that the typical American political values of liberty, equality before the law, individual responsibility and laissez-faire (called 'the Creed' by Huntington) originate from Anglo-Protestant culture. He warns that 'a multicultural America will, in time, become a multi-creedal America, with groups with different cultures espousing distinctive political values and principles rooted in their particular cultures' (Huntington 2004, p. 340). Public education, according to liberal nationalists, has an important role to play in fostering national identity (and thus indirectly in enhancing solidarity and social trust) by offering a national curriculum that stresses national heritage and shared values and that is taught in a common language to diverse social and ethnic groups.

The liberal nationalist argument raises a host of interesting questions for this study. Would the ethno-cultural composition of a state's population also matter for social cohesion? In liberal nationalist thinking it would because people are presumed to trust members of their own national group more than others, and interpersonal trust is considered to be a vital component of social cohesion, as we have seen in chapter 1. Would countries with relatively homogeneous populations by extension also exhibit higher levels of institutional trust and civic co-operation, some of the other elements of the social cohesion syndrome identified in that chapter? If a relation can indeed be established, does education then have a role to play in decreasing cultural diversity and thereby indirectly promoting social cohesion? To put it more provocatively, should education abandon the promotion of multiculturalism and (re)instate monolingual education and a single standardized curriculum? Would a renewed emphasis in schools on the core values of the nation and on the key events and heroes of national history enhance trust, engagement and tolerance within national boundaries? Does patriotic education contribute equally to these civic attitudes or does it impact differently on them? What is, for instance, the relation between patriotic education and tolerance?

The first half of this chapter examines different elements of national identity and their effects on social cohesion. Using ethnographic data and international survey data on social attitudes the analysis will first establish the degree of ethno-linguistic homogeneity of national populations and their levels of national pride and will then relate these to measures of social cohesion. The analyses of this section will be performed on aggregated country-level data.

The second part of the chapter turns to education and explores how various thematic components of citizenship education relate to civic attitudes and tolerance among youngsters. Our analyses will make use of data from the comprehensive IEA Civic Education Study.

National identity and social cohesion

Despite a wealth of theoretical literature on liberal nationalism supporting, refuting or refining the argument (see, for instance: Kymlicka and Straehle 1999; Patten 1999; Moore 2001; Abizadeh 2004) there have been remarkably few studies examining the relation between national identity and democracy or social cohesion at the empirical level. This has no doubt partly to do with the difficulty in measuring the elusive concept of national identity. There are no criteria that *all* national identities use in supporting their claim of distinctiveness. Some use political symbols like a constitution, a monarchy or certain slogans (*liberté, égalité, fraternité*) to stress their singularity whereas others rely on cultural traits (language, religion or customs) or ascriptive features (race, descent). Some identities differ on many markers while others are distinguishable only by state allegiance (for example: the Walloons and the French; Chileans and Argentineans). Moreover, like other social phenomena, national identities are subject to change. In the twentieth century, for instance, many cultural groups evolved from dormant communities to independent nations (Slovaks, Ukrainians, Finns, Eritreans). On the other hand some strong regional identities in the early 1900s – or 'ethnies' to use Smith's term (Smith 1995) – have not made it into nations (Bavarians, Occitans, Bretons).

Nonetheless, of the many markers that can be used to underpin national identity, language is of paramount importance. Indeed, there are relatively few cases where a certain national identity is centrally based on more than one language (the Swiss and Canadians are oft-cited exceptions). Moreover, liberal nationalist theory itself assigns great value to a common language as a mechanism facilitating both a unified national identity and the democratic process. An active democracy, it is argued, requires collective political discussions, and these are only feasible if participants speak the same language. Thus, for a democracy to be truly participatory and 'grassroots' in nature, politics should be monolingual and in the vernacular since 'the average citizen only feels comfortable debating political issues in their own tongue' (Kymlicka 1999, p. 70).

A measure that establishes the degree of linguistic and ethnic diversity in a country is the Ethno-Linguistic Fractionalization (ELF). It takes both the number of ethnic groups and the size of each group into account with values approaching one denoting high diversity and values close to zero denoting homogeneity. To calculate the ELF value for a country, one can use either several criteria to define ethnic groups (racial distinctions, ancestry, religion, language) or just one. We chose the variety of the ELF that identifies ethnic groups only by language as this is the crucial cleavage in liberal nationalist philosophy. This variety thus essentially measures the linguistic diversity in a country.[1]

The ELF has mostly been used by economists interested in the effect of ethnic heterogeneity on economic performance in developing countries. Both Easterly and Levine (1997) and Masters and McMillan (1999) have, for instance, found a strong negative relationship between ethno-linguistic diversity and economic growth in African countries. Interestingly, Collier (1998) observes that this relationship only holds in countries with non-democratic regimes. In democratic countries the negative effect of heterogeneity on economic growth almost disappears, leading him to conclude that 'the lack of political rights is economically ruinous in ethnically highly fractionalized societies' (ibid., p. 8). He explains the beneficial influence of democracy by pointing out that democratic institutions have the potential to pacify costly disputes between ethnic groups. Heterogeneous societies, he argues, might thus benefit more from democracy than homogeneous societies because the need for ethnic conflict resolution is not as prominent in the latter. In addition, he finds ethno-linguistic heterogeneity to be correlated with the risk of violent conflict but not in a monotonic way. Societies most likely to engender armed conflict are those with middle levels of ethnic diversity. Highly fractionalized African countries are actually more peaceful than homogeneous ones, he observes. The explanation, in his view, might be that the co-ordination cost of rebellion is much higher in heterogeneous societies (agreements have to be made across ethnic boundaries) than in homogeneous ones. Collier's conclusions clearly contradict the liberal nationalist argument. Instead of seeing democracy as a variable affected by ethno-linguistic heterogeneity, he regards it as an important independent condition modifying the effect of ethno-linguistic diversity. In similar vein, it can be argued that democracy is the crucial condition keeping multinational Canada, Belgium and Switzerland intact, while the lack of it caused the multicultural Soviet Union, Yugoslavia and Czechoslovakia to disintegrate once the communist party lost its monopoly on power at the end of the 1980s (Moore 2001). Thus, both the causal direction of the link between democracy and ethno-linguistic heterogeneity and the nature of the relation between heterogeneity and armed conflict (and therefore social cohesion) are very much open to debate.

Before examining the relationship between ethno-linguistic heterogeneity and social cohesion, we will operationalize the concept of social cohesion and provide a quick scan of social cohesion levels in a number of countries. Following Green, Preston and Sabates (2003), we took two items on trust (interpersonal and institutional) and two items on civic co-operation from the 1995 wave of the World Values Survey (WVS) to represent social cohesion:

Interpersonal trust: 'Generally speaking, would you say that most people can be trusted or that you can't be too careful in dealing with people?'
(1) Most people can be trusted, (2) Can't be too careful, (3) Don't know

Institutional trust: 'I am going to name a number of organizations. For each one, could you tell me how much confidence you have in them?' (Parliament)
(1) A great deal, (2) Quite a lot, (3) Not very much, (4) None at all

Civic co-operation: 'Please tell me for each of the following statements whether you think it can always be justified, never be justified, or something in between.'
Never justifiable 1 / 2 / 3 ... 9 / 10 always justifiable
(2 items) *Avoiding a fare on public transport*
Cheating on taxes if you have a chance

Table 4.1 presents the aggregated country scores on these items, as well as the ELF (i.e. ethno-linguistic diversity), World Bank data on Gross National Product per capita, and another WVS item tapping national pride ('How proud are you to be [nationality]?' (1) very proud, (2) quite proud, (3) not very proud, (4) not at all proud). We included national pride to examine whether a subjective indicator of national identity relates differently to social cohesion than an objective one (ELF). Perhaps the most noticeable result in this table is the difference between developed nations and other nations on interpersonal trust, the former being generally more trusting of other people than the latter (compare, for instance, Norway's 64.8 per cent to Brazil's meagre 2.8 per cent). Interpersonal trust is the exception, however, as pronounced contrasts between the developed world and other countries do not appear on the other three items of social cohesion. If we consider institutional trust, for instance, we see that the Ghanaians are the most trusting of parliament (2.44) and the Macedonians the least (0.76). The Western countries are all close to the international mean on this measure.

Table 4.1 Country aggregate scores on ELF, national pride, GNP per capita and four indicators of social cohesion

	ELF (1985)*	National pride (0–3)**	GNP per capita (1995)	Inter-personal trust (% saying most people can be trusted)	Institu-tional trust (0–3)**	Never allowed to cheat on transport (%)***	Never allowed to cheat on tax (%)***
Developed countries							
West Germany	.14	1.54	—	39.9	1.18	38.5	39.5
United Kingdom	.39	—	18,700	29.1	—	—	—
Switzerland	.59	1.93	40,630	37.8	1.33	58.4	52.5
Spain	.46	2.55	13,580	28.7	1.20	66.2	67.7
USA	.42	2.76	26,980	35.6	1.19	66.6	73.6
Finland	.13	2.33	20,580	46.9	1.21	62.4	57.1
Sweden	.14	2.34	23,750	56.6	1.41	46.9	48.9
Norway	.06	2.40	31,250	64.8	1.74	69.9	47.3
South Korea	.00	—	9,700	30.3	1.17	49.1	71.4
Taiwan	.27	1.82	—	41.9	1.31	58.7	63.7
Japan	.01	1.78	39,640	46.0	1.10	77.3	80.6
Australia	.44	2.70	18,720	39.9	1.19	62.8	62.0
Regional average	*.25*	*2.22*	*24,353*	*41.5*	*1.28*	*59.7*	*60.4*
Former communist countries							
East Germany	.01	1.67	—	24.3	.93	51.1	53.1
Poland	.04	2.66	2,790	16.9	1.21	67.5	54.6
Croatia	.42	2.36	3,250	23.6	1.50	26.1	36.6
Slovenia	.18	2.51	8,200	15.5	1.05	54.1	53.9
Macedonia	.51	2.58	860	7.5	.76	60.8	57.2
Bosnia	.70	2.40	—	26.9	1.60	51.7	55.9
Bulgaria	.23	2.32	1,330	23.7	1.35	59.2	63.3
Moldova	.55	2.10	920	21.9	1.23	42.1	37.6
Russia	.33	1.95	2,240	23.4	.91	32.9	42.6
Ukraine	.42	1.80	1,630	28.8	1.18	25.8	36.8
Belarus	.37	2.05	2,070	23.0	1.05	30.3	37.5
Estonia	.53	1.88	2,860	21.1	1.32	47.5	40.9
Latvia	.61	1.78	2,270	23.9	.99	25.0	30.6
Lithuania	.35	1.80	1,900	21.6	1.16	42.1	44.1
Armenia	.13	2.21	730	23.5	.95	36.4	39.9
Georgia	.49	2.48	440	21.5	1.15	45.2	49.2
Azerbaijan	.31	2.57	480	19.4	1.92	44.9	44.4
Regional average	*.36*	*2.18*	*2,131*	*21.6*	*1.19*	*43.7*	*45.8*
Asian countries							
Turkey	.26	2.70	2,780	5.5	1.35	—	—
China	.13	2.26	620	52.6	—	76.1	79.9
India	.88	2.59	340	33.0	1.67	74.5	72.1
Bangladesh	.04	2.75	240	20.5	2.17	94.0	91.7
Pakistan	.54	2.84	460	20.4	—	—	—
Philippines	.75	2.66	1,050	5.5	1.68	35.0	38.1
Regional average	*.43*	*2.63*	*915*	*22.9*	*1.72*	*69.9*	*70.5*

Table 4.1   Continued

	ELF (1985)*	National pride (0–3)**	GNP per capita (1995)	Inter-personal trust (% saying most people can be trusted)	Institu-tional trust (0–3)**	Never allowed to cheat on transport (%)***	Never allowed to cheat on tax (%)***
Latin American countries							
Dominican Republic	.10	2.67	1,464	25.2	.82	69.1	68.6
Colombia	.05	2.81	1,910	10.70	.90	49.4	72.0
Venezuela	.26	2.92	3,020	13.7	.83	72.0	70.6
Peru	.48	2.74	2,310	4.9	.85	44.3	59.5
Brazil	.07	2.46	3,640	2.8	.93	55.3	46.4
Argentina	.29	2.44	8,030	17.5	.78	62.5	72.1
Uruguay	.25	2.68	5,170	21.7	1.24	70.4	78.3
Chile	.17	2.41	4,160	21.4	1.20	56.4	62.8
Mexico	.21	2.42	3,320	26.4	1.28	48.2	52.9
Regional average	*.21*	*2.62*	*3,669*	*16.0*	*.98*	*58.6*	*64.8*
African countries							
Ghana	.69	2.91	390	22.4	2.44	65.2	74.5
Nigeria	.86	2.55	260	19.5	1.31	59.9	69.5
South Africa	.89	2.79	3,160	17.6	1.91	60.3	62.3
Regional average	*.81*	*2.75*	*1,270*	*19.8*	*1.89*	*61.8*	*68.8*
Total average	—	*2.38*	—	*25.64*	*1.26*	*54.4*	*57.1*

Notes:

* The ELF values listed here are copied from column 11 of the table in the source (Roeder 2001) and pertain to ethnic groups defined by language.

** These data are country average scores of Likert scale responses. The average scores were reversed to facilitate interpretation (0 not at all–3 a great deal).

*** The percentage of respondents in each country stating that cheating on public transport/taxes is never justifiable.

Sources: Roeder (2001) (second column); World Development Report (1997) (fourth column); World Values Survey 1990 (third and fifth to ninth columns).

On the two civic co-operation items *intra*-regional differences are in fact more prominent than *inter*-regional ones. Compare, for instance, Germany's scores (very low) to those of Spain (high), the Philippines (very low) to Bangladesh (very high), and Latvia (very low) to Bulgaria (high). National pride levels also vary substantially within the group of developed countries and that of former communist states: contrast West Germany (very low) with the USA (very high), and Latvia (very low) with Poland (high). Ethno-Linguistic Fractionalization shows considerable intra-regional variation as well. Compare Switzerland (0.59) to Norway (0.06), India (0.88) to Bangladesh (0.04), and Bosnia (0.70) to Poland (0.04).

Nonetheless, distinct regional patterns can also be discerned. As noted before, all developed countries have scores on interpersonal trust that are higher than the international mean. By contrast, with the exception of Ukraine and Bosnia, all former communist countries display lower than average scores on this measure. Most remarkable is the set of responses shown by the Latin American countries. With the exception of Mexico, they combine (much) higher than average national pride levels with (much) lower than average interpersonal and institutional trust scores. The three African nations also follow this pattern but their institutional trust scores are higher than the international mean.

In sum, social cohesion levels vary across indicators, regions, and countries within regions. A straightforward pattern cannot be identified.

We can now proceed with investigating the link between ethno-linguistic diversity and social cohesion, using Table 4.1 as the data base for our analyses. A first remarkable result is that ethno-linguistic diversity does not show a significant correlation with national pride (see Table 4.2). This is difficult for liberal nationalists to explain. They expect national pride levels to be higher in homogeneous societies as the state in these societies would be able to mobilize high levels of identification and loyalty among the population by equating itself with the dominant nation. In heterogeneous societies, by contrast, the state would by necessity have to remain culturally neutral, which in the logic of liberal nationalist theory would impede a close identification with the national level by the various cultural groups. Our finding that subjective expressions of national belonging (national pride) are not related to objective ethno-linguistic conditions in a country thus cannot be reconciled with the liberal nationalist argument, which does assume these conditions to have an impact on people's sense of unity and solidarity.

However, more embarrassing for the liberal nationalists is our finding that ethno-linguistic diversity is not meaningfully related to any of the four social cohesion indicators. Heterogeneity is negatively correlated with interpersonal trust and with the two civic cooperation items, which is in line with liberal nationalist theory, but these correlations are not significant. On top of that it also shows a significant positive relation with institutional trust, meaning that the more linguistically diverse a country the higher the level of institutional trust among its citizens. This finding is opposite to what the liberal nationalist argument would predict. Equally puzzling for the liberal nationalists is the relation between national pride and the four indicators of social cohesion. The table shows strong positive correlations of national pride with the two items of civic cooperation, which is what liberal nationalists would

Table 4.2 Correlations between ELF, GNI per capita, national pride and four indicators of social cohesion

	ELF	National pride	GNI per capita	Interpersonal trust	Institutional trust	Never allowed to cheat on transport	Never allowed to cheat on tax
ELF		.16	−.20	−.23	.33*	−.18	−.15
National pride			−.24	−.36*	.26	.45**	.50**
GNI per capita				.67**	−.01	.28	.14

Notes:
* Correlation is significant at the 0.05 level (2-tailed).
** Correlation is significant at the 0.01 level (2-tailed).
NB: the number of countries (N) in the cells ranges from 41 to 47.
Source: Table 4.1.

expect, but a negative correlation with interpersonal trust and no significant correlation with institutional trust. Thus, whether subjectively (national pride) or objectively conceived (linguistic diversity), national identity is not linked to social cohesion in any comprehensible way. National pride and linguistic diversity even show different patterns of correlations with the social cohesion items.

The high correlations between national pride and the two civic cooperation items are worth considering in more detail. Possibly, national pride and civic co-operation are both highly responsive to drastic short-term changes in a country's economic performance. It seems no coincidence, for example, that most of the post-Soviet countries, all of which experienced a severe economic crisis in the transition to a market economy, combine low levels of national pride with low levels of civic co-operation (see again Table 4.1). People in these countries may blame the state for being incompetent and indifferent to the fate of its citizens, and their identification with the state and preparedness to respect the law may dwindle accordingly. Interpersonal trust, on the other hand, might be closely associated with more structural characteristics of a society, such as the level of socioeconomic development. Notice, for instance, the strong positive correlation between GNI per capita and interpersonal trust. It must further be noted that the pronounced inter-regional differences found in Table 4.1 could well mean that the correlations between conditions may be very different from one region of the world to another.

We have to note here that our findings do not match those of Knack and Keefer (1997) in their study on social capital. Examining the very same relation and also using WVS data, they found that ethnic heterogeneity was not only a significant negative predictor of interpersonal trust but also of civic co-operation, controlling for GDP and primary and secondary education (Knack and Keefer 1997, pp. 1281, 1282).[2] They used WVS data on ethnicity to establish the degree of ethnic heterogeneity in a country (the WVS asked respondents if they identified with an ethnic group and if so with which). However, these data are highly problematic as large groups of respondents answered the question on ethnicity with 'not applicable' in 16 of the 39 countries of the survey (percentages of more than 40 per cent). Moreover, the set answers to the question differed from country to country. In some countries these answers included the category 'I feel a [nationality] citizen first, and a member of some ethnic group second', while in other countries this category was omitted. Because of these problems, we chose to employ ELF as a measure of ethno-linguistic heterogeneity.

The data for all the countries combined might also obscure a difference between advanced societies and developing countries in the impact of heterogeneity. Here the argument can run in different directions. Modernization theorists would argue that ethno-cultural groups in (post-)industrial societies have been so eroded by processes of industrialization, state penetration and assimilation that these identities have become peripheral and are destined to fade away in the near future (Deutsch 1966; Parsons 1975; Gellner 1983). Thus, for them pronounced ethno-linguistic cleavages are characteristic of pre-modern developing societies. The ethnic competition perspective, on the other hand, contends that the ethno-cultural identities that have survived state- and nation-building processes in modern societies are actually more deeply entrenched than those in developing societies. Scholars embracing this perspective see modernization as having reinforced ethno-cultural awareness by bringing ethnic groups in contact with each other and forcing them to compete for the same resources (Hannan 1979; Nielsen 1985). Gellner (1983) in fact to some extent subscribes to this perspective by pointing out that modernization and standardization need not always have resulted in assimilation and homogenization. Crucial in his view was access to the high culture of the dominant group. In cases where minorities felt excluded from this culture counter-nationalisms developed, which either led to the disintegration of states or have continued to trouble states after the Second World War.

If the modernization argument is correct, one would expect heterogeneity to have a stronger negative impact on social cohesion in developing countries than in modern societies. If the ethnic competition perspective is correct, the reverse applies. We tested these hypotheses by splitting the sample in two using a GNP per capita of US $2,500 as a cut-off point and performing correlations for each of the two groups of countries.

The results of this analysis showed that neither in poor (GNP pc < $2,500) nor in rich countries (GNP pc > $2,500) did linguistic diversity correlate significantly with any of the four indicators of social cohesion.[3] In sum, the argument that a country's ethno-linguistic make-up matters for levels of social cohesion, whatever the level of development of that country, is not sufficiently supported by empirical data.

In fact, this conclusion is only reinforced by data from the European Values Study, a survey conducted in 1981, 1990 and 1999. The 1999 wave of this survey, which was held in 33 European countries, asked the question 'To what extent do you feel concerned about the living conditions of your fellow countryman?,' with answers ranging from 1 (very much) to 5 (not at all) on a Likert scale. The liberal nationalist logic would predict that levels of concern are much higher in homogeneous states as compared to heterogeneous states because the national unit to a large degree coincides with the political unit in homogeneous states, making it easier for citizens to express feelings of solidarity with compatriots. In heterogeneous states, by contrast, the national unit is a subgroup of the political unit, which means that people will tend to see ethnically different compatriots as little more than persons they happen to share a society with. Miller (1995, p. 83), for instance, argues that national identity motivates people to care about co-nationals because 'nations are communities of obligation, in the sense that their members recognize duties to meet the basic needs and protect the basic interests of other members'. However, performing a regression analysis of the EVS item *concern about fellow countryman* using ELF and GDP per capita as explanatory variables, we found that neither ethno-linguistic diversity nor income per capita are anywhere near significant predictors of this item for the group of European countries.[4] Thus, heterogeneity is not at all related to concern for fellow countryman, refuting the liberal nationalist argument once again.

The fact that there does not seem to be a relation between a state's ethno-cultural make-up and social cohesion at the present time does not exclude the possibility that the two conditions were related in the past. Indeed, processes like individualization, dealignment, the proliferation of different lifestyles and internationalization may have undermined the bonding capacity of national identity, transforming nationally homogeneous states into societies that are de facto as culturally diverse as heterogeneous states. If this reasoning were valid one would expect declining levels of solidarity and trust in all homogeneous states over the last two decades. A comparison of the three waves of the WVS (1980, 1990 and 1995) on the item of interpersonal trust, however, shows diverging trends (Table 4.3). Among the eight relatively homogeneous states (ELF < 0.3) that participated in all three waves, there were four states in which people became more trusting (Norway, Sweden, West Germany, Japan) and four where they became less trusting (Finland, Argentina, Hungary and South Korea). Although a sample of eight states is too small to base any definite statements on, it does suggest that there are no clear patterns. Norris (2002) in fact arrived at the same conclusion comparing a much larger group of countries. To double check whether there was perhaps a relationship between heterogeneity and interpersonal trust in the near past, we performed a regression analysis for the 1980, 1990 and 1995 waves of the WVS with ELF and GNP per capita as predictor variables. The results of this analysis showed that only GNP per capita was significantly related to interpersonal trust in all three waves.[5] Thus, also for the recent past there are no indications of an effect of ethno-linguistic heterogeneity on interpersonal trust as a vital element of social cohesion. Unfortunately we cannot assess whether the liberal nationalist argument actually does hold true for periods further back in time because there are no cross-national survey data available for these periods. Yet, our finding that the present empirical evidence does not suggest a link between heterogeneity and social cohesion is important. It means that the liberal nationalist argument, however theoretically sound and appealing it may appear, is not capable of explaining the actual variation in social cohesion levels across countries, neither now nor in the recent past. We have to turn to different factors to understand the processes that affect social cohesion.

Table 4.3 Interpersonal trust in ethnically homogeneous countries in three waves of the World Values Study (percentage saying 'most people can be trusted')

	1980 wave	*1990 wave*	*1995 wave*	*Change*
Norway	61.5	65.1	65.3	+
Sweden	56.7	66.1	59.7	+
West Germany	32.3	37.9	41.8	+
Japan	41.5	41.7	42.3	+
Finland	57.2	62.7	48.8	−
Argentina	26.1	23.3	17.6	−
Hungary	33.6	24.6	22.7	−
South Korea	38.0	34.2	30.3	−

Source: Norris (2002). This table is a selection of the one presented by Norris.

Education: the role of curriculum content

So how does education come into all of this? How does it connect to national identity and social cohesion? Miller (1989, 1995), a vocal defender of the liberal-nationalist discourse, has outspoken views on the role of education. In his opinion, schools have an important role to play in fostering national identity. A national curriculum and instruction in national history are essential components of this assignment as they allow children of various cultural backgrounds to acquire a common overarching national identity:

> The principle of nationality implies that schools should be seen, *inter alia*, as places where a common national identity is reproduced and children prepared for democratic citizenship. In the case of recently arrived immigrants whose sense of their national identity may be insecure, schools can act as a counterweight to the cultural environment of the family. It follows that schools should be public in character, places where members of different ethnic groups are thrown together and taught in common. It follows too that there should be something like a national curriculum, a core body of material that all children should be expected to assimilate. (Miller 1995, p. 142)

Interestingly, Miller contends that the nation-building project in schools need not be culturally neutral because national identity itself is not. Minority cultures do not have to feel offended by curriculum policies reflecting the culture of the dominant group as long as the common curriculum in some way acknowledges their historical role in the making of the nation:

> If we are attempting to reform national identity so that it becomes accessible to all citizens, we do this not by discarding everything except constitutional principles, but by adapting the inherited culture to make room for minority communities. Thus, rather than abandoning the teaching of national history in schools, we establish a common curriculum which gives due weight to the place that these communities have occupied in the making of the nation. If religion has played a large part in constituting national identity, we do not turn our backs on it by enacting purely secular policies, but try to strike a balance between the claims of the community's historic faith and the claims of dissenters.[...] In the matter of language policy, we do not opt for neutrality or *laissez-faire*, but instead decide which

language or languages are going to be the national ones, and then ensure that every citizen learns these as her first and second language – a policy that is also compatible with protecting the languages spoken by ethnic minorities if the communities in question desire this. (Miller 1995, p. 189)[6]

True to his argument, he strongly rejects radical multiculturalism, which in his opinion leads to policies that keep people locked in their small cultural identities and deprive them of the possibility to broaden their view and develop their talents in the wider society.

Both advocates of multiculturalism and liberal nationalists would agree with the statement that education matters for the transmission of values and identities. Despite their differences they expect the school to foster inclusive identities, civic attitudes, tolerance and social trust. Yet, is schooling still effective in an era when it has to compete with many other sources (such as TV, the Internet, magazines, peer groups, family) for access to the pupil's mind. Does the kind of curriculum content make a difference? If so, do the various citizenship modules socialize youngsters in the intended values or are there indications that they have unwanted side-effects? These questions are central to the following section.

There have been remarkably few comparative cross-national studies of citizenship education and values and identity formation among youngsters. One favourable exception is the IEA Civic Education study. This comprehensive survey study was carried out in 28 countries among fourteen-year-olds in lower secondary education. Respondents were administered a test measuring civic knowledge and skills and a questionnaire tapping civic engagement and attitudes. The study found that students with high civic knowledge scores expressed a higher willingness to engage in political activities. Another major result was that schools that model democratic practice were more effective in conveying civic knowledge and engagement than schools with traditional teaching modes (Torney-Purta *et al.* 2001; Torney-Purta 2002). Although the report on the study of fourteen-year-olds offers a good description of the survey results, little analytical work has to date been done with this rich data source. One of the purposes of the current study and of the study on tolerance in chapter 3, which also made use of the IEA data, is to draw the attention of the academic community to this valuable underexplored educational database.

We used this data source to examine the effect of schooling as reported by the students. More precisely, the questionnaire asked students to state to what extent the school had influenced their skills and attitudes on a number of topics dealing with civic education. We will first review these data on reported school effect and then examine to what extent they are linked with items in the survey tapping civic dispositions. While we identified one of these dispositions – institutional trust – as a component of a social cohesion syndrome (chapter 1), the others – political engagement, national pride, and tolerance – seem to constitute standalone notions (see chapter 3 for the discussion on tolerance). Naturally, by relying on subjective accounts of the school effect, we cannot make claims about the actual effect of school education nor about the exact amount and kind of course content. Yet student perceptions of the effect of various elements of citizenship education are likely to reflect curriculum priorities. Moreover, they are likely to say something about the receptiveness for learning and therefore about the effectiveness of schooling. It must further be noted that the current chapter, while obviously strongly related to chapter 3, does not duplicate that study. It also looks at tolerance but only as one of four civic dispositions, and it specifically evaluates the link between the reported effect of citizenship education and these dispositions, a matter that was not addressed in chapter 3.

Figure 4.1 presents regional aggregates of student respondents agreeing and agreeing strongly with a number of statements relating to civic education topics (see Appendix 4A for the countries included in each of the four regions). These statements are:

1. In school I have learned to be a patriotic and loyal citizen of my country (patriotism).
2. In school I have learned to understand people who have different ideas (pluralism).
3. In school I have learned to be concerned about what happens in other countries (internationalism).
4. In school I have learned about the importance of voting in national and local elections (elections).

Set answers: <strongly agree> <agree> <disagree> <strongly disagree>

We refer to these statements by the terms in parentheses. The figure shows that students in all four regions consider schools to be far more effective in cultivating pluralism than any of the other three civic education elements. Most noticeable, however, are the distinctive regional patterns, particularly on patriotism and elections. Whereas north-western Europe has the lowest scores on these two topics of all four regions, southern Europe combines the highest score on patriotism with the second-highest score on elections, and the non-European

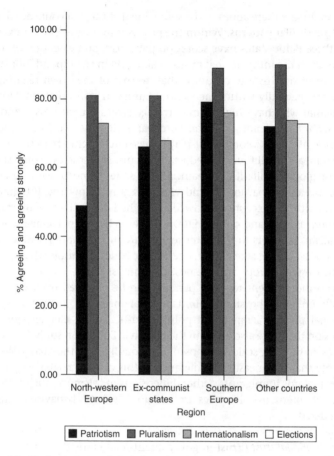

Figure 4.1 Student views of their learning in school about a number of civic education topics (regional aggregates)

Source: IEA Lower Secondary Civic Education study.

countries combine the highest score on elections with the second-highest score on patriotism. The post-communist countries fall in between these two extremes. Students thus have very different views on the degree to which the school influenced their outlooks depending on the region of the world and the topic of citizenship education.

Although the differences between the regions were all significant,[7] the aggregate data of Figure 4.1 may hide important intra-regional contrasts. Appendix 4A, which presents the same information as Figure 4.1 by country, indeed shows considerable variation between countries within a region. In fact there appear to be subregional clusters of countries demonstrating similar patterns. Within the post-communist world, for example, the three Baltic states have scores on patriotism and elections which are lower than the international mean, making them correspond more to the pattern of north-western Europe than to that of their own region. They contrast markedly with some Central European states (Poland, Slovakia, Romania) who have higher than average scores on patriotism and elections. Similarly, among the non-European states, the two Latin American states (Chile and Colombia) display scores much higher than the international mean on all four civic education items. Nonetheless, some striking intra-regional similarities remain. All the states of north-western Europe have values on patriotism and elections way below the international mean (with the exception of Sweden for the latter). Likewise all states in southern Europe and outside Europe have higher than average scores on pluralism. Students in the latter regions are in fact more positive on the effect of schooling across the range of civic education topics than those in north-western Europe and the post-communist states.

Even more salient regional patterns can be observed from Figure 4.2, which presents the standardized regional mean on institutional trust, national pride, tolerance and political participation, elements of social cohesion that were also asked in the IEA Civic Education study. These civic values, in turn, are scales composed of various items in the survey. We have to note that our measure of tolerance in this chapter relates only to attitudes towards immigrants. Other dimensions of tolerance, such as acceptance of alternative lifestyles or socially 'deviant' behaviour, are not considered.

Institutional trust ('trust in government-related institutions')
   'How much of the time can you trust each of the following institutions?'
   (1) national government, (2) local government, (3) courts, (4) the police, (5) political parties, (6) national parliament.
   Answer categories: never – only some of the time – most of the time – always

National pride ('positive attitudes towards one's nation')
   (1) 'The flag of this country is important to me'
   (2) 'I have great love for this country'
   (3) 'This country should be proud of what it has achieved'
   (4) 'I would prefer to live permanently in another country'
   Answer categories: strongly disagree – disagree – agree – strongly agree

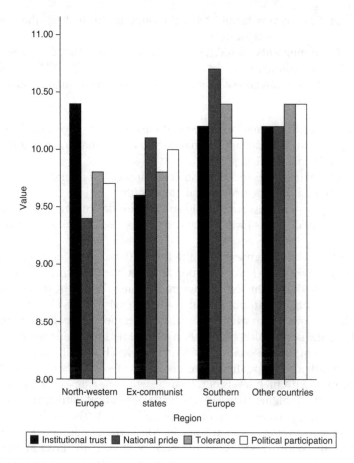

Figure 4.2 Standardized regional means of four civic attitudes
Source: IEA Lower Secondary Civic Education study.

Tolerance ('positive attitudes towards immigrants')
   (1) 'Immigrants should have the opportunity to keep their own language'
   (2) 'Immigrants' children should have the same opportunities for education that other children in the country have'
   (3) 'Immigrants who live in a country for several years should have the opportunity to vote in elections'

   (4) 'Immigrants should have the opportunity to keep their own customs and lifestyle'
   (5) 'Immigrants should have all the same rights that everyone else in a country has'
       Answer categories: strongly disagree – disagree – agree – strongly agree

Political participation ('expected participation in political activities')
   'When you are an adult, what do you expect that you will do?'
   (1) 'Join a political party'
   (2) 'Write letters to a newspaper about social or political concerns'
   (3) 'Be a candidate for a local or city office'
       Answer categories: I will certainly not do this – I will probably not do this – I will probably do this – I will certainly do this

With the value 10 representing the international mean, it can be seen that north-western Europe demonstrates a pattern which is almost opposite to that of the former communist states. While the former combines very high institutional trust levels with very low levels of national pride and lower than average values on tolerance and political participation, the latter unites higher than average national pride scores, very low levels of institutional trust and average levels of political participation. Southern Europe shows a combination of extremely high levels of patriotism with high levels of tolerance, while the non-European countries combine higher than average levels of political participation with higher than average levels of tolerance. As with the evaluations of school effectiveness, respondents in southern Europe and the non-European countries are generally more positive than those in north-western Europe and the post-communist countries, showing higher than average scores on the four civic attitudes. Particularly striking is the difference on tolerance between southern Europe and the non-European countries, on the one hand, and north-western Europe and the former communist world, on the other, the former showing higher and the latter lower than average values. Remarkably, Torney-Purta *et al.* (2001) could not find a relation between aggregate country-level scores on tolerance (i.e. attitudes on immigrants) and the percentage of foreign-born students in the sample, which runs counter to the commonly held view that the presence of immigrant groups fuels anti-foreigner sentiments (see chapter 3). Looking at *intra*-regional differences (see Appendix 4B), it can be noticed that the country patterns on the four civic attitudes are much less varied in north-western Europe than in the other three regions. The countries in the former all show lower than average scores on political participation, average or higher than average scores on institutional trust and lower than average scores on national pride (Finland excepted).

The next step is to relate the civic education items to the four civic attitudes measures. Table 4.4 presents binary correlations between these variables. The correlations are based on the country aggregate scores shown in Appendixes 4A and 4B. The table shows that all four civic education items (pluralism, internationalism, patriotism and elections) correlate positively with tolerance. This means that countries with relatively high levels of students reporting that school has been effective in teaching them about the four civic education topics also have high average tolerance scores. The civic education items also correlate positively with political participation, with only internationalism not showing a significant correlation. By contrast, institutional trust is not significantly correlated with any of the civic education items but is showing a strong relation with GNP per capita (the larger the GNP the higher the mean score on institutional trust). It can further be noted that reported learning about being a patriotic citizen and the importance of elections show by far the highest correlations with national pride, tolerance and political engagement, suggesting that these civic education practices are the most effective in fostering civic attitudes. As could perhaps be expected, pluralism ('understand people with different ideas') shows a strong positive correlation with tolerance. We have to note, however, that causality is difficult to prove as the IEA survey was cross-sectional and the data on civic education items relied on student reportage.

At first sight, the positive correlation between learning about being a patriotic citizen and the three of the four civic attitudes would seem to support Miller's argument that instruction in patriotic values and national history contributes to social inclusion and a widening of one's horizons. Remarkably, learning about being a patriotic citizen even correlates positively with tolerance, suggesting that an emphasis on national history and culture is actually furthering positive attitudes towards immigrants. At this point, however, we have to be cautious. The correlations are based on national aggregates and these may obscure altogether different relations at the individual level.

So let us look in more detail now at the relations at the individual level. Table 4.5 presents the results of regression analyses of institutional trust for each region using the four civic education elements as independent variables. Again we need to remind the reader that some of the terminology that we will employ in the ensuing section (predictor, factor)

Table 4.4 Correlations between civic education items and civic attitudes based on country aggregate data (N = 28)

	Civic education items					Civic attitudes			
	Patriotism	Pluralism	Internat-ionalism	Elections	Institutional trust	National pride	Tolerance	Political participation	GNP per capita
Patriotism	—	.55**	.18	.73**	-.11	.81**	.56**	.66**	-.56**
Pluralism		—	.62**	.58**	-.03	.33	.50**	.53**	-.11
Internationalism			—	.44*	.35	.06	.38*	.29	.22
Elections				—	.18	.48*	.75**	.72**	-.29
Institutional trust					—	.03	.24	-.18	.64**
National pride						—	.51**	.37	-.48*
Tolerance							—	.56**	-.08
Political participation								—	-.38*

Notes:
* Correlation is significant at the 0.05 level (2-tailed).
** Correlation is significant at the 0.01 level (2-tailed).
NB: the correlations are based on the country scores presented in appendixes 5.A and 5.B (N = 28).

Table 4.5 Regression of four civic education items and three individual background factors on institutional trust by region (individual-level data)

	North-western Europe	Ex-communist states	Southern Europe	Other countries
Civic education items (betas)				
Patriotism	.10**	.13**	.15**	.08**
Pluralism	.07**	.07**	.05**	.05**
Internationalism	.09**	.02**	.08**	.08**
Elections	.13**	.14**	.15**	.09**
Background factors (betas)				
Education mother	.01	−.01	.01	−.01
Education father	.02	−.00	.04**	.04**
Total test score respondent	.06**	.06**	.00	.08**
Explained variance (adjusted R^2) in %	7.7	7.3	9.4	5.1

Notes:
* Correlation is significant at the 0.05 level.
** Correlation is significant at the 0.01 level.

does not imply that we attribute causality to the civic education elements, as the cross-sectional nature of the IEA data rules this out. The use of this terminology is simply specific to regression analysis, a technique that allows us to examine the link between each of the civic education elements and the civic attitudes in isolation.

If we then turn to the table we can see that, remarkably, the four elements are all positive predictors of institutional trust in the four regions. There are no negative correlations. As we can see, learning about elections is the strongest predictor in all regions, with learning to be patriotic following close behind. These results are in line with the liberal-nationalist idea that patriotism contributes to social and institutional trust. Yet there are regional differences in the strength of learning to be a patriotic citizen as a positive predictor. Whereas patriotism competes with elections for the strongest predictor of institutional trust in southern Europe and the post-communist states, it is vying with internationalism for second place in north-western Europe and in the non-European countries. Performing the same regression analysis at the subregional level, we found that patriotism is even the weakest predictor among the four civic education items in Germany, Norway and Sweden. In Sweden it is not even a significant factor. In Denmark and the French-speaking community of Belgium it is a significant positive predictor only at the .05 level.[8] This suggests that an emphasis on patriotism in the school curriculum is not a cure for declining levels of institutional trust in all subregional contexts.

It can further be noted that the education predictors explain some of the variance in institutional trust, but not a particularly impressive amount. This squares with other studies that have found education to have a small, but significant impact on youngsters' knowledge and attitudes. Generally these studies have shown that family background and age are the strongest predictors (Atkin 1981; Niemi and Junn 1998; Hahn 1998; McGlynn *et al.* 2004). Introducing background variables in the regression analysis (see Table 4.5), we found, however, that the education level of the mother was unrelated to institutional trust. The education level of the father was only a significant positive predictor in southern Europe and in the non-European states. By contrast, the total score of the respondent on a test measuring civic knowledge and competencies was a significant positive predictor of institutional trust (i.e. the higher the test score the higher the level of trust) in north-western Europe, the former communist bloc and in the non-European countries, but not in southern Europe. This once more underlines the salience of regional differences.

Passive institutional trust is one thing, but political activism is quite another. Indeed, regression analyses of political engagement using the same educational predictors show quite a different pattern (Table 4.6). As could perhaps be expected given the conceptual proximity, this time elections is by far the strongest predictor of political participation in all regional contexts. Patriotism is a rather insignificant factor, competing with internationalism for second place but losing out to internationalism in the non-European countries. Most striking, however, are the negative correlations between pluralism (understanding people with different ideas) and political engagement. This seems to confirm the popularly held belief that (future) politicians are bad listeners, certainly to those with different opinions. The regional differences, visible in the previous table, have by and large disappeared, which is most likely due to the preponderance of elections as the prime predictor. Looking at the background factors, however, there is a conspicuous regional contrast, with the education level of the father and the total test score being important positive predictors only in north-western Europe. Comparing the regression analyses of Tables 4.5 and 4.6, the conclusion is warranted that the four elements of civic education relate quite differently to the two civic attitudes discussed so far. This suggests that a standard formula of citizenship education benefiting all aspects of civic culture equally is not possible.

Table 4.6 Regression of four civic education items and three individual background factors on expected participation in political activities by region (individual-level data)

	North-western Europe	Ex-communist states	Southern Europe	Other countries
Civic education items (betas)				
Patriotism	.06**	.08**	.05**	.08**
Pluralism	−.02	−.02**	−.02*	−.04**
Internationalism	.06**	.06**	.04**	.10**
Elections	.18**	.17**	.16**	.19**
Background factors (betas)				
Education mother	.01	.01	.02	−.01
Education father	.05**	.01	.03*	.02
Total test score respondent	.08**	.02**	.00	−.01
Explained variance (adjusted R^2) in %	6.2	5.5	4.0	8.3

Notes:
* Correlation is significant at the 0.05 level.
** Correlation is significant at the 0.01 level.

Last but not least we show the results of the regression analyses of tolerance (Table 4.7). Unsurprisingly, pluralism is the strongest positive predictor of tolerance in three regions and is almost the strongest predictor in north-western Europe. Pluralism is thus a positive factor at both the individual and national levels, which reinforces the findings of the country-level analyses of chapter 3. Of the three background factors, the test score is the most important predictor, showing a strong positive relation with tolerance in all four regions.

Still, in none of the three regression analyses do regional differences surface as clearly as in Table 4.7. First of all, the education of the mother shows a remarkable varying correlation with tolerance across regions: in north-western Europe it is a positive predictor but in the former communist countries a negative one. Thus, the conventional wisdom that the more educated the family, the more understanding youngsters are towards immigrants does not apply in all regional contexts. Secondly, going back to the civic education items, we see that internationalism is the strongest predictor in north-western Europe but comes only in third place in southern Europe. Undoubtedly most interesting, however, is the relation between patriotism and tolerance. As we can see, patriotism is a significant positive predictor in southern Europe but a significant

Table 4.7   Regression of four civic education items and three individual background factors on tolerance by region (individual-level data)

	North-western Europe	Ex-communist states	Southern Europe	Other countries
Civic education items (betas)				
Patriotism	−.10**	.02*	.14**	.03*
Pluralism	.17**	.19**	.19**	.26**
Internationalism	.18**	.08**	.09**	.08**
Elections	.02	−.00	.02	.07**
Background factors (betas)				
Education mother	.04**	−.04**	.01	−.02
Education father	.06**	.01	.02	−.00
Total test score respondent	.11**	.17**	.17**	.14**
Explained variance (adjusted R^2) in %	10.8	7.9	13.0	12.7

Notes:
* Correlation is significant at the 0.05 level.
** Correlation is significant at the 0.01 level.

negative one in north-western Europe – that is, the higher the effectiveness of schools in teaching patriotic values as reported by students in north-western Europe, the less positive the attitudes towards immigrants are among these students. In the other two regions patriotism is only a moderately positive predictor. These results could be an indication that in the core of the developed world a focus on patriotism in the school curriculum is not conducive to ethnic tolerance while in more peripheral areas it is. Using data from the 1995 edition of the ISSP survey, Hjerm (2004) in fact also found a negative correlation between national senti-ment and tolerance at the individual level in a good number of countries. Clearly liberal nationalist theory has a problem here: instead of the hoped-for beneficial effect, patriotic education actually might produce the opposite in the shape of increasing intolerance.

At this point it must be noted that the notions of patriotism and national identity are likely to be understood rather differently across the world. In Western Europe, certainly in those states that have suffered from the Second World War (both as occupier and occupied states), the concepts have become associated with authoritarianism, fascism, racism and other negative phenomena. By contrast, in the former communist countries, Greece and Cyprus and the Latin American states, patriotism and nationalism may (still) carry the positive connotations of heroism and liberation from totalitarian or colonial rule. These differential interpretations could explain why the average levels of national pride are much higher in the latter states than in the former (see once more Figure 4.2). Given that it is not done to call oneself a patriot or nationalist in Western Europe, certainly not in educated circles, the people who continue to do so are more likely to belong to the marginalized, poorly educated strata of society where xenophobic sentiments may be stronger. In eastern Europe intellectuals and dissidents played a key role in the democratic nationalist opposition movements that toppled the communist regimes. As a consequence, nationalism there is associated with socioeconomic reforms, democracy and opening up to the wider world. The IEA data used for this study most likely reflect these different understandings. Liberal nationalist theory is seriously flawed for not taking these regionally different understandings of national identity into account. In many countries of Western Europe attempts to introduce patriotic values in the curriculum are likely to be met with suspicion, contempt and ridicule.

Conclusion

This chapter has shown that liberal nationalist theory fails the test of empirical corroboration in a number of ways. First, contrary to the theory's expectation, we could not find a link between the degree of ethno-linguistic homogeneity of a country and aggregate measures of social cohesion. The absence of a relationship was evident in both rich and poor countries, both now and in the recent past. Liberal nationalists could argue that the measure we used to establish the degree of homogeneity (the Ethno-Linguistic Fractionalization index (ELF)) is not a good indicator of national unity as it fails to account for national identities that are grounded in markers other than language and ethnicity. This criticism would, however, not be consistent given that liberal nationalists themselves attribute great value to language. Moreover, stressing the fact that national identity can also rely on other markers – say political ones – undermines the conceptual distinction between state and nation, and dilutes the liberal nationalist argument that multilingual states have handicapped democracies and lower levels of interpersonal trust and solidarity.

Secondly, this study has shown that relations between educational variables and civic attitudes at the national level are not necessarily reproduced at the individual level. At the national level, the liberal nationalist argument seems to be confirmed: instruction in patriotic values shows stronger positive correlations with civic attitudes than some of the other citizenship education components do. Yet, shifting the analysis to the individual level, patriotic education appears to be related to only *one* aspect of civic culture – institutional trust. It only marginally correlates with political participation and, worse, appears to be detrimental to tolerance. In other words, the more effective schools are in promoting patriotism (as reported by students), the more they also seem to be promoting less positive attitudes towards ethnic others, which is an unforeseen effect that should be disturbing for liberal nationalists. If the aim is to promote tolerance, schools seem to be better off teaching pluralism and internationalism (developments in other countries) as these components do correlate positively with tolerance.

Critics might argue that the data presented in the current chapter are not able to establish the direction of causation. It cannot be excluded, for instance, that students who judged the school to be very effective in transmitting patriotic values are more nationalistic and xenophobic in the first place. In this case the causal direction runs the opposite way: *attitudes → reported school impact* instead of *reported school impact → attitudes*. We have to concede that causation may indeed have run in all kinds of unexpected and opposite directions. Given their cross-sectional nature, the IEA study data simply were not robust enough to establish causality. They did, however, show the close relationship between the teaching of patriotic values and intolerance in many Western European countries. Whatever the direction of causality, the close connection itself ought to give liberal nationalists a feeling of discomfort.

Thirdly, liberal nationalists fail to realize that national identity and related concepts like national pride and patriotism carry very different connotations across the globe. Whereas these concepts have been stained with fascism, racism, military aggression and other negative notions in Western Europe, other parts of the world (eastern Europe, southern Europe and Latin America) have associated national pride with positive concepts like emancipation, equality and democratic reform.

This brings us to the most important insight this analysis has produced: the pronounced contrasts between different regions of the world. Not only do *levels* of national homogeneity, national pride, school effectiveness and social cohesion vary substantially across the world, but the *relations* between these concepts at the individual level also do. Both the WVS and IEA Civic Education data showed pronounced differences between (north-) western Europe, the former communist countries, southern Europe and Latin America. The lesson we can learn from this is that one has to be careful in proposing an easy standard educational formula to solve social problems, such as waning civic attitudes and declining social cohesion levels, all around the world. The various regions of the world have experienced different historical trajectories resulting in different social problems, different perceptions of these problems and different understandings of conceptual tools at a given point in time. This fact does not preclude general solutions but suggests that these solutions have to be tailor-made to the region in question.

5
Comprehensive Schooling and Educational Inequality

The major argument of this book is that educational inequality matters in terms of the social effects of education and may, indeed, be one of its major determinants. This chapter focuses on the production of inequality in school systems, reviewing the evidence on the differences in levels of educational equality across countries, and assessing the school system factors which may explain these variations. The chapter concludes by asking whether one can identify different (supra-national) regional patterns in the characteristics of national school systems and their distributional outcomes.

The debate over comprehensive schools and educational inequality

Reducing educational inequality has been one of the organizing agendas of educational reform in the past half-century and, until quite recently at least, probably the dominant force in the most developed countries. To this end, various forms of comprehensive – or non-selective – education have been developed in the compulsory school systems in different developed countries, so that now the vast majority are, at least formally, comprehensive. North America (the USA and Canada) has had common compulsory school systems for a long time; since the 1960s most of the current European Union states have followed suit, with only a handful (Austria, Belgium, Germany, Luxembourg and, arguably, the Netherlands) remaining predominantly selective in the lower secondary phase. The majority of developed East Asian states, including Japan, South Korea and Taiwan, also have comprehensive systems in the state sector.

This development of multiple forms of comprehensive schooling, alongside the few remaining selective systems, should, in theory, have provided ample opportunity for comparative study to analyse the genealogy and regional distribution of different models of compulsory schooling. Given the increasing availability of comparable international data, it should also have made possible comparative assessment of the validity of the claims that comprehensivization would lead to reduction in inequality of educational opportunity. However, until recently, comparative analysis has been surprisingly mute about the different forms of non-selective schooling and their effects on class reproduction.

This situation may now be changing. Two recent and ongoing international surveys by the OECD – the International Adult Literacy Survey (IALS) and the Programme for International Student Assessment (PISA) – provide much-improved, cross-national comparative data on learning outcomes and have already produced a groundswell of reassessment among policy makers of the effects of different educational policies, particularly in relation to educational inequality. The surveys are important because they provide direct measures of skills among adults (IALS) and young people (the 15-year-olds surveyed by PISA) in literacy, numeracy and basic science (in the case of PISA) which are considerably more reliable than previously used proxy measures such as years of schooling, levels completed and qualifications attained (UNDP 2002). They allow better estimation of the effects of different school systems on educational inequality across countries. Taken together, the data show rather clear patterns of variation in levels of inequality across countries, which cluster both in terms of regions and system types.

International research has been unable to date to show conclusively that comprehensive reform does increase educational equality. In fact, most surveys until recently have shown relatively stable rates of educational inequality through the first six or seven decades of the twentieth century, including through the first years of comprehensive systems (Bothenius, Lehman and Peshcar 1983; Garnier and Raffalovich 1984; Handl 1986; Featherman and Hauser 1978; Halsey, Heath and Ridge 1980). Shavit and Blossfeld's classic 1983 study, *Persistent Inequality*, includes the findings from 13 separate country studies, seven of which are for western developed countries. Each of the studies analyses the impact of social origin (in terms of parental occupation and education) on both years of schooling and survival rates at key educational transition points, for successive cohorts between the early 1900s and 1960. The editorial conclusion is that 'despite the marked expansion of all educational systems under study, in most countries there was little change in socio-economic inequality of educational opportunity' (1983, p. 97). Only Sweden and the Netherlands showed a marked decline in the impact of social origin on educational attainment over the period.

The authors could find no evidence that major educational reforms made an impact on educational equality, even in Sweden where there were reductions in levels of inequality over time. Jan Jonsson, who was co-author of the Sweden study in the Shavit and Blossfeld collection, did re-examine his data for Sweden in a later publication (Jonsson 1999) and, using more data points, was able to show a continuing decline in educational inequality through the first decade of comprehensivization in Sweden. School reforms, he says, were in part responsible for the reductions in inequality, which were not only across social classes but also in terms of regional differences and gender. However, Esping-Andersen (2003), using different data, argues that diminishing educational inequality in Sweden has little to do with structural reforms in the school system. Following Bourdieu's thesis, he argues that a low level of cultural capital among parents plays the major part in lowering children's educational achievement. This occurs, he says, through less cognitive stimulation in the early years; through failure to pass on the cultural codes which are valued in schools; through less parental ability to navigate school systems to the benefit of the child; and through making children more risk-averse in relation to future educational decisions. Universal childcare in Sweden, says Esping-Andersen, counteracts this by providing supplementary socialization in culturally mixed environments. Education systems, comprehensive or otherwise, don't seem to make much difference.

The evidence from PISA and IALS

The PISA and IALS surveys tell a different story. The surveys show that levels of educational equality, measured in terms of the distribution of tested skills in areas such as literacy, numeracy and basic science, vary very substantially across countries both for adults and for young people. They also show that variations in skills inequality across countries follow distinctly regional patterns which can be related to, among other regional factors, the education system types which predominate in those regions.

The IALS study (OECD 2000) gives clear evidence of regional variation. The Nordic countries, for instance, including Denmark, Finland, Norway and Sweden, were all among the most equal in their distributions of adult literacy while the English-speaking countries, including the USA and the UK, were usually among the most unequal (Green 2003). However, although all the Nordic countries are notable for having almost entirely unstreamed comprehensive education in the compulsory years, by comparison with the rather incomplete and quite differentiated comprehensive school systems in English-speaking countries, the data tell us relatively little about the effects of different system characteristics since they show the educational outcomes of national systems in different periods.

A number of factors determine the distributions of skills within the adult population in addition to the effects of compulsory schooling. The distribution of skills among adult immigrants will have an effect, as will the distribution of post-school learning. Distributions of adult skills are also affected by differences between cohorts receiving their compulsory education at different times and in different educational systems, so that systems which have undergone more rapid change will produce greater variation in levels of skill between different cohorts. (This may, for instance, partly explain why the UK comes out as the third most unequal of the countries since there may be large cohort differences between those who have and those who have not had the benefit of the massification of upper secondary education which came later than in many countries.) Using the figures for the whole adult sample will tell us relatively little about the effects of comprehensive schooling since a large proportion of the sample in each country were educated at a time when the school systems were selective.

One can look at the data across countries for particular age cohorts before and after comprehensive reforms. Figure 5.1 shows that in most countries the distribution of prose literacy skills (as measured by the standard deviation) is more unequal for those aged 46–55 (schooled in the 1950s and early 1960s) compared to those aged 26–35 (schooled in the 1980s). This may reflect growing equality of educational outcomes in these countries. On the other hand, Sweden, Germany and Switzerland show more inequality among the younger age groups and Great Britain shows practically no difference. The national trends vary and, in any case, the procedure reduces the sample size rather substantially, which lowers reliability. The PISA data, however, based on tested skills of fifteen-year-olds, can give a much better guide to the effects of the school system.

The OECD PISA survey of skills in reading, numeracy and basic science skills of 15-year-olds in 32 countries provides the most recent evidence on how far different compulsory school systems generate equal or unequal outcomes in the performance of their students. The OECD

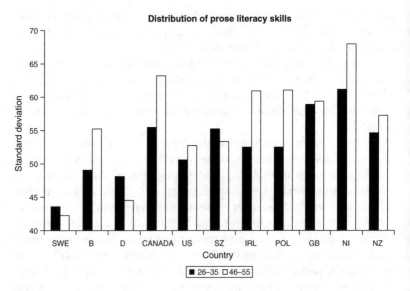

Figure 5.1   Distribution of prose literacy scores for different age groups

provides the standard deviations for scores between the 5th and 95th percentiles for students tested in each country in each of three domains (OECD 2001a: table 2.3a, p. 253, for the combined reading literacy scale; table 3.1, p. 259, for the mathematical literacy scale; and table 3.3, p. 261, for the scientific literacy scale). The data show that countries do differ very substantially in how widely skills are distributed among 15-year-olds. For instance, students in Japan falling within the lowest sixth of international achievement are 42 points behind those who performed in the top sixth of international scores, while the gap between the same groups in Germany was 120 points (OECD 2001a, p. 189). There are also very regular patterns as regards the relative position of different countries on different measures of equality in education.

Taking a basic standard deviation measure of skills dispersal (averaging the standards deviations for the three tests conducted in reading, mathematical and scientific literacy), we find that the most unequal of the 23 advanced states in the sample are (in descending order) Belgium, Germany, New Zealand, the USA and Switzerland (with the UK coming close after). The most equal (in descending order) are Korea, Finland, Japan, Iceland, Canada and Ireland. Sweden is 10th most equal and Denmark 14th (see OECD 2001a, tables 2.3a–3.3). It is notable that all the most equal education systems have comprehensive education systems at lower secondary level. Among the least equal countries, three have selective secondary systems and two, the US and New Zealand, have highly marketized comprehensive systems, where the emphasis on school choice substantially undermines principles of non-selectivity (Lauder *et al.* 1999).

The alternative measure of inequality, based on the strength of social inheritance (in terms of parental wealth, occupation, education and cultural capital combined) in determining educational outcomes, suggests a similar country patterning. The advanced states where social inheritance appears to have the greatest impact are: Germany, Switzerland, UK, USA, Belgium, France, Australia and New Zealand. The countries where the effect is least are: Korea, Japan, Iceland, Spain and Sweden. Denmark, Finland and Norway are again in the lower half but closer to the middle of the range (OECD, table 8.1). The country groupings are similar again. East Asian and Nordic states tend to predominate among the more education-equal countries. Anglo-Saxon countries and countries in the region proximate to Germany tend to be most unequal. Among the unequal group, five of the ten systems are selective at secondary level, and four are highly marketized comprehensive systems. All the more equal countries have comprehensive systems.

Breaking down the social inheritance syndrome into the separate effects of parental wealth and occupation, also repeats the pattern. Parental wealth has the highest impact on educational outcomes in the USA, Luxembourg, New Zealand, Portugal and Germany, and the lowest effect in the Netherlands, Japan, Finland, Italy and Norway. Parental occupational status has the strongest effect in Germany, Switzerland, Luxembourg, Portugal, the UK and Belgium, and the lowest in Korea, Finland, Canada and Italy. The major changes to the pattern here are that Norway is closer to the more equal end of the spectrum in the parental wealth measure than in previous measures, and Portugal has found itself in the more unequal group of countries in both the above measures, whereas on the previous measures both countries were closer to the middle. The regional clustering is still apparent.

Another interesting aspect of regional patterning becomes apparent when we analyse the effect of school intake mix on variations in achievements between schools. According to the OECD analysis, school status, measured in terms of the average level of parental occupations, wealth and 'cultural capital', has a major impact on the performance of individual students internationally – more, even, than the effects of the individual students' own background characteristics in many countries (OECD 2001a, p. 210). However, school intake mix has a much larger impact on the differences in outcomes between schools in the English-speaking countries than elsewhere. For the OECD countries taken together, school status explains 34 per cent of the variance in average outcomes (on combined literacy measures) between schools, whereas in the English-speaking countries its impact is much higher: explaining 64 per cent of the between-school variance in Australia, 59 per cent in Ireland, 70 per cent in New Zealand, 61 per cent in the US and 61 per cent in the UK (OECD 2001a, p. 197). In Japan and Korea the impact of school status on differences in school outcomes is much lower (explaining 11 and 17 per cent of between-school variance respectively). Intake effects are also moderately low in Scandinavian countries, except in Sweden where the differences in outcomes between school are very low in any case.

A second report on PISA by the OECD (2002) provided a more detailed examination of the effects of school-level factors on student achievement in test scores. They compute an intra-class correlation coefficient as a measure of the total variance in literacy scores within each country accounted for at the school level. The coefficient is equal to the between-school variance divided by the sum of the between-school and within-school variance, where 0 represents a situation where all the school achievement means are the same and 1 represents a situation where all schools differ in means whereas within schools all students score the same. Their analysis for each country shows that Finland, Iceland, Norway and Sweden each have intra-class correlations of below 0.15 (that is the schools account for less than 15 per cent of total variance in scores between students). Denmark is slightly higher at 0.19. Predominantly English-speaking countries, on the other hand, have intra-class correlations of between 0.15 and 0.30 (the USA – 0.29; the UK – 0.22; Australia – 0.18; Canada – 0.18; Ireland – 0.18 and New Zealand – 0.16). However, between-school variation is greatest in the German-speaking countries and countries proximate to them (Austria – 0.60; Belgium – 0.60; Germany – 0.59; Switzerland – 0.43; Luxembourg – 0.31; the Netherlands – 0.50). The results for southern European countries are rather mixed and do not show a clear regional pattern, with Spain having rather low variation between schools and Italy rather high variation (OECD 2002, pp. 148–50).

The conclusion drawn by the OECD is that greater social segregation in school intakes increases educational inequality whereas increasing the heterogeneity of intakes, and narrowing the gaps between schools, reduces it (OECD 2000, p. 201). The Nordic and East Asian countries would appear to have considerably less segregation in school intakes

than most of the English-speaking and German-speaking countries and
the effect of intake differences on inequalities between schools is much
lower. Since 36 per cent of the total variation in student performance is
attributable to the variation between schools, this leads to substantially
lower levels of overall inequality in outcomes.

The regional clustering is not perfect, of course, but the patterns above
suggest strong regional/historical affinities in terms of levels of educational equality. The Nordic and East Asian countries form two rather
well-delineated regional groups with relatively low levels of inequality.
The English-speaking countries (excepting, to some extent, Ireland and
bilingual Canada) form another with higher levels of inequality. A third
group with rather high levels of inequality include some German-
speaking countries and other multilingual countries which are geographically close to Germany and may be expected to share certain
influences, although the Netherlands is not so clearly in this group. A
fourth group includes France and the Mediterranean states, which
appear to occupy an intermediate position relative to other countries in
terms of levels of inequality. Clearly each group of countries have a
number of sociopolitical characteristics in common which may in part
explain the commonalities in levels of educational equality. However,
education system characteristics are also regionally patterned and it
would be hard not to conclude that these may also play a part.

How can we explain the marked regional differences in inequality of
outcomes with reference to the common regional characteristics of education systems? The positive cases of East Asia and the Nordic states
offer a good place to start.

Comprehensive schooling in East Asia

Japan has long been known to produce rather equal outcomes in education. Studies by Merry White (1987) and Ronald Dore and Mari Sako
(1989) both emphasize the success of Japanese schools in encouraging
the majority of children to achieve and the relatively low variation in
performance outcomes between children. William Cummings, whose
research focused mainly on primary schools in Japan in the 1960s, entitled
his major study *Education and Equality in Japan* and claimed that 'Japan's
distribution of cognitive skills is probably more equal than in any other
contemporary society' (1980, p. 6). Even official studies for the UK
government, which are not usually noted for their strong endorsements
in international reports, also frequently note this characteristic. The DFE
report *Teaching and Learning in Japanese Elementary Schools* (DFE/Scottish

Office 1992, p. 19) concluded that: 'A pervasive and powerful assumption of Japanese elementary education is that virtually all children are capable of learning and understanding the content prescribed in the Course of Study, provided they work hard enough and receive adequate support from their families, peers and teachers' (although it should be noted that some Japanese scholars maintain that up to a third of Japanese children are unable to keep up with the class by the last years of primary education: see Ichikawa 1989).

This common perception of high average standards and relative equality of outcomes has been repeatedly confirmed by International Evaluation of Educational Achievement (IEA) surveys. In the IEA survey of science attainment in 19 countries (Coomber and Reeves 1973) Japanese children at 11 and 14 years achieved the highest average scores with among the lowest levels of variation between individuals. A second science survey conducted in the mid-1980s found Japanese 14-year-olds still had the second highest average scores with the lowest levels of variations between schools (IEA 1988). Attainment spread is greater at the higher grades in Japan, as one would expect, but the evidence does confirm the frequent observations of outsiders that compared with many other countries, Japan does achieve relatively equal outcomes in the compulsory years of education (Ichikawa 1989).[1]

The achievement of relative equality within Japanese schooling is the result of a host of quite specific social and educational factors, some of which go back to the early modernization period, but most of which are specifically postwar phenomena.

Learning in Japan has always carried high social esteem, partly because of the value placed upon it within the Confucian tradition and partly because of the relative absence of public socializing agencies other than the school. Education was quite widespread in pre-industrial Tokugawa Japan; the school was both a repository of Confucian learning and a place for the education and socialization of children, thus combining two functions which in most western societies were divided between the school and the Church (Dore 1997, 1982; Passim 1965). Economic and social modernization after the Meiji Restoration in 1868 gave schools further prominence. They were to become the essential vehicles of ideological unification and modernization in a concerted process of state-led nation-building engineered by the Meiji reformers. At the same time, they were called upon to generate the knowledge and skills that were vital for Japan's nascent industrialization process. Like all subsequent late-developing countries, Japan was particularly dependent on education for economic growth since this rested precisely on the ability to learn from other countries (Dore 1997). From its inception in 1872, the public education system was thus already conceived as a key institution for the attainment of national goals in citizen and human capital formation (Green 1997, 1999). This alone would have guaranteed its strong emphasis on universality and inclusiveness, as demonstrated by the rapid achievement of full enrolment in elementary schools by 1910 and the relatively socially mixed nature of their intakes (Dore 1997; Passim 1965). However, other historical social factors to do with class formation have also combined to emphasize equality in Japanese education.

Modernization virtually eliminated the old elites in Japanese society, something it did not do in countries like Germany and Britain, and postwar Japan has emerged as one of the less class-divided of advanced societies: for all its vertical divisions of gender and economic sector, the Japanese labour market has had a narrower distribution of income than in any other of the developed economies (although this is now widening) (Perkin 1996). Nation-building, the lack of old elites and non-educational vehicles of social mobility, and relative economic and cultural homogeneity have thus all combined historically to produce an environment favouring educational equality.

However, it is only in the period since the Second World War that an education system has emerged with specific institutional characteristics favouring equality. Most important of these has been the creation of the 6-3-3 public system of elementary, secondary and high schools first proposed by the American occupying powers after the war and readily accepted then by a Japanese population eager to embrace a new democracy in education. Envisaged as a fully comprehensive system, and strongly supported as such by the influential teaching union *Nikkyoso*, this was never fully realized at the upper end since the postwar high schools rapidly became both selective and specialized under the pressure of increasing demand. Nevertheless, public elementary and lower secondary schools remained both non-selective and neighbourhood-based, providing relative equality of access to children from all social groups.

Other institutional factors have been important in fostering equal opportunities in education. Centralized control has been used to equalize funding between schools, just as frequent rotation of teachers and heads between schools has worked to ensure consistency in the other key area of resourcing. Mixed ability classes throughout the compulsory years and automatic promotion between grades have enhanced uniformity of school experiences and standards for each age cohort of children

(Ichikawa 1989). This uniformity has been further reinforced through central control over curricula, assessment methods and textbooks, all of which are tightly prescribed by the Ministry of Education through its detailed Course of Study for each year of schooling and which teachers tend to follow quite closely.

Lastly, but not least, there has been a strong equalizing force from the prevailing view in Japan that achievement is largely the product of effort rather than innate ability (Takeuchi 1991). This belief is widely held by teachers in public schools (White 1987) and appears also to leave its mark on children. A review of research by Susan Holloway (1988) on concepts of ability and effort among schoolchildren strongly suggests that Japanese children are much more likely than their American counterparts to ascribe both their successes and failures to levels of effort rather than ability. Not only have Japanese children traditionally been encouraged to believe that they can all do well if they try hard enough, but they have also been encouraged to help each other in the process, with the faster ones commonly helping the slower ones in group tasks which are subsequently assessed on group rather than individual performance (White 1987).

Although there are less data in English on equality of outcomes in Taiwan and South Korea, except the PISA data already noted for the latter, it would not be at all surprising if these two countries showed similar properties in this regard to those of Japan. South Korea and Taiwan both experienced long periods of Japanese occupation when their school systems were substantially remoulded after the Japanese pattern. After independence, school reforms were highly influenced by the US model, as was the case in Japan until the mid-1950s, and they also, particularly in the case of South Korea, followed Japan as a model for educational reform (Brown, Green and Lauder 2001). The other two of the four tigers in East Asia, Singapore and Hong Kong, were much more influenced by their British colonial legacy and share more features educationally with the UK than with Japan, and so, unsurprisingly, do not exhibit the same patterns as the other two in relation to structures designed to equalize outcomes. Japan, South Korea and Taiwan all developed a 6-3-3 school system for primary, lower secondary and high school education, following the American model. They also adopted a system of unstreamed neighbourhood comprehensive schools in lower secondary education in the state sector, although a much more stratified system of private evening crammer schools (*Juku* in Japan) exists alongside this in Japan and Korea. These shared characteristics no doubt go some way to explaining the similarly high levels of educational equality in Japan,

South Korea and Taiwan (although we have only the near universalization of upper secondary education to go on for the last), but there are also other important social and cultural characteristics, which cannot be explored here, which may also help to explain the obvious educational affinities.

In any case, it would seem that there are sufficient commonalities in the histories and structures of the educational system in these three East Asian states to justify a claim that they do to some extent represent a dominant East Asian model, from which Singapore and Hong Kong inevitably diverge, and that this model is exceptionally favourable towards educational equality. Current reforms in all the states may be undermining this model (Green 1997), but they had not gone so far in the years covered by the PISA surveys at the time of the first PISA survey in 2000 to undermine the equality effect visible in the data in that study.

The Nordic model

In some ways the Nordic states offer an even more convincing case of a regional model of compulsory schooling which favours egalitarian outcomes. All the Nordic states, including Denmark, Finland, Norway, Sweden and Iceland, share the same basic institutional structure. This comprises nine or ten years learning in the primary/lower secondary phases of compulsory education in mixed ability classes in all-through, non-selective, comprehensive schools. In contrast to East Asia, the selective private sector is also relatively weak in each country, with in Denmark, for instance, 89 per cent of children in state schools. The 'private' schools here, as elsewhere in Scandinavia, are, in any case, largely state funded (80–85 per cent in Denmark) and therefore also largely controlled by the state (Wiborg 2004a, 2004b). High schools are differentiated in most Nordic states – Sweden being the exception with its integrated academic/vocational *Gymnasieskola* – but upper secondary education has near universal enrolments in all of these countries. School choice has been introduced in Denmark and Sweden, but its salience at the secondary level is limited since most children stay in their initial primary school through the secondary level and its impact has mainly been limited to the major urban areas. Measures to increase private schools have not substantially enlarged that sector in any of the countries (OECD 1994; Green, Wolf and Leney 1999).

The Nordic states all then share an exceptionally egalitarian structure of schooling, with all kinds of selection delayed until the upper secondary phase. It cannot be a coincidence that all the Nordic countries on which we have data are also alike in the relatively low levels of inequality in their educational outcomes. Other societal factors will also contribute to this common regional phenomenon, but the chances are they are working through education in having their effects.

Why has this very particular common regional pattern emerged in the Nordic states? A number of preconditions existed in the nineteenth century which helped with the early introduction of linear educational ladders, as opposed to the parallel education systems that persisted – often until the mid-twentieth century – in other European states such as the UK, France and Germany. The Scandinavian states shared a common Lutheran religious heritage which was favourable to the establishment of universal literacy and they were also early to introduce state regulation of education in the early part of the nineteenth century, thus creating the basis for later systematic reforms (Skovgaard-Petersen 1976; Sjöstrand 1965; Dokka 1967). However, there were other countries in Europe, such as the German states, which shared a dominant Protestant heritage and which also developed early state education systems, but they were much slower than the Scandinavian states to begin to unravel their elitist parallel systems of elementary and secondary education for different groups.

The Scandinavian states had three distinct advantages. First, when state systems of education first developed it was within political systems which had already evolved substantial elements of popular democracy due to long-standing historical traditions (Boli 1989). Secondly, their social class systems were distinctively favourable to populist politics since they combined relatively weak landowner and bourgeois classes with a strong class of independent peasant farmers who were able to form alliances with the smaller nascent working classes of the industrial areas (Anderson 1994; Isling 1984; Esping-Andersen 1985). Thirdly, populations in these largely agrarian societies were relatively dispersed which provided pragmatic arguments for common schooling.

The combination of these factors allowed the early evolution of consolidated single education ladders in Denmark, Norway and Sweden. The relative numerical weakness, and hence political weakness, of the landowner and bourgeois classes meant that social representation in the traditional Latin school was rather less skewed towards the higher classes than in many other countries, thus making it easier to combine these schools with the primary schools. In addition, the relative political weakness of the upper classes in the lobbies for the Latin schools meant that it was much harder for them to defend their elite status than it was in other countries. The strong independent peasant interests were thus the major force in propelling the liberal parties in the latter decades of the nineteenth century progressively to transfer the lower secondary classes from the elite Latin schools to new middle schools which then provided a single educational ladder from the primary schools through to the upper secondary schools. This happened first in Norway (1869) and somewhat later in Denmark (1903) and Sweden (1905), countries which, unlike Norway, had bicameral parliaments which allowed the landowner interests to block reforms in the upper house for some time.[2]

The second major wave of reform occurred under social democratic governments in all these countries and dates largely from after the Second World War. As Esping-Andersen (1985) argues, the social democratic parties have been exceptionally influential in the Nordic states since the 1930s. This was due partly to their powerful organizational apparatuses and partly to their ability to weld political alliances between the industrial working class, small farmers and sections of the middle classes. It has been these social democratic parties, often in coalition with liberal allies, which have pushed through the particularly radical comprehensivization of school systems during the middle decades of the twentieth century. Norway abolished its middle schools in 1936, progressively integrating them with the primary schools to create a nine-year, all-through comprehensive school by 1969. Denmark abolished its middle schools in 1958 and by 1975 had completed its own transition to a nine-year comprehensive school system. Sweden introduced its nine-year comprehensive system in 1962, after extensive trials during the 1950s, and then after 1969 started to integrate its high schools as well. All three countries progressively eliminated streaming and setting in all subjects so that the comprehensive schools are now almost entirely mixed ability.

The Nordic model of compulsory schooling shares with the East Asian model the key equality-favouring characteristics of mixed ability comprehensive schools, but it has, in addition, the integration of primary and lower secondary education into one school. This may make it even more favourable to reducing inequality in that it eliminates school choice at lower secondary phase entry except in the unusual cases of school switchers (whose families have usually moved residence). Moreover, unlike the East Asian model, it also has an almost all-encompassing state sector so that this model applies almost universally throughout compulsory schooling. The Scandinavian states, and the Nordic states more generally (the non-Scandinavian Nordic states having similar structural characteristics to the others, although we have not shown this here), have adapted a peculiarly radical form of comprehensive schooling which may go some way to explaining why they have relatively equal outcomes in the IALS and PISA studies.

The less egalitarian systems, according to our outcomes data, include the countries in the German-speaking region, some of the anglophone countries and the Mediterranean states. How can we explain their relative low performance in inequality reduction?

The model in the Germanic region

The 'Germanic' model is perhaps the best place to start, since the countries included in this set all share very similar institutional structures in their education systems and since they are notably similar in their rather high levels of educational inequality among 15-year-olds.

Austria, Belgium, Germany, Luxembourg, Switzerland (in the German-speaking areas) and, arguably, the Netherlands are the only states in western Europe to retain selective secondary school systems. These are based largely on the German model where children are tracked at the age of 11 or 12 into different types of school for different ability levels. Parents do have a choice, officially, as to where children go during the end-of-primary-level orientation phase, but children will be reallocated to other schools over time if their performance does not conform to the academic standard of the chosen school, so the system is effectively allocating by ability to different school types. In Germany the proportion in each type of school changes over time, but in the late 1980s in the FRG 25 per cent of 14-year-olds were in lower-level *Hauptschule* (taking grades 5–9/10) as against 55 per cent in the academic or more vocationally oriented higher schools, the *Gymnasien* (grades 5–13) and the *Realschulen* (grades 5–10 or 7–10) (Leschinsky and Mayer 1999, p. 24). There are also some nominally comprehensive schools coexisting with the selective system in some *Länder*, but only 9 per cent of children in the 7th grade in the unified FRG were in these schools in 1997/8. The new *Länder* have dumped the old GDR comprehensive model (with the comprehensive *Polytechnische Oberschule*) and adopted the FRG's traditional selective system, although in some cases rolling up the *Hauptschule* and *Realschule* into a single institution (in Saxony, Thuringia and Saxony Anhalt) (Pritchard 1999). Germany thus retains a selective system in all states except, arguably, in Berlin, where the comprehensive *Gesamtschulen* do now predominate. The other states named above have similar systems, although Switzerland only in the German-speaking regions.

Why Germany, and these other geographically and culturally proximate states, practically alone in all of western Europe, retained a selective system, and despite various attempts to reform it in Germany in the 1970s, has continued to be something of a mystery to educational research. It is certainly the case that most of the countries concerned are constrained in their reform efforts by being federal systems – that is to say, systems where the individual regions substantially control school education and find it difficult to agree nationwide reform. However, regional control is much weaker in the states outside Germany, so this does not seem to provide a satisfactory answer. Comparative logic would suggest that the reasons will lie in the examination of those distinctive societal characteristics which these countries have in common.

Germany, Austria, Belgium, Switzerland and the Netherlands all retain strong apprenticeship systems as well as selective school systems. It seems likely that these distinctive facts are connected and that the reasons for the two overlap. Apprenticeship systems have traditionally provided acceptable progression routes and employment opportunities for graduates of the least-favoured schools, the *Hauptschulen*, in ways that post-school provision in countries without strong apprenticeship systems has generally not (Green, Wolf and Leney 1999). This may well explain why the pressure for eliminating the low-status schools, not least from among middle-class parents whose children were consigned to them, has not reached the levels in these countries that it did in other countries where governments were forced to concede that selection by ability at the end of primary schooling was socially unacceptable. We therefore need to identify what common conditions in these states have led to the retention both of selective schools and of strong apprenticeship systems.

Various factors have no doubt contributed. Firstly, most of the countries which still practise selection have been influenced by German language and culture, not least the traditions of cultural particularism and differentionism associated with ethno-cultural German models of citizenship (Brubaker 1992; McLean 1990). This, arguably, encourages differentiated forms of schooling. However, at the same time, the neo-corporatist states like Austria, Germany and Switzerland have retained strong craft traditions, have high levels of unionization and manifestly robust traditions of social partnership which have enabled the extension of the privileged status of skilled workers widely throughout the workforce, thus underpinning notions of 'equality of productive capacity' (Streeck 1997) and working in favour of income equalization. This relative professional egalitarianism of the skilled has served to legitimate a school system which differentiates young people into different tracks leading, usually, to different occupational destinations, but where each track retains its own identity, status and social value (OSA 1994; Streeck 1997; Brown 1997). In other countries, with more universalist cultural traditions, and with weaker craft traditions and weaker occupational identities for manual and junior white-collar workers, such legitimacy for selective organization has not been sustainable, and comprehensive reforms have followed.

The survival of strong apprenticeship systems also depends on more specific characteristics of labour market organization and regulation associated with social partnership. Germany, and to a lesser extent the other countries, have strong occupational labour markets and a degree of labour market co-ordination which allows companies to provide apprentice training without excessive cost, still allowing mobility between firms (Marsden and Ryan 1995). Sectoral agreements on pay in skilled jobs reduce the danger of poaching of trained employees and, therefore, increase the incentive of employers to invest in training (CEDEFOP 1987; Brown, Green and Lauder 2001).[3] Social partnership in labour market relationships, within a strong framework of central government regulation, have thus proven indispensable to the survival of strong apprenticeship systems, and no countries without these have retained them – although many, like the UK, have tried.

These shared regional characteristics in the German-speaking area no doubt provide a large part of the explanation for the survival of the selective secondary systems and the apprenticeship systems with which they articulate. The selective education systems must surely contribute substantially to the high levels of variations in outcomes among 15-year-olds observed in the PISA study. However, paradoxically, the apprenticeship system, which may be seen to legitimate the school system in producing this inequality, probably also contributes to a mitigation of its effects in later life. Germany is both one of the most unequal in its outcomes at 15 years, according to PISA, and one of the most equal in adults' skills, according to IALS. The early universalization of upper secondary education through the apprenticeship system may have had an effect here in reducing inter-cohort differences. However, it is also likely that the further three to four years of education that lower-achieving young people from the *Hauptschulen* receive within the dual system, especially in compulsory Mathematics and German lessons in the *Berufsschule*, substantially improves their basic skills so that the skills gaps between German adults are not as great as they would otherwise have been.[4]

The Mediterranean states

Despite their widely shared Napoleonic legacies of centralized control and curricula encyclopeidism (McLean 1990), the educational systems in France and the Mediterranean states are clearly too various to be considered as a single model. It should not surprise, therefore, that the outcomes for Mediterranean states on the PISA inequality measures are fairly diverse. However, for the most part they do seem to occupy intermediate positions which may relate to certain common school system features.

The Mediterranean states have all adopted comprehensive lower secondary school systems during the past forty years – although some, like Greece and Spain, only relatively recently – and they all have institutionally differentiated upper secondary systems.[5] In the lower secondary schools these countries are distinguished by their use of grade repeating, whereby students falling too far behind the average standard for their class are obliged to stay down and repeat a year. This is generally defended on the grounds that, unlike streaming, it reinforces the same norms for all students, allowing lower achievers more time to meet the standards set for all. Whether it has this – potentially equalizing – effect on outcomes or, alternatively, simply labels children and reinforces failure, is hotly debated. However, it is also the case that most Mediterranean states have retained some forms of setting in core subject areas.

In France, for instance, streaming has been progressively eliminated officially since the 1978 Haby reforms. However, school principals still have sufficient latitude to organize some classes according to ability and, according to research, some 40 per cent of schools do this in order to make classes more homogeneous and easier to teach. Research by Duru-Bellat and Mingat (1999) suggests that the gain to lower-achieving pupils from learning in mixed ability classes in France is stronger than the loss to the more able pupils. Although they may have relatively little to lose from mixed classes, it is the middle-class parents who are more likely to push for ability grouping. In addition to the continuation of setting, France, and some of the other southern European states, have also experienced the introduction of some moderate school choice policies. These, in France, are carefully controlled so that the area committees which review school choices made by parents are bound to reject these choices where they would detract from the overall provision of schooling, as where exit from a particular school is damaging its quality (OECD 1994; Green, Wolf and Leney 1999). However, research by Trancart (1993 cited by Duru-Bellat and Mingat 1999, p. 99) does suggest that even this limited introduction of school choice has already widened disparities between schools in terms of intakes and average achievement levels.

The Mediterranean states do not have a single model of comprehensive schooling and one would not expect them to perform as a group in terms of the level of equality of outcomes. However, as comprehensive systems with substantial elements of internal differentiation – through grade repeating and setting – one would expect them to achieve only middling levels of equality, and considerably lower levels than those achieved in the East Asian and Nordic systems and this is in fact where most of them fall in terms of the PISA data.

The systems in predominantly English-speaking countries

The systems in the English-speaking countries are again too diverse to classify as a single model, even in the most general terms. However, there are clear similarities in the systems of those states which have the more unequal outcomes – that is to say, of the USA, the UK and New Zealand. These countries all have nominally comprehensive school systems, but where comprehensivization has been radically incomplete in certain ways and where it is now being substantially undermined by streaming, setting and school choice and diversification policies (Whitty, Power and Halpin 1988). Equality within comprehensive schooling in the US was always substantially undermined by the continued existence of a large private school sector and by the huge disparities between states and even education districts in curricula, school structures and levels of school finance (Carnoy 1993; Winkler 1993). Not only has there never been a national comprehensive curriculum in the USA, there has never been a national structure of comprehensive schools either.

The same can be said of the UK, which now has four different education systems in its constituent countries. Scotland had generally had more uniform educational structures, but in England and Wales there was never a single national model of comprehensive schooling. Circular 10/65 had required LEAs to develop comprehensive systems but, according to the typically voluntaristic mode of educational legislation prior to 1988, they were free to chose different models and they did so, with the majority opting for a combination of 11–16 and 11–18 comprehensive schools. This left a major inequality between schools containing sixth forms and those without, as the sixth form became the main signifier of superior quality. Additional differentiation occurred in those areas which kept some of their grammar schools. Arguably, England and Wales did not complete their comprehensive reforms until 1988 when there appeared the first national curriculum and when a single lower secondary exam, GCSE, was beginning to operate. However, by that time in England and Wales (and to a lesser extent Scotland), as in the USA, a new movement towards introducing market competition into the school system was about to undercut the comprehensive nature of the school system in new ways.

School diversification and school choice policies in New Zealand, the UK and the USA have now substantially undermined the comprehensive principle of non-selection, although in the UK the effects are varied – as between systems in Scotland and England, for instance. Many comprehensive schools in these countries now legally or illicitly select their intakes and national policies actively encourage greater differentiation between schools. On some estimates only 40 per cent of children in England and Wales go to genuinely non-selective schools (Benn and Chitty 2004). New Zealand's schools have gone in the same direction (Lauder, Hughes and Watson 1999). Given their incomplete original comprehensivization, and the subsequent undermining of comprehensive education through the introduction of quasi-markets in education, it is therefore not surprising that the education systems in these countries, despite being nominally comprehensive, show high levels of inequality in outcomes in the PISA study, and also wide distribution of skills among adults in the IALS study.

Conclusions

We have not sought to conduct rigorous statistical tests here on which factors are most responsible for equalizing educational opportunities across the countries, although this might well be done. However, comparative logic would suggest that where there are relevant common characteristics shared by the country systems which demonstrate the egalitarian outcomes and which are absent in those systems which do not, we may be able to identify the key mechanisms. The problem with this approach, as always, is that there may be many characteristics which are present in the 'positive' cases and absent in the 'negative' cases, including some which we have not observed (Ragin 1981). However, in the analysis above we can see a number of contenders.

It might plausibly be argued that it is economic equality (low income differentials) which provides the best explanatory variable. Certainly, the countries in the sample above with higher levels of educational equality are also countries with lower levels of income inequality (see chapter 6), and this may provide part of the explanation for greater educational equality. However, the correlation does not invariably hold. Germany, for instance, is one of the most income-equal countries in

Europe (Perkin 1996), but is not so equal educationally at the school level. If we concede that there is a connection in most cases – and research has repeatedly shown that income distribution and skills distribution are highly correlated across countries (Nickell and Layard 1998; Green, Preston and Sabates 2001) – then this does not rule out an education effect since income effects are likely, in part at least, to be working through and mediated by education structures. Countries with very unequal incomes are likely to generate divided education systems as those with more purchasing power lobby for the opportunity to buy better schooling, as with private schools or school choice.

In a similar vein we might argue that it is countries with high levels of social cohesion which are more likely to generate educational equality. Since social solidarity is a central motif of social democratic government, particularly in Scandinavia, this argument fits well with the outcomes in the Nordic countries. It might also be said to fit well in Japan whose cultural traditions place a high premium on the group or collectivity, the *iemoto* (family-like) grouping being a basic organizational principle (Perkin 1996). However, the argument fits less well in cases like South Korea, which has only recently matured into a democratic system and which has had years of rather intense class conflict since decolonization. Again, if social cohesion and social solidarity is an explanatory factor in some of the cases it no doubt works through education. Research, again, shows a high correlation across countries between aggregate levels of social cohesion and levels of educational equality, as we demonstrated in chapter 1. It is very likely that solidaristic ideologies are a necessary precondition for achieving egalitarian educational reforms.

In terms of education system factors, what the more equal countries have in common, which is absent in the less equal countries, are the structures and processes typically associated with radical versions of comprehensive education: non-selective schools, mixed ability classes, late subject specialization and measures to equalize resources between schools. That these features should work towards lowering educational inequality should be no mystery. The great French sociologist, Raymond Boudon, gave the most cogent explanation of this some thirty years ago in his famous 'positional theory' of social reproduction in schooling (Boudon 1974).

Inequalities in educational achievement by different social groups arise partly because of the unequal learning advantages given to children from different social backgrounds. This is the standard argument of Bourdieu and cultural capital theory (Bourdieu 1980). Children from families with higher levels of education and more cultural capital have acquired more of the cultural 'habitus' and the language codes required in the school system to get on. They are likely to have more confidence and higher aspirations and have the assistance of their parents in knowing how to navigate the system. However, school structures also make a difference.

Children from less affluent families not only tend to have less of the advantages from their families that make it easier for them to achieve, they are also more likely to make educational choices that will make achieving less likely. Where they are positioned in the social structure affects the logics of their choices (both rational and otherwise) and they are more likely to make less academically aspiring choices than middle-class children of similar ability. Middle-class children may have more to lose in pursuing non-academic routes which are likely to lead to downward mobility than working-class children for whom choosing a non-academic route will likely lead to social class maintenance. Regardless of cognitive ability, children from less well-endowed backgrounds will perceive greater positional risks in choosing long academic routes not only because of fear of failing, but also from concern that success may entail costs. These may include deferring earning and building debt and also, ultimately, the emotional strains of cultural dislocation as academic success brings mobility from their class of origin. Duru-Bellat and Mingat's analysis of streaming at the end of lower secondary in 1990 in France, for instance, well illustrates how this works. Looking at transition to different types of *lycée* they show that while 25 per cent of the social class differences in transitions to high or low streams could be attributed to ability, a further 25 per cent derived from the choices made by parents and their children which are unrelated to achievement (Duru-Bellat and Mingat 1999).

Education systems are not neutral in terms of these social class effects arising from positional choices. As Boudon (1974) rightly argues, systems which provide more and earlier 'branching points' provide more opportunity for social class differences to assert themselves through the early educational career choices made by students which will affect their later achievement. The East Asian and Nordic countries in this study which demonstrate lower levels of inequality have systems which minimize all the significant branching points. They limit choice between schools (the Nordic countries having no choices at all at lower secondary phase entry, except for school switchers), minimize the difference between classes and have no separate tracks at all before the end of compulsory schooling. Less branching, less inequality.

Limiting choice in education is clearly not a very fashionable position in this day and age. However, the research still seems to suggest that it is the most effective way of reducing inequality. PISA has provided the most powerful evidence of this to date. As the surveys are repeated over the years, allowing more rigorous testing over time, they may well lead to a major scholarly reassessment of the impact of comprehensivization on educational inequality, giving more credence to the claims of its advocates. If research does finally return this verdict it would be highly ironic at a time when comprehensive systems are being systematically dismantled in many countries. But it would hardly be the first time that such wisdom only comes with hindsight. As Hegel once said: The Owl of Minerva only flies at dusk.

6
Models of Lifelong Learning and the 'Knowledge Society': Education for Competitiveness and Social Cohesion

Policy debates frequently invoke lifelong learning as a key to achieving both national economic competitiveness *and* social cohesion. The European Commission's targets for education and training, for instance, are considered central to the overall Lisbon strategy for 'a competitive and knowledge-based economy ... with more and better jobs *and greater social cohesion*' (Fontaine 2000). But how far is it possible to achieve a competitive and dynamic 'knowledge economy' which is also a 'knowledge society' with high levels of social cohesion? And if it is, what forms of lifelong learning are most likely to promote this, and combined with what policies in other economic and social domains? This chapter seeks to examine these questions by analysing the different national and regional models of the knowledge economy and knowledge society in Europe and the contribution that lifelong learning makes in each.

Models of the knowledge economy and knowledge society

Debates about the knowledge economy frequently revolve around two models which are seen as the major alternatives for competitive economies in the globalized world. In abbreviated policy discussions these are referred to as the 'neo-liberal' or 'Anglo-Saxon' model, represented by the USA and some other English-speaking countries, and the 'social market' model, represented by various countries in northern Europe, and notably by Germany. The comparative global literature on political economy and skills often displays a similar dualism but with different regional models taken to represent the basic antinomies (see Lloyd and Payne 2004, for an overview). Hutton (1995) contrasts the 'shareholder' model of Anglo-American capitalism with the 'stakeholder' model said to be represented by Germany, Japan and some other northern European states. Albert (1993) contrasts the liberal market model of Anglo-American capitalism, with its culture of hire and fire, takeovers and companies as 'commodities', with the 'Rhine Model' capitalism of Germany, Austria and Switzerland, where companies are considered 'communities' and where social partnership mediates shareholder power. More recently, Dore (2000) contrasts the 'stockmarket capitalism' of the USA and other Anglo-Saxon economies with what he calls the 'welfare' or 'relational' capitalism of Germany and Japan. In each case a similar set of contrasts are being applied, although with different national exemplars.

Shareholder/stockmarket economies are said to give primacy to market mechanisms and to the overriding rights of investors; stakeholder/welfare economies balance the rights of shareholders and other stakeholders in the enterprise and society, and they moderate the effects of the markets through regulation and interest group intermediation between concerted social partner bodies or other interests. In the shareholder model innovation and competitiveness are achieved, it is argued, through flexible labour markets, low levels of regulation, high rates of employment, long working hours and lower rates of social expenditure. These are said to promote high productivity and rapid growth, but come at the price of poorer public services, greater inequality and low levels of social cohesion. In the stakeholder or social model, social expenditure is higher and there is more regulation of labour and other markets, which tends to enhance public services and promote equality and social cohesion. However, regulation, high social costs and lower employment rates may lower overall productivity and growth. The stakeholder model is often identified with the social market economies of 'core' Europe, and is sometimes seen as contributing to the distinctive nature of 'social Europe'.

Each of these models of competitiveness has been associated with different skills formation strategies (Brown, Green and Lauder 2001; Crouch, Finegold and Sato 1999). The liberal Anglo-Saxon model is typically associated with skills formation systems that create polarized skills distributions, combining high skills elites with a substantial number of poorly qualified low-skilled employees. Labour markets with such polarized skills profiles are said to match the needs of sectors and companies which operate different competition strategies: the high skills elites serve the knowledge-intensive, high skills industries which compete on quality and innovation and generate high value-added to enterprises; the low skilled serve the sectors and companies which compete on price rather than quality and which rely on the flexible and low-cost labour which the low skilled provide. The European social market model, by contrast, is associated with skills formation strategies which generate high levels of skills distributed throughout the workforce. Social market economies, such as that in Germany, are said to compete primarily on the diversified quality production of their manufacturing industries, which produce a wide array of high-quality, high-priced goods for the international markets (Streeck 1997). These sectors are said to rely not only on the high skills of the elites but also on the wide dispersion of intermediate-level skills throughout the workforce.

In line with the rather binary models provided by some of the political economists, policy makers often come to see the relationship between these two models of economic competitiveness as being characterized by a series of 'trade-offs' where mutually incompatible benefits have to be weighed against each other: job creation and low unemployment against income equality and job quality; long work hours and high incomes against leisure time and quality of life; innovation and economic dynamism against the regulation of standards and the environment.

A high national income in terms of GDP per capita, so it is argued, depends on high labour productivity, long working hours and high rates of employment. High rates of employment may be achieved, on the US model, through flexible labour markets, but these reduce job protection and work quality for the employed and tend to increase wage inequality. Longer working hours can raise average incomes but reduce leisure time, creating the paradox of the high-skilled elites in the USA, described by Robert Reich (2001), who have a surplus of disposable income but no time to enjoy it. Low levels of regulation may increase opportunities for innovation and stimulate economic dynamism, but they may also lower product and service standards and pose a threat to the environment.

Social market economies, on the other hand, may achieve high levels of labour productivity through high skills and high capital investment and they may also use greater regulation to achieve higher quality of work, better product and service standards and higher environmental protection. They may also achieve greater equality of incomes for the waged. On the other hand, labour market regulation is likely to reduce job growth and employment rates, which will lower national income and create greater inequalities between the waged and the unemployed, albeit while maintaining relative wage equality. So-called 'third way' politics, as practised in the UK, seek to square the circle through combining flexible labour markets with policies for 'social inclusion' where equity is equated with opportunities for labour market participation. But, as critics point out, 'social inclusion' in economic terms does not necessarily increase equality where it fails to address low pay. Economic competitiveness, to this way of thinking, would still seem to be at odds with social cohesion.

Research into recent trends in western economies, however, suggests that the various binary models which pit economic competitiveness against social cohesion need to be rethought and that there are possible models of the knowledge society which combine both. These are most obviously represented in recent years by the Nordic states and also, in some respects, the Netherlands. On most indicators, which we will examine later, these countries perform highly not only on overall productivity but also on social outcomes.

Recent research by de Mooij and Tang (2003) provides some indication of how they may achieve this. In their detailed analysis of the varying components of productivity across major economies, the two authors confirm that there is, to some extent, a trade-off between competitiveness and social cohesion in the effects of different labour market policies. Countries like the USA and the UK, which boost their overall productivity through high rates of employment, do tend to have higher rates of income inequality. At the same time, several countries with lower rates of inequality, such as France, also have rather lower employment rates which bring down their overall productivity despite, in the French case, having very high levels of labour productivity per hour. This is conventionally explained in terms of the effects of different labour market mechanisms. Flexible labour markets tend to allow higher job growth and increase the rate of employment by making it more economical for employers to hire new labour. But they only achieve this through reduced worker protection, which allows wage differentials to rise and, by drawing the less qualified to work at low wages, which also increases wage inequality.

However, as de Mooij and Tang show, some labour market regulatory mechanisms appear to escape this trade-off. In their cross-national statistical analysis they find that benefit duration, union density and employment protection do have statistically significant negative effects on participation, while at the same time increasing income equality. This fits with the classic trade-off argument. However, some labour market policies and institutions seem to escape this trade-off. Strong trade unions, as measured by union coverage, may tend to increase unemployment at the same time as reducing inequality, but centralized unions, conducting concerted cross-sectoral bargaining, tend to reduce unemployment and promote pay equality. Also, Active Labour Market policies, including, among other things, assistance with job search and training for the unemployed, boost employment rates and lower unemployment rates at the same time as mitigating income inequality. Centralized trade union bargaining and Active Labour Market policies have, of course, been notable features of many of the Nordic countries which achieve both high productivity, high rates of employment and also low levels of income inequality.

The evidence also suggests that lifelong learning regimes may play a part in this. The Nordic countries, as we demonstarted in chapter 5, have high aggregate levels of attainment and skills both among the young people (in PISA surveys) and amongst adults (in IALS) and show more equal distributions of skills than countries in other regions. The wide distribution of skills achieved in these countries no doubt plays its part in the levels of labour productivity achieved across different sectors of their economies, which forms an important component of the overall productivity outcomes. At the same time, widespread uptake of adult learning – and particularly the training provided for the unemployed and those about to be made redundant through Active Labour Market policies – promotes the higher employment rates which also contribute to overall productivity. Relative equality of incomes is no doubt due partly to labour market institutions, including minimum wage laws and mechanisms for concerted and centralized pay bargaining. Nevertheless, given the exceptionally strong correlations in cross-country studies between skills equality and income equality (Checchi 2001; Green and Preston 2001a; Nickell and Layard 1998) it seems likely that education also plays a substantial role. The relatively equal distribution of skills in Nordic countries helps to maintain relatively low levels of income inequality, not least because where increasing participation rates bring less qualified people into the labour market, these are not much less qualified than the majority, thus mitigating pressures for low wages which would raise income disparity.

If the analysis provided by de Mooij and Tang is correct, we need to modify the customary models of political economy to include three, not just two, types of the knowledge economy in the developed western world. These would include: the neo-liberal or market model of the USA and some other English-speaking countries; the social market model of countries in what de Mooij and Tang (2003) call 'core Europe' (that is, in their sample, Austria, Belgium, France, Germany, Luxembourg and the Netherlands) and the social democratic model of the Nordic states. The differences between the traditional antagonists, the neo-liberal and the social market, remain much as described in the literature. However, a further distinction is made between the social market model and the social democratic model, on the basis that the latter generally achieves higher rates of employment, and therefore often higher overall productivity, while also displaying higher levels of equality and social cohesion. An examination of some of the primary social and economic indicators does seem to show that such a threefold patterning exists.

We can examine the differences in these three models and the countries they represent by examining the various components of overall productivity or GDP per capita, which include labour productivity (output per hour), employment rates and average hours worked. De Mooij and Tang (2003) do this in terms of the size of the gap with respect to the USA for various European states on each of these measures. What their analysis shows is that while the USA still has a commanding lead in terms of GDP per capita over all the European states except Luxembourg, the size of the gap varies substantially for different states, and reflects different combinations of strengths and weaknesses as regards the different components of productivity. In Figure 6.1 we adopt a similar approach but include where possible figures for all European states for the later year of 2003.

Figure 6.1 shows that in 2003 there were a number of countries in Europe achieving higher rates of labour productivity than the USA. These include: Austria, Belgium, Denmark, France, Germany, Ireland,

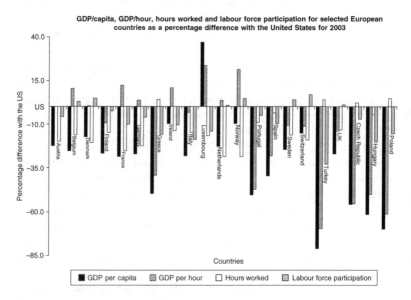

Figure 6.1   Components of GDP per capita

Luxembourg, the Netherlands and Norway. However, all European countries, including those with higher labour productivity, lag behind the USA in terms of GDP per capita (with the exception in 2003 of Luxembourg). Different groups of countries lag behind for different reasons.

The countries furthest behind the USA in GDP per capita are in central or southern Europe. These include Greece, Portugal, Spain and the Czech Republic, which trail the USA by between 35 and 60 percentage points and, further down, Turkey, Hungary and Poland, which trail the USA by more than 60 percentage points. Low labour productivity is the major cause of the gap in all cases, but this is compounded, except in the Czech Republic and Portugal, by considerably lower employment rates.

Low labour productivity is not necessarily, however, the major cause for the lag behind the USA in other European states. Austria, Belgium, Denmark, France, Germany, Ireland, Luxembourg, the Netherlands and Norway all have higher labour productivity than the USA but all, except Luxembourg, lag behind in GDP per capita, with gaps ranging from 28.4 per cent (France) to 9.6 per cent (Ireland). These, and other countries with labour productivity quite close to the US levels, fall behind the USA in overall wealth for different reasons. Average hours worked are more than 10 per cent lower than in the USA in all EU states – except in the Czech Republic, Greece and Poland, where they are higher, and in Portugal and Spain where they are within 10 per cent. Labour force participation rates are lower than in the USA in 14 of the selected European countries, with the exceptions being Belgium, Denmark, the Netherlands, Sweden, Switzerland and the UK. Overall wealth deficits with the USA are therefore due to different combinations of reasons in different countries.

Core European countries, including broadly all those in western (non-Nordic) continental Europe, except the so-called consolidation states of Spain, Portugal and Greece, all have higher labour productivity than the USA, but all – except Luxembourg – fall behind in wealth due to lower employment rates and short working hours, or both. Two groupings emerge. The majority grouping are those with employment rates more than 5 per cent below US levels and include Austria (−5.5 per cent), France (−10 per cent), Germany (−5.9 per cent) and Italy (−18 per cent). These have levels of per capita GDP between 22 per cent (Austria) and 28 per cent (France) behind the USA. The minority group include two countries (Belgium and the Netherlands) whose employment rates are higher than those in the USA but which fall behind in levels of wealth due to substantially shorter working hours. These two, although geographically part of 'core' Europe, perform more like the Nordic countries, as we shall see.

The two English-speaking countries, the UK and Ireland, conform more to the US pattern than the core European countries in some respects in having working hours closer to US levels and, in the UK case, having higher employment rates. However, they perform differently overall. Ireland has considerably higher GDP per capita than the UK and the core European countries, because its labour productivity is very high, at more than 10 per cent above US levels. The UK achieves a lower GDP per capita, at around the level of Germany, Italy and France at the lower end of the core countries, because labour productivity is 13 per cent adrift of the US levels and further behind most of the core countries.

The Nordic countries (Denmark, Finland, Norway and Sweden) present a different pattern from the other groups. They have higher employment rates than most of the core European countries, with all except Finland exceeding the USA on this measure. However, like the core European countries, with the exception of Sweden, they have considerably shorter working hours than the English-speaking countries. In general, the Nordics combine the strengths of core Europe countries in high labour productivity (all except Sweden outperform the UK and the USA) with the strengths of the English-speaking countries in high employment rates. Consequently, overall performance in GDP per capita is higher for the Nordic group of countries than for core Europe or for the UK, Denmark, Norway and Sweden all have higher GDP per capita than the UK, and Denmark and Norway substantially outperform any of the core Europe states.

Clearly, the regional patterning that emerges from this analysis is not perfect. Luxembourg does not fit with any other group; Ireland is more similar, overall, to core Europe than the UK, having high labour productivity and low employment rates. The Netherlands, and even Belgium, are closer in some ways to the Nordic group than core Europe in having relatively high employment rates as well as high labour productivity. So one might talk of a Nordic group plus the Netherlands and a core Europe group plus Ireland; with Luxembourg standing apart from all groups and the UK only forming part of a group with some other non-European English-speaking countries. Nevertheless, what is clear is that in terms of the components of productivity one can identify two major and distinctive models of competitiveness in the north-west of continental Europe and not one as is usually supposed.

The economies in the Nordic countries also stand out from those of the rest of northern Europe on measures of competitiveness and innovation used by the World Economic Forum in its *Global Competitiveness Report* (World Economic Forum 2004). For the 25 leading countries in the sample of over 100 for which WEF has indicators, we can see from Figure 6.2 that the USA comes highest in the overall rankings with 2nd place in Business Competitiveness, 1st place in Innovative Capacity and 5th place in Internet Use. Other leading English-speaking countries do rather less well: UK (6, 3, 18); Canada (12, 12, 10); Australia (11, 15, 14). The core Europe countries generally lag substantially behind the USA on all the measures: Austria (17, 16, 17); Belgium (15, 17, 23); Germany (5, 5, 15); and France (10, 10, 25). After the USA, it is the Nordic region which does particularly well on most of the indicators. Norway performs less well than the others, but Finland, Sweden and Denmark are ranked 1st, 3rd and 4th respectively on Business Competitiveness, 2nd, 7th and 8th on Innovative Capacity and 7th, 2nd and 11th on Internet use.

Country	Business Competitiveness	Innovative Capacity	Internet Use
Finland	1	2	7
United States	2	1	5
Sweden	3	7	2
Denmark	4	8	11
Germany	5	5	15
United Kingdom	6	3	18
Switzerland	7	9	24
Singapore	8	6	4
Netherlands	9	11	6
France	10	10	25
Australia	11	15	14
Canada	12	12	10
Japan	13	4	12
Iceland	14	18	1
Belgium	15	17	23
Taiwan	16	13	20
Austria	17	16	17
New Zealand	18	23	9
Hong Kong	19	25	13
Israel	20	14	27
Ireland	21	19	29
Norway	22	22	8
Korea	23		
Italy	24	21	28
Spain	25	24	33

Figure 6.2   WEF Economic Competitiveness Rankings

OECD figures on research and development (R&D) investment also show the Nordic countries standing apart from other countries in Europe. Figure 6.3 plots changes in business investment in R&D against changes in multi-factor productivity (MFP) for the period between the 1980s and 1990s. As the OECD analysis shows, these two measures are significantly correlated, although some countries, such as the USA, have seen significant improvements in MFP without such high increases in investment. What is interesting again about the distribution is that four of the Nordic countries (Denmark, Norway, Finland and Sweden) all lie in the top right-hand quadrant, with the four among the top seven out of 16 developed countries on MFP growth, and with Denmark, Finland and Sweden among the top four in growth in investment in R&D.

Social indicators also show a marked regional clustering. Figures 6.4 and 6.5 group countries into four clusters. The English-speaking group includes the USA, the UK and Ireland, where there are data on the latter. The Nordic group includes Denmark, Finland, Norway and Sweden. The southern European group includes Greece, Italy, Portugal and Spain and the 'core Europe' group includes Austria, Belgium, France, Germany, Luxembourg, the Netherlands and Switzerland, or whichever of these countries feature in the particular figure. On each of the social indicators

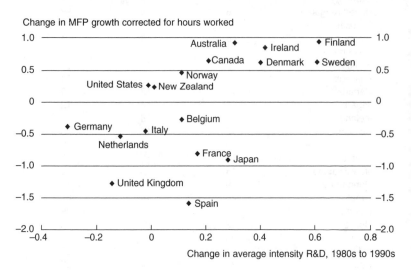

Figure 6.3   Changes in multi-factor productivity growth and R&D

Source: Figure 111.2, p. 43 in OECD (2001) *The New Economy: Beyond the Hype*. Paris: OECD.

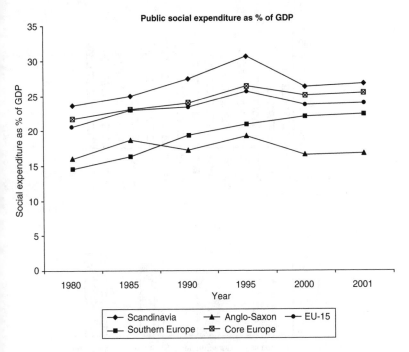

Figure 6.4 Public social expenditure as percentage of GDP by region

Source: OECD (2004), Social Expenditure Database (SOCX, www.oecd.org/els/social/expenditure).

shown in the different figures there is a marked variation in the average levels for each group.

Figure 6.4 shows the average total public social expenditures as a percentage of GDP for various years between 1980 and 2001 for countries within each group. The English-speaking countries show a relatively flat trend on this measure and for the period from 1990 have the lowest average level of spending as a proportion of GDP. The southern European countries start in 1980 with a lower average level than the other groups, but have the faster rate of increase and overtake the English-speaking countries in the late 1980s. The core Europe countries have a rising average level of spending relative to GDP which starts somewhat higher than the average for southern European and the English-speaking countries, and remains so until the end of the reference period. The highest average level of spending relative to GDP is among the Nordic countries. This starts higher in 1980 than in any other group and rises more rapidly until the mid-1990s. After this it declines quite

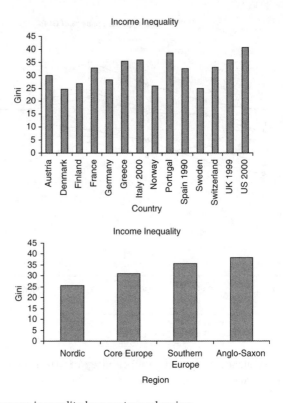

Figure 6.5   Income inequality by country and region

sharply but remains higher on average than for any other of the groups. The regional boundaries of the three northern European groups conform closely to the typologies used in Esping-Andersen's study of the *Three Worlds of Welfare Capitalism* (1990), where he distinguished between liberal Anglo-Saxon countries, neo-corporatist Christian Democrat countries of northern Europe, and Social Democratic Nordic countries. The relative levels of social spending which characterize each group are also, of course, consistent with his original analysis of the levels of welfare universalism attributable to each model.

Income inequality displays the same patterns of regional variation. As Figure 6.5 shows, there are marked differences in the levels of income inequality, using the standard gini measure, for each of the country groups. The English-speaking group of countries has the highest average level of inequality followed by the southern European group. Core

Europe is rather more equal than these two groups. But it is the four Nordic states which have the lowest levels of inequality by quite a substantial margin. The countries in each of the groups are relatively closely clustered in terms of the measure: the Nordic countries have gini coefficients between 24.7 and 26.9, the core Europe group between 28.3 and 33.1, the southern Europe group between 32.5 and 38.5, and the English-speaking group between 36 and 40.8. There are overlaps at the top and bottom ends for core Europe and southern Europe and between southern Europe and the English-speaking group, but the groups still appear relatively distinct overall.

Figure 6.6 plots countries on two axes for income inequality and a combined measure for social cohesion. The income inequality measure is the gini coefficients from the World Bank *World Development Report* (2005), as in the earlier figures. The social cohesion measure, as discussed in chapter 1, is a combined factor which amalgamates data from the World Values Survey for trust in others, trust in institutions, and civic cooperation, with data from Interpol on levels of violent crime (treated inversely). Although Germany and Norway are outriders, the plot shows a clear correlation between levels of income inequality and levels of social cohesion on this combined measure. The countries with higher income inequality, like the USA, the UK and Portugal, have rather lower

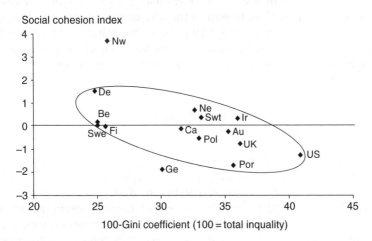

Figure 6.6 Income inequality and social cohesion

Source: A. Green, J. Preston and R. Sabates (2003) *Education, Equity and Social Cohesion: A Distributional Approach*, Wider Benefits of Learning Centre Report 7. London: Institute of Education.

levels of social cohesion on this measure. The Nordic countries have the lowest levels of income inequality and are above the average on social cohesion, with Denmark and Norway measuring highest of all the countries. The core Europe countries tend to fall somewhat between those of the other two groups on both measures, but with Germany coming particularly low on the social cohesion index.

The various data represented above on economic and social characteristics do seem to suggest a pattern of regional clustering with considerable similarities between countries in each group on most of the indicators and marked differences between the averages on each measure for the countries in each group. The grouping of the countries could certainly be adjusted at the margins on various of the measures, but the pattern overall suggests there is some sense in classifying them into the four regional/cultural groups designated as Nordic, Core Europe, southern Europe and English-speaking (or Anglo-Saxon), although given that only the USA and the UK are very close on a number of measures, the last might be better termed Anglo-American. The patterns by and large do support the broad distinctions in characteristics which the comparative political economy models seek to capture, and the countries taken to represent these models do conform broadly with the regional clusters adopted here. The analysis of the cross-country data also gives strong support to the notion that we should treat the Nordic countries as a separate group from the core Europe countries. The Nordic countries can be distinguished from most of the core Europe countries in having higher rates of employment, higher social spending relative to GDP, lower levels of income inequality and higher levels of social cohesion. The Netherlands stands somewhere between the two groups on most of these measures.

Lifelong learning systems and models of the knowledge economy/society

Lifelong learning systems can be classified by region/group in the same way that economic and social systems were above. Comparative analysts traditionally classify education systems in Western Europe into four regional groups which include France and the Mediterranean states; Germany, German-speaking countries and other countries proximate to Germany; and the Nordic states and the English-speaking countries (McLean 1990). The groups are not distinctive in every respect and the traditional classification of education systems into groups differs in some respects from the way this has been done for the economic and social models. French education, for instance, has more in common with education in other Mediterranean states than it does with education in the group of core European countries, not least because historically the Napoleonic plan of French education had considerable influence in some southern European countries, like Greece and Italy, and France still retains that influence today. Switzerland has a French system of education in its French-speaking areas and a German-style system in its German-speaking areas, and therefore cannot be classified into a single group. There is also considerably more diversity within the southern European education systems than in some of the other groups, which makes the cluster relatively diverse in its outcomes. Nevertheless, the education systems of the different regions have sufficient in common and are sufficiently distinctive from those in the other groups for the exercise to make sense (Green, Wolf and Leney 1999). The following regional/group characterizations are based on analysis of the constituent national education systems along three dimensions: institutional structures, modes of governance and regulation, and knowledge and curricula traditions.

France and the Mediterranean states form the least definable grouping, but they still have many characteristics in common. They have the most centralized of all European education systems, particularly in the cases of Greece and Portugal, but also in respect of France, Spain and Italy, where centralized control is only partially attenuated by a devolution of some powers to regional government which is in turn offset by the 'deconcentration' of central powers to the regional outposts of national education ministries (Lauglo 1995; Lauglo and Mclean 1995) (see Figure 6.7). Central government typically hires teachers, often posting them to schools, inspects them, and pays their salaries, albeit in some cases via their regional bodies. Post-school education and training are also quite centralized in their systems which, although often utilizing social partner-based organizations to collect and distribute levies for training, typically frame the rights and responsibilities for employees and employers for training in national law (Green, Hodgson and Sakamoto 2000). In terms of their institutional structures all the countries in southern Europe (excluding Malta) have comprehensive primary and lower secondary schools, with grade repeating in the latter, and typically retain most post-compulsory education in school-based programmes in general or specialist vocational high schools, with only rather residual apprenticeship systems. Knowledge traditions in southern European education typically follow the French idea of encyclopeidic education (McLean 1990), with a broad range of subjects followed right through to the end of the upper secondary schooling in both

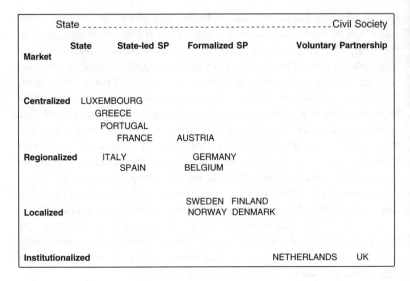

Figure 6.7 Modes of regulation
Source: Green, Hodgson and Sakamoto (2000).

academic and vocational tracks (Green 1998). Examination systems and diplomas are largely state controlled, utilize 'grouped' awards requiring competence in a range of subjects (like the French *Baccalauréat* or the Italian *Maturita*), and tend to be relatively well integrated across the general and vocational lines, with common elements of the curricula and status equivalences and so on.

The German-speaking countries, and countries geographically proximate to Germany, have education systems which are easily distinguished from others in Europe. Regulation and control of school systems is typically on a regional basis (as with the German *Länder*) with the central state playing a lesser part than in southern Europe. Post-compulsory education and training is largely through apprenticeship systems which are organized through a system of formalized social partnership. In terms of institutional structures these countries are all very distinctive. They all have selective secondary schooling, with different types of school for those of different abilities, albeit that some comprehensive *Gesamtschulen* are allowed to exist alongside these in some German *Länder*. Most of the countries and regions of countries in this group (Austria, Germany, German-speaking Switzerland, the Netherlands) also have strong apprenticeship systems which form the dominant pathway from school to work. Higher education systems are also typically bifurcated between general universities and technical universities (Teichler 1993). School knowledge traditions tend to be more specialized and differentiated in these states, arguably following the more culturally particularistic traditions of the region, and examinations systems are less integrated and allow more specialization than in the southern European states, not least in the high degree of specialization in vocational diplomas.

The English-speaking countries (including the UK, the USA and Ireland) are not so easy to classify since there is considerable (sub-national) regional variation in both the USA and the UK, with distinctive differences between states in the USA and between England, Scotland, Wales and Northern Ireland in the UK where each of these now have their own systems. Nevertheless, there is enough in common between constituent systems in each case to make certain broad generalizations. Historically, these countries have had highly decentralized education systems, giving local authorities, schools and teachers considerable autonomy (Green 1990). This has changed in recent years in the UK as powers formerly allocated to the local education authorities have been transferred up to central government or down to schools. However, the UK and the USA have in common their provisions for high levels of school autonomy, with devolution to schools of budgets and powers of teacher hire and fire, and their proliferating measures for increasing school diversity and school choice, as part of the programme to introduce a competitive quasi-market into public sector education. All three countries have formally comprehensive primary and secondary schools in the state sector, but school choice and diversity policies are increasingly eroding the non-selective nature of these – although arguably more in England than in Scotland, in the UK case. Secondary schools are characterized by a high degree of tracking, particularly after the end of compulsory schooling where children can go to a wide variety of different types of upper secondary general and vocational programmes. In curricula terms these countries have historically encouraged high levels of specialization and individualization in learning and continue to have much more early specialization than elsewhere. In the UK, and most particularly England, this has meant a largely unintegrated upper secondary examination system, albeit with new attempts to create credit frameworks, where young people can take a multiplicity of examinations in single elective subjects.

The Nordic countries have some differences between their education traditions, but they undoubtedly represent the most homogeneous of the groups. Regulation of school education is largely at local level in all states, but within a strong central government framework which operates a policy of 'steering by goals'. Post-compulsory education and training tends to involve high levels of public funding, but also strong social partnership traditions with regard to work-based learning (Rubenson, forthcoming). Most distinctive, as we saw in chapter 5, are the institutional structures of the Nordic compulsory school systems which share a unique system of mixed ability teaching virtually throughout the compulsory school years which takes place in combined primary/lower secondary neighbourhood comprehensive schools. Limited school choice operates in Sweden and elsewhere, but there are very few private schools in the Nordic countries and rather little school diversity by comparison with the non-Nordic countries. Encyclopedic knowledge traditions and broad curricula prevail, although with a greater inclination towards individualization and customizing of programmes in recent years than one would find in southern European countries.

Perhaps most significantly, adult learning, often funded by the state, is more prevalent in the Nordic countries than in any other region (OECD 2003). Kjell Rubenson, in his paper on the *Nordic Model of Adult Education* (Rubenson, forthcoming), points out that Nordic countries have a long tradition of diverse forms of adult learning, including the Folk High School and study circles, which developed historically in close connection with the social movements, and which are currently strongly underpinned by the social partners and the social democratic state. Major recent reforms in Norway, Sweden and Finland, including the 2 billion euro 1995 Adult Education Intiative in Sweden and the 1999 Norwegian Competence Reform (see also Payne 2005 for some of the limitations of the latter) have provided extensive new opportunities for adults without completed secondary education to gain secondary-level qualifications and underline the propensity in Nordic countries to give equal priority to both general education and vocational training in adult education. Other characteristics common to the Nordic states noted by Rubenson include the high levels of state subsidy for adult education and training, often specifically targetted to the unemployed and those with low levels of qualification, and the high rate of employer funding for training, evidenced by the fact that 73 per cent of those in the IALS survey undergoing adult learning during the previous year had received funding from their employers (OECD 2000, p. 2). As with school education, adult education in the Nordic countries is also relatively evenly distributed. Although some groups benefit more than others, Rubenson's analysis shows that relative to other countries in IALS, participation in adult learning is more evenly distributed in the Nordic states, not least because of the higher representation of those with lower qualifications and those over 55.

The impacts of lifelong learning systems on the knowledge economy/society in different regions

How do these regionally distinctive lifelong learning systems articulate with the different forms of knowledge economy/knowledge society we have identified in the different regions? We may start with the outcomes they produce in terms of skills.

A traditional argument about skills formation and economic competitiveness (Crouch, Finegold and Sato 2000; Brown, Green and Lauder 2001) is that different systems of skills formation tend to follow the skills requirements of the national economies and their different sectors, either serving their needs well or, in another scenario, replicating their pathologies (Finegold and Soskice 1990). The systems of skills formation in the UK and USA are said to produce exceptionally polarized high skills/low skills labour forces. These contain abundant high skilled elites which serve the needs of the knowledge-intensive, high skills sectors of high value-added production and services, such as design, media, pharmaceuticals, IT, aero and defense engineering and so on. On the other hand, the abundant low-skilled workforce meets the needs of the sectors which compete on costs and efficiency by providing cheap and flexible labour (Keep 1998).

Other sectors, like banking and chemicals, seem to require highly polarized skills sets in their employees and thus can also be said to be well served by the skills formation systems (Brown, Green and Lauder 2001). In the typical binary contrast, countries like Germany, and other core European states, are seen to compete economically mainly through highly diversified quality production in manufacturing (Streeck 1997) which requires more evenly distributed skills and, in particular, a large body of skilled craft workers and technicians. The skills formation systems in these countries generally achieve this in as much as the majority of the workforce – generally over two-thirds – are qualified at intermediate levels with relatively smaller skilled elites and low skilled workforces (Brown, Green and Lauder 2001).

But how do the skills formation and social-economic models articulate in the more differentiated tripodic typology of knowledge economies and knowledge societies proposed here? And what are the mechanisms and characteristics of the putative regional lifelong learning systems which promote and support the features of the different models?

Three aspects concern us here: first, the overall proportion of high skilled employees turned out in each type of system; secondly, how skills are distributed through the workforce; and thirdly, how far adults are involved in learning. Each of these education output characteristics relates to the features of the different knowledge economy/society models we have distinguished. Lifelong learning systems which produce a high volume of high-skilled employees will be promoting high skills, high labour-productivity economies. Systems which produce a relatively even distribution of skills will be promoting the more income-equal type high skills economy. Systems with strong adult learning cultures are likely to support high employment rates since they are associated with the Active Labour Market policies which seem to achieve this.

To take the overal level of skills first, data from IALS seem to suggest that the proportion of high skilled jobs in the economies of different countries are broadly consistent with what would be predicted by the three regional models of the knowledge economy/society. Figure 6.8 shows the proportion of workers in high skilled jobs at the time of the IALS surveys conducted between 1994 and 1998. Denmark, Finland, Norway and Sweden are all in the survey and they form the group of countries with the highest average proportion in high skilled jobs. Core Europe is represented here by Austria, Germany, the Netherlands and Switzerland and these have on average a rather lower proportion of high skilled jobs. The predominantly English-speaking countries here include Australia, Canada, Ireland, New Zealand, the UK and the USA and they have the lowest proportion in high skilled jobs. The regional distributions are therefore consistent with the tripodic model of knowledge societies/economies which predicts skilled

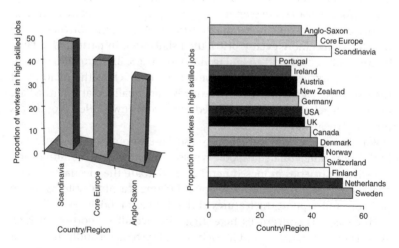

Figure 6.8   Proportion of workers in high skilled jobs by country and region

elites in the English-speaking countries, a higher overall level of skills in the high labour-productivity core Europe countries, and a somewhat higher level still in the more egalitarian Nordic countries.

The OECD analysis of the IALS data shows that there is a significant correlation between average literacy levels by country and the main measure of economic competitiveness: GDP per capita (OECD 2000, p. 80). There is also a strong cross-national correlation between aggregates for literacy levels and the proportion of workers in high skilled jobs, taken to include legislators, senior officials and managers, professional and associate professionals. In terms of achievement levels, IALS also shows that there are very clear regional patterns, at least with regard to the Nordic and English-speaking countries which belong to the only regional/cultural groupings well enough represented to make a judgement. The average scores for Nordic countries, as shown in Figure 6.9, are among the highest of all the 22 countries on all the measures of literacy and numeracy.

For prose literacy, Denmark, Finland, Norway and Sweden had average scores in country rank positions 1, 2, 3 and 8 respectively. For document literacy their averages were the highest (Sweden – 1; Norway – 2; Denmark – 3; Finland – 4) for all countries. Their averages were also among the highest in Quantitative Literacy (Sweden – 1; Denmark – 2; Norway – 4; Finland – 7). By contrast, the English-speaking countries, with the exception of Canada, all had averages in the bottom half of the country rankings on all measures. For prose literacy rank positions were:

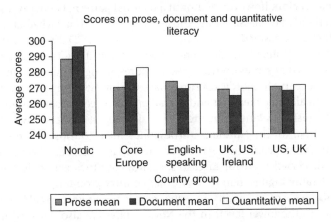

Figure 6.9 Mean literacy scores by region

New Zealand – 7; Australia – 9; USA – 10; UK – 13 and Ireland – 14. For Document Literacy the ranking were: Australia – 11; New Zealand – 14; USA – 15; UK – 16 and Ireland – 17. For Quantitative Literacy the rankings were: Australia – 12; USA – 13; New Zealand – 15; UK – 17; and Ireland – 18. Germany and the Netherlands had average scores on all measures in the middle of the top half of rankings. Switzerland's average scores are in the middle on all.

Figure 6.9 shows the mean scores for each country averaged by country grouping. Nordic countries have the highest average scores on prose, document and quantitative literacy. Core Europe countries average higher than English-speaking countries on document and quantitative literacy, but lower on prose literacy. The USA/UK/Ireland group performs similarly to the UK/USA group, and both have lower mean scores on all measures than the other country groups in the sample.

Turning to the question of educational equality and skills distribution we now have rather strong evidence from the IALS and PISA surveys, as we saw in chapter 5, about how the different regions compare in terms of skills distribution and equality in education.

Differences between regions in degrees of dispersal of literacy scores are very marked in the IALS survey. In terms of the range between the 5th and the 95th percentiles of scores, across the three measures for reading, writing and numeracy, the Nordic countries all fall into a group which OECD classify as having 'consistently small' dispersal in scores. Canada, the UK and the USA fall into the group classified as having 'consistently large' dispersal, although Australia and New Zealand have 'consistently moderate or varying' degrees of dispersal. Countries in the German region, however, do not fit a regional pattern. Germany and the Netherlands are classified as 'consistently small', but Switzerland and Belgium are classified as 'moderate or varying' (OECD 2000, p. 14).

Figure 6.10 shows the differences between country groups in terms of the dispersal of scores on the three measures, using standard deviations. As can be seen, the Nordic countries have the lowest average degree of dispersal on all three measures and overall on the three measures combined. The English-speaking countries have degrees of dispersal which are higher than for the Nordic countries, but similar to those for the group of core Europe countries. Scores for the UK and the USA, however, are more dispersed than for English-speaking countries generally and are considerably higher than for any other country grouping.

High levels of inequality in outcomes in the English-speaking states relative to the lower levels in the Nordic states are also reflected in the measures for socioeconomic gradients which show the impact of

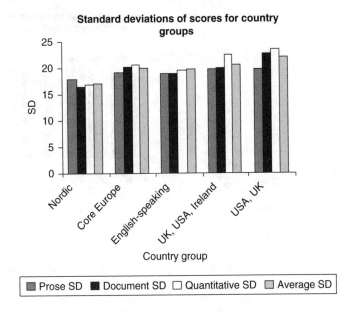

Figure 6.10 Distribution of literacy scores by region

parental education on individual outcomes. The OECD groups countries according to the steepness of the gradient for document literacy scores of the population aged 16–25. Australia, Canada, Ireland, New Zealand, the UK and the USA all have gradients of a similar steepness with an average gap of 30 percentage points in the scores of an average young person whose parents had eight years of schooling and someone whose parents had twelve years of schooling (OECD 2000, p. 30). By contrast, the four Nordic countries all have a much shallower gradient. The OECD gloss that: 'The striking degree of homogeneity in these results [for the Nordic countries] points to the existence of a degree of commonality in Nordic approaches to education and society' (p. 32).

Similar country clustering on education inequality measures can be found in the data from the PISA survey for 15-year-olds, as we saw in chapter 5. Figure 6.11 shows the degrees of dispersal in scores (in standard deviations) for each type of skill and all the skills combined in terms of the averages for each region or country cluster. The Asian group (comprising Japan and Korea) have the lowest average dispersal in scores for all types of skill combined by a long margin. Next come the Nordic countries (including Denmark, Finland, Iceland, Norway and Sweden), followed by the southern European countries (Italy, Greece, Spain and

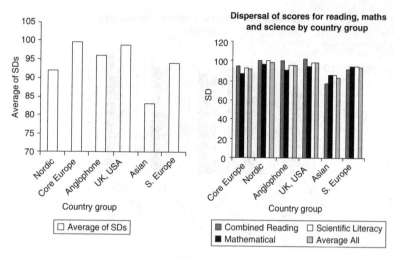

Figure 6.11 Dispersal of scores for reading, Maths and Science by country group

Portugal). The Anglophone (or part Anglophone) countries together (including Australia, Canada, Ireland, New Zealand, the USA and the UK) have lower degrees of dispersal than core Europe countries (Austria, Belgium, France, Germany, Luxembourg and Switzerland), which are the most dispersed along with the USA/UK group.

The patterns above suggest regional affinities in terms of levels of educational equality. The Nordic countries form one rather well delineated group with, in general, rather low levels of inequality in skills both among young people and adults. The English-speaking countries, excepting the Republic of Ireland and Canada, form another, with very high levels of inequality for both youth and adult skills. Germany, Belgium and Switzerland, representing core Europe in these samples, also have rather high levels of inequality, although Germany comes out more equal on the measures of adult skills than 15-year-olds' skills, possibly due to the mitigating effects on low skills experienced by the young people who go through the apprenticeship system.

Recent research by Blanden, Gregg and Machin (2005) from the London School of Economics also supports this regional patterning of inequality. Using comparable longitudinal data for cohorts born in the 1950s and 1970s they find that inter-generational mobility in Britain and the USA is substantially lower than in Canada and the Nordic countries, with Germany apparently somewhere in between the two groups (although the sample size qualifies the validity of this finding for Germany). They also found that the strength of the social inheritance effect, particularly as regards the link between family income and higher education participation and attainment, was at the heart of the explanation of Britain's low mobility culture.

Again the regional patterns in lifelong learning show a close relationship to the regional models of the knowledge economy/society. The group with the lowest level of income inequality, the Nordic countries, is the same as the group with the lowest level of educational equality. Likewise the group with the higher levels of educational inequality (the English-speaking group minus perhaps Canada and Ireland whose rankings are ambiguous) is the same as the group with high levels of income inequality.

A final connection between regional lifelong learning models and models of the knowledge economy/society relates to the distribution of adult learning. One claim made for the distinctiveness of the Nordic model of the knowledge society is that it achieves high levels of employment at the same time as low levels of income equality. According to the analysis of de Mooij and Tang (2003), this may be partly explained by the prevalence of Active Labour Market policies which appear, unlike other forms of labour market intervention, to promote employment without reducing wage equality. The data on adult participation in learning in Figure 6.12 would seem to support this explanation. Adult learning, as measured here, can, of course, come in many forms. All forms are likely to be beneficial to raising employment since they counteract

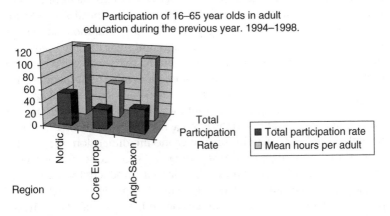

Figure 6.12 Proportion of adults participating in adult education

the tendency towards obsolescence of skills among older workers and thus increase their chances of maintaining employment. Some of the adult learning here, however, is likely to be in the form of targeted measures for the unemployed or soon-to-be-made unemployed, which generally go under the title of Active Labour Market policy. It is notable from Figure 6.12 that rates of participation in adult learning, on both total rates and mean hours, are highest in the Nordic group of countries. According to Rubenson's evidence, cited earlier, access to adult learning is also more equal in these countries which combine high employment rates and low income equality. English-speaking countries, which have generally high employment rates (except Ireland) but lower levels of income equality, come between the Nordic countries and Core Europe on both measures of participation. The core Europe countries, which have substantially lower rates of employment, although greater income equality than the English-speaking countries, have the lowest average participation rates.

What processes contribute to the economic and social effects in each model?

The model proposed here suggests a number of hypotheses about the role of lifelong learning in the development of the different types of knowledge economy/society, which we have characterized as liberal Anglo-Saxon; neo-corporatist core European; and social democratic Nordic.

Firstly, the type of knowledge economy/society is defined in terms of its overall productivity and social outcome properties whose proximal determinants are variously labour productivity, employment rates, wage equality, skills distribution and socialization. The liberal Anglo-Saxon model of the knowledge economy tends to combine moderate labour productivity with high employment rates and high income inequality, producing medium to high overall productivity on the economic dimension and, on the social dimension, moderate social spending and lower measures of social cohesion. The neo-corporatist core European model of the knowledge society combines high labour productivity with lower employment rates and lower wage inequality producing moderate to high overall productivity on the economic dimension and, on the social dimension, higher social spending and social cohesion outcomes. The Nordic model combines high labour productivity with high employment rates and relative wage equality, producing high overall productivity on the economic dimension and, on the social dimension, high social spending and high social cohesion.

Secondly, lifelong learning plays a central part in generating each of the proximal causes of the different models, in conjunction with, inter alia, the effects of welfare regimes and labour market regulation. In a linear representation of the causal chain (Figure 6.13 – straight arrows), lifelong learning systems produce different types of skills distribution and differential forms of socialization which affect employment rates, productivity, income distribution and social cohesion either directly or indirectly. Here we ignore the process of socialization and identity formation, even though this is undoubtedly part of the process of determining the different regimes of social cohesion, and we concentrate on the distribution effects. Three dimensions of lifelong learning outcomes seem to be crucial to each of the causal chains: the overall output of skills for the labour market; the distribution of these skills; and the rates of participation in adult learning. We have identified three ways in which the different outcomes of lifelong learning may impact on the knowledge economy model, although these cannot be considered entirely separately.

First, in the obvious case, lifelong learning systems that introduce high average levels of skill into the labour market are likely to contribute to high overall labour productivity as skill is converted into productive outcomes, with the assistance of capital investment and other production factors. Secondly, lifelong learning systems generate different levels of inequality in the distributions of skills they pass on to the labour market.

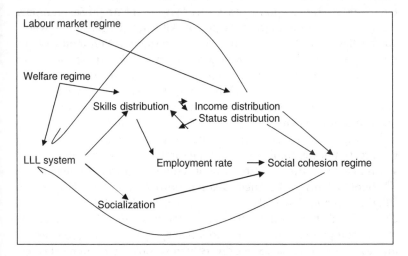

Figure 6.13   Education effects on social cohesion: pathways

These different skills distributions, in conjunction with different forms of labour market regulation, will affect levels of income and status inequality among employees which, together with the redistributive effects of welfare systems on overall household incomes distribution, will finally impact on levels of social cohesion. Thirdly, lifelong learning systems will impact on employment rates which affect both overall productivity and social cohesion. In particular, lifelong learning systems with high levels of adult participation in learning, especially through Active Labour Market policy, will promote high rates of employment which are one, although partial, means of raising social cohesion through 'social inclusion'.

So what are the structures and processes of the lifelong learning systems in each model which produce the salient effects?

The lifelong learning systems in the liberal Anglo-Saxon model tend, as we have seen, to produce moderate aggregate levels of skills in the labour market with a high degree of skills polarization between elites and the low skilled. These outcomes may contribute respectively towards the rather moderate average levels of labour productivity, the high level of income inequality and the lower level of social cohesion. The moderate aggregate levels of skills are the product of skills polarization since the high skills of the elites are balanced by the lower skills of the less qualified (assuming that there is a limit to how far you can raise the overall average without attenuating the bottom end), so the question resolves itself into one of skills inequality and the problem of the 'long tail of underachievers' in these systems. Why do the Anglo-Saxon model systems produce such a high degree of skills inequality? One possible answer lies in the effects of their welfare systems which tend to have rather poor provision of pre-school education for those on lower incomes and which do little to support the incomes of families with no or low wages. As repeated research shows, children of low-income families – which in the countries following this model are disproportionately likely to be sole-parent families – are more likely to underachieve in education, especially if there is inadequate pre-school education to mitigate the effects of lower human and cultural capital in the home. However, it seems likely that there is also a school system effect working here.

School systems in the Anglo-Saxon countries, and particularly in the UK, the USA and New Zealand, are notable for their high levels of school diversity and choice and for having regulatory systems, based on quasi-market competition and local school management, which are likely to increase school diversity. Since diversity in schools seems, in most cases, to mean diversity in school standards, these systems, although nominally comprehensive in structure, tend to produce high levels of between-school variation in achievement (see OECD 2002) which is likely, other things being equal, to increase overall inequality in outcomes. As far as school choice is linked to ability to pay – or to cultural capital endowment associated with occupation and income – then such systems are likely to increase the degree of social background determination in school achievement, thus reducing social mobility and increasing social inequality in education. This, as we have seen, may have negative effects on income inequality and – ultimately – on social cohesion.

On the other hand, the lifelong learning systems in the Anglo-Saxon countries tend to provide quite good opportunities for adult learning, as implied by the relatively high rates of participation achieved. Although the evidence suggests that such opportunities are closely linked to initial levels of education – thus in effect exacerbating the inequalities inherited from the school system (Brown, Green and Lauder 2001; EC 1999, 2002) – the existence of high rates of adult learning, even if unevenly distributed, and particularly where associated with Active Labour Market policy, is likely to boost employment rates through making excluded workers more employable. High employment rates will reduce the number of the socially excluded, and thus are likely to have some positive effects on social cohesion. However, the effects in the case of the Anglo-Saxon model countries may be limited because high wage inequality, even in conditions of near full employment, may still be detrimental to social cohesion.

The lifelong learning systems in the core Europe countries seem to work differently. They produce aggregate levels of skills which are as high, if not higher than in the Anglo-Saxon countries, depending on the country case, which will have positive effects on labour productivity. They also appear to produce rather narrower distributions of skills, at least among the adult workforce, which are conducive towards creating rather higher levels of income equality which will be beneficial to social cohesion. However, this may seem paradoxical since their compulsory school systems produce very unequal outcomes. A number of explanations may be offered. The compulsory school systems do produce very unequal outcomes (except in the case of France) because, excepting France, all the countries in this group have selective and differentiated school systems which, by their nature, are intended to produce a diversity of outcomes. However, the inequality of outcomes measured among 15-year-olds, is not reflected in the adult population overall. This is probably due to two causes. One is that change in qualification rates in a number of these countries has been rather slow relative to other country groups and there is therefore less inter-cohort variation in skills levels within the adult population. The second is that all these countries, again excepting France, have strong apprenticeship systems which provide an additional three years of general (as well as vocational) education to the majority of young people who participate in them. This is likely to have a substantial effect on mitigating the variation in literacy and numeracy skills levels observed among the 15-year-olds, although further testing of 18- and 19-year-olds would be necessary to test this assumption. The net impact of these two system effects is a level of adult skills inequality which is higher than for the Nordic countries but rather lower than for the Anglo-Saxon countries. This, combined with forms of labour market regulation that reduce wage inequality (that is, in most of the countries, various combinations of minimum wage, sectoral pay bargaining and setting of wage rates for occupations, company co-determination and so on), serves to reduce overall wage inequality and promote social cohesion.

However, in the core European countries, another process occurs which may not be so beneficial for overall equality and social cohesion. Labour market regulation, in the form of statutory laws on Licence to Practise and sectoral agreements on pay and qualification for skilled occupations, have adverse consequences in terms of overall income equality as well as beneficial effects on wage equality. Firstly, strong labour market regulation raises the costs to employers of creating new jobs and is therefore likely to be associated with higher levels of unemployment. Secondly, because labour market sectoral agreements serve to define most jobs as skilled, and to enforce qualification requirements for entry into these jobs, they create strong barriers to employment to the unqualified. While apprenticeship systems generally provide a rather smooth transition to employment for those who participate, for those who cannot secure apprentice places, and who have not otherwise acquired general education qualifications which will help them get jobs, employment prospects are very bleak. Typically, the proportion without at least skilled qualifications (at ISCED level 3) in these countries are rather smaller than in the Anglo-Saxon countries (Brown, Green and Lauder 2001). On the other hand, those at this level are probably rather more disadvantaged, owing to the greater barriers to their employment. The core European countries, which have high labour market regulation as well as highly tracked lifelong learning systems, therefore create something of a 'curate's egg' situation in terms of social inclusion and equality. Relatively high levels of wage equality are achieved, but at the cost of increased division between the employed and unemployed which are only partially attenuated by generous benefit systems. This may in part explain why levels of social cohesion are not as great in many cases as would be suggested by the relatively high degrees of wage equality.

The Nordic countries, finally, seem to offer a rather different set of relationships. They produce high aggregate levels and narrow distributions of skills in the labour force, which will contribute to the high levels of labour productivity at the same time as reducing wage inequality. High participation in adult learning will promote employment rates which, along with high productivity rates, yield high overall productivity levels. High rates of employment, together with low income inequality, and strong redistributive effects from welfare systems, will reduce overall inequality and support social cohesion.

Lifelong learning systems seem to contribute in two ways to the beneficial outcomes in both economic and social domains. Firstly, they produce relatively equal skills levels both among 15-year-olds and adults. This may be partly due to the Esping-Andersen welfare effects. Labour protection and regulation policies reduce the incidence of low-income families whose children would be statistically more likely to underachieve in education. Universal state provided pre-school education also provides an early socialization which offsets the depressing effect on educational aspirations and achievement of lower reserves of human and cultural capital in the family (Esping-Andersen 2003). Consequently, underachievement linked to social class – and particularly in the Anglo-Saxon countries, to low-income, sole-parent family backgrounds – is reduced, thus increasing overall equality in educational outcomes. However, it would also seem highly likely that there are education system effects as well. What is notable about the relatively egalitarian Nordic (and indeed Asian) education systems, is that they all have completely comprehensive and non-selective school systems in the state sector, with mixed ability teaching throughout, and, in the Nordic region at least, very small elite private sectors in education. In the Nordic case the egalitarian structures are compounded by the typically neighbourhood basis of school admissions (OECD 1994). Since primary and lower secondary schooling is integrated in all through schools, the issue of school choice at lower secondary entry age is removed except where families move area. Given that lower levels of income inequality in the Nordic countries usually means rather less social class differentiation between neighbourhoods, where schools admit children on a neighbourhood basis this is likely to mean rather low levels of social differentiation between schools and consequently lower levels of variations in performance between schools, as we saw in chapter 5 (OECD 2002).

The other notable effect from the lifelong learning system would appear to be from the high levels and relatively even distribution of participation in adult learning taking place in the Nordic countries. This partly relates to the Active Labour Market measures which encourage re-skilling of the unemployed and about-to-become unemployed, which may well have positive effects on employment rates and consequently on social inclusion. It also relates to the rather widespread provision of state-funded general adult education (not least in the uniquely Nordic day and residential folk high schools) which may contribute towards adult employability but which also serve, in the case of the *Folkehojskole*, as forums for promoting community spirit, political awareness and social cohesion (Boucher 1982; Rubenson 2002). It is important to note here how lifelong learning systems in the Nordic countries interact in positive ways with the labour market regime, not only through Active Labour Market policies but also through the combination of relative labour market flexibility with employment protection, a combination which, in relation to Denmark, has been refered to as 'flexicurity' (Lundvall 2005).

Taken together, the egalitarian school systems and the pervasive adult learning opportunities would seem to maximize the potential effects on lifelong learning both through social inclusion (in the labour market), socialization and income equalization.

Reverse effects

The discussion thus far hypothesizes a one-way causal chain linking lifelong learning systems with different economic and social outcomes. This is, of course, a simplification. Correlational analysis of cross-sectional data suggests that there is an association between different variables which represent the links in the chain, and provisional analysis of time series data suggests that the association may be causal. Theoretical deductions and comparative logic also suggest a causal relationship. But we have no clear evidence as yet on which way the causality may run. The likelihood is that causality runs in both directions between many of the variables (as suggested by the curved arrows in Figure 6.13).

At the level of ideology and politics it is highly likely that social cohesion impacts on lifelong learning systems at the same time as lifelong learning systems contribute towards social cohesion. Lifelong learning systems are the product of policy choices that are shaped by politics and ideology. Issues of system design that affect equality are, and always have been, contested and highly political, as in the post-1960s debates about comprehensive schooling (Benn and Chitty 2004) and in current debates about school choice and diversity. Countries, like those in the Nordic region, which have achieved highly egalitarian comprehensive systems have done so over many years of political contestation and under the influence of powerful social liberal and social democratic ideologies underpinned by exceptionally cohesive social structures (Wiborg 2005). In these cases it is not hard to see that 'social cohesion' is, in effect, one of the conditions for the kind of political mobilization that allows equality-favouring policies in education to be adopted in the first place. So the causality may be seen to run both ways.

In terms of the lifelong learning system/income equality relationship it is highly likely that income inequality contributes towards the generation of unequal outcomes in education at the same time as unequal outcomes affect income inequality. Countries characterized by more unequal social structures are likely to have more unequal education systems. High-income elites are liable to lobby for elite private schools or for selective state schools, so as to pass on their advantages to their children, and these will increase the inequality of educational outcomes. Income inequality is likely to increase residential segregation among social groups, which will lead to wider variation in the social mix of intakes between schools, even in systems with neighbourhood-based admissions policies, and this will lead to higher between-school variation in achievement of students (Ball 2003). Highly unequal income endowments among families are also likely to be associated with variations in educational aspiration and 'cultural capital' among parents, which will condition the choices of educational paths made by students and thus reproduce social inequality in educational outcomes (Boudon 1974; Bourdieu 1986).

Daniele Checchi (2001) has analysed the reciprocal relations using lagged time series analysis for a group of 97 countries for which we have data for years between 1960 and 1995 on trends in both educational inequality and income inequality. His findings show that there are correlations between the two but that the relationships are region-specific and nonlinear. For the OECD countries, which most concern us here, there was a general trend towards increasing educational inequality during the period, accompanied, after 1975, by increasing income inequality. In Checchi's analysis causation runs both ways, although the effects are lagged: 'current income inequality affects future educational inequality, which, according to human capital theory, will shape future income inequality' (p. 45).

Conclusions

The analysis conducted here suggests a threefold typology of knowledge economies and knowledge societies which calls for revisions in the traditionally binary approach to analysis of models of economic competitiveness and social cohesion. Rather than focusing only on the differences between the neo-liberal and social market models of the knowledge economy, with the typical policy deductions of zero-sum trade-offs between policies and characteristics associated with each, we should assume that there are at least three models of the knowledge economy/society in Europe and that the Nordic model is in fact quite distinct from the social market model of the core European states and better able to combine the benefits of economic competitiveness and social cohesion than either the core European model or the neo-liberal model. In this sense the Nordic countries come closer to the Lisbon Goal than either of the other two groupings and more than has currently been acknowledged in policy debates about the future of Europe.

If this is the case it has important ramifications for lifelong learning policy. European debates assume, rightly, that increasing European competitiveness requires improving employment rates (Kok 2004); they also acknowledge, although with diminishing emphasis, that maintaining social cohesion requires not only social inclusion through employment but also reasonable levels of income equality. Lifelong learning, as the Nordic examples show, can play a vital role in achieving both of these. However, it can only do so if we acknowledge, more than is currently the case, that increasing educational equality matters as much as raising overall standards.

7
Conclusion: Some Remarks on Future Research

The analysis in this book remains provisional and incomplete, like most academic endeavours. We have set out some novel hypotheses which we think have important policy implications and find considerable support for them both from theory and in our empirical tests. However, there remains more research to be done to determine the multiple causations of social cohesion and to understand the mechanisms and processes through which education influences socially cohesive outcomes. The analysis here has involved a number of interconnected parts.

Defining social cohesion

First of all, we have sought to understand what social cohesion means in modern developed societies at a time of rapid globalization. We have approached this both by examining theories of social cohesion and by investigating the patterns in the data across countries for different indicators of social cohesion. Our first conclusions are, in a sense, frustratingly indeterminate. We cannot define a single form of social cohesion nor find adequate empirical measures for such a definition. In fact, it would appear that there are multiple types of social cohesion – different social cohesion regimes, as we call them – which can be found in different times and places. Only much deeper historical investigation could throw substantially more light on the ways in which we may define these different forms. Nevertheless, we are able to clarify some of the common components of these different forms by analysing the patterns of variation for their measures across countries and this we can use to interrogate some of the different theories of social cohesion.

We started from the currently dominant theories of social capital and examined how far these can be applied to cohesion throughout whole societies. What we found is that the cluster of characteristics by which social capital theorists define individual social capital as a coherent syndrome make little sense when it comes to the consideration of whole societies. Social capital theory argues that individuals who associate more with others tend also to be more tolerant, more trusting in other people and institutions, give more to charity and be more politically engaged. Social groups and communities made up of such people tend to co-operate more effectively than other groups and communities which do not contain as many people like this. The key to the process, according to leading theorists like Putnam, is the regularity of associational activity which helps to build trust and reciprocity.

Scaled up from communities to societies as a whole, the theory closely resembles the notion of democracy in the liberal theories of de Tocqueville and others, where it is the vibrancy of civil association – and the dynamism of civil society – which vouchsafes a healthy democracy. However, empirical tests of the theory at the level of societies does not confirm the core assertions regarding the relationships between the different components. As we demonstrated in chapters 1 and 3, standard measures for the different components of social capital do not generally co-vary across countries. In particular, levels of tolerance and associational activity show no relation across countries to levels of trust and crime, so that some countries may have very active civil association and low levels of trust, like the USA, while others, like the Nordic countries, will have high levels of trust, but only moderate to low levels of association.

As we suggest in chapter 1, the empirical problem here is that association is a crude quantitative measure that cannot distinguish adequately between the kinds of association that promote trust and tolerance and those that may do the opposite. Social capital theory, consequently, is able to show that trust and association may go together in intra-group settings, but not that association necessarily leads to inter-community and inter-group harmony and solidarity. As we argue in chapter 1, social capital does not necessarily translate up from the level of the community to the level of whole societies and therefore cannot be an adequate way to conceptualize social cohesion.

This problem of the non-correspondence between levels, between community and society, points to a deeper difficulty in liberal theories of democracy and social cohesion. Vibrant associational life and a strong civil society are not necessarily enough to guarantee a cohesive society. A strong civil society – with dense associational networks between the state and individuals' families – may generally be a good thing, and most democracies have needed to develop this to work effectively.

However, civil association can take many different forms, many of which may well not contribute towards cohesive societal relationships. One thinks, for instance, of countries with high levels of inequality and deep class and racial divisions where many associations may spring up, whether to fight for greater equity for particular groups, or to repress certain other groups, as in the case of racist organizations. Whether the causes of these organizations are just or oppressive, their forms of association represent conflict rather than cohesion. High levels of association may well be indicative of struggles which, over time, create more cohesive societies, but association in this case can hardly be equated with cohesion in a synchronic analysis. Likewise there are many forms of association which represent only the self interest of particular groups and therefore do little to generate cohesion at large. As Fukuyama (1999) has argued, much of the associational activity measured by Putnam in countries like the USA may well be of this sort. More generally, it can be argued that as societies become more individualized and as identity becomes more focused around the particularities of lifestyle, locality and ethnic group, associational activity reflects this by becoming more narrow in its aims – more morally miniature as Fukuyama says – and less encompassing in its memberships, thus contributing less to overall societal cohesion.

While liberal theories have emphasized civic association as the primary source of social integration what they have lacked is an analysis of the roles of the state and the major institutions in society. This has been for the fairly obvious reason that their ideological roots – at least in the American case – lay in decidedly anti-statist beliefs. Social democratic theory, on the other hand, from Durkheim onwards, has shown much greater appreciation of the importance of the state and the major societal institutions in underpinning social cohesion. In its modern forms this has typically not only involved a stress on the welfare institutions, but also on the whole apparatus of social partnership between employer and employee organizations. This perspective allows a way through the problem which has confounded Putnam of distinguishing between associational activity that promotes cohesion and associational activity that increases social divisions. Social democratic theories of social partnership are based on notions of the importance of organized interest group intermediation in concerting and reconciling interests and mediating social conflict. The key to this process is the existence of encompassing interest group organizations. In the positive reading of such organizations one can see a way of distinguishing forms of association which serve to generate cohesion and those which do not. It is the organizations with encompassing memberships, concerting wide interests, and negotiating with other such organizations for consensual solutions, which may be seen as the basis for the positive link between association and social cohesion which has eluded the social capital theorists.

Understanding such processes, of course, requires much more qualitative analysis and less reliance on crude quantitative measures. This book has only made a start in doing such work and thus in exploring the institutional bases of social cohesion. However, the analysis we have conducted not only shows this to be an important dimension, but also gives some other clues as to how we may begin to define and distinguish different forms of social cohesion.

Our cross-country statistical analyses suggest that there are some core traits of at least one form of social cohesion. While measures for association and tolerance show no co-variance with other measures of social cohesion, there are at least four measures that do seem to be related. Trust in others, trust in institutions, civic cooperation and, inversely, crime, are all associated and, we would argue, form a coherent set of characteristics which many would recognize as central to social cohesion. Trust would appear to be one of the most robust and generalizable elements here, not least because its patterns of variation across countries are so consistent, because countries vary so widely on the measure, and because it is statistically correlated with so many other factors which theory would suggest are effects of social cohesion (not least of which being economic growth). In addition, the fact that trust in institutions appears as one of the core measures is consistent with the emphasis from social democratic theory, with which we concur, on the importance of institutions. We do, then, seem to have a core set of properties by which we may begin to define social cohesion and a set of indicators by which to measure them. However, other problems emerge at this point.

Tolerance would be identified by many as a key constituent of socially cohesive societies. However, on the conventional measures (of ethnic and cultural tolerance, and so on) it does not co-vary across countries with our other 'core' measures. A simple solution at this point would be to say that tolerance is in fact a distinct phenomenon that, despite common perceptions, is not related to social cohesion. One line of argument, favoured by liberal nationalists, would be that trust is actually a product of ethnic homogeneity which, by extension, we could argue, does not necessarily imply tolerance at all. If societies which value trust believe that they can only be trusting if they share a very homogeneous culture then one might well expect them to be intolerant of other cultures. However, our empirical tests in chapter 4 substantially undercut this line of reasoning. There would appear to be no relationship between ethno-cultural homogeneity and trust across countries and equally no relationship between ethnic diversity and levels of patriotism. Patriotism and tolerance are also not highly correlated. Diverse societies can be patriotic and show a high level of trust, just as homogeneous societies can be distrusting or lacking in patriotic pride.

We are therefore left with a paradoxical and open-ended definition of social cohesion. There would appear to be an identifiable core of characteristics which form the main constituents of social cohesion – trust, cooperation, low crime – but also other characteristics, like tolerance, which may also be constitutive, but which are to some degree in tension, or at least not fully consonant, with the first set of characteristics. This leads us to the conclusion that we should talk not of social cohesion as a single, unitary property, but of different types of social cohesion which combine different constituent elements in different configurations. This is fairly unsatisfactory for statistical analysis but may well be much closer to historical realities. We tend to think of tightly knit countries, like the Nordic states, as the most socially cohesive. However, we should also recognize other possibilities. We could, for instance, argue that there have been examples of diverse and fairly loosely bonded societies which are not highly trusting and law-abiding, but which show a degree of tolerance to other cultures and lifestyles, where such tolerance, while more *laissez-faire* than engaged, and somewhat short of what may be called social solidarity, represents the mode and extent of such social cohesion as exists. These cases are, of course, worth identifying. So for now the way forward would seem to be to conduct more qualitative and historical analyses of different social cohesion regimes, recognizing that each will have different configurations of constituent elements, and that these configurations will be highly dependent on context. As far as statistical analysis is concerned, without better theory, the most that can be done is to continue to identify relationships between each of the different indicators, taken separately, and the different relevant contextual variables across countries and regions.

Education, equality and social cohesion

The main purpose of the studies in this book has been to identify how education impacts on different aspects of social cohesion. The model proposed at the outset assumed that education may impact in two different ways: the first, indirectly, through the way it distributes skills, and hence incomes, opportunity and status among adult populations; and the second, through how it socializes students through the formation of values and identities.

Our findings in relation to the first pathway – our distributional model – appear to be quite clear-cut. As chapters 1 and 2 demonstrate, while there are no apparent relationships between aggregate levels of education and social cohesion indicators across countries, there are quite strong and significant correlations between measures of educational equality, income equality and a wide range of social cohesion outcomes, including general and institutional trust, crime, civil liberties and political liberties. More education-equal countries tend to be more income equal and rate higher on a range of social cohesion measures. Furthermore, educational equality appears to have a positive relationship with social cohesion outcomes independently of income distribution. Both cross-sectional and time series data were analysed, with the analysis of the latter adding considerable weight to the initial evidence, albeit that the relationships it demonstrated were nonlinear. We can therefore say with some confidence that, barring explanations in terms of 'third causes', which we have not yet found, there would seem to be some kind of causal relationship between how skills are distributed and levels of cohesion in societies. However, we still cannot be clear about the directions of causality or the exact mechanisms through which education has its effects, and without specification of these explanations the argument remains incomplete.

We can only speculate on the mechanisms based on extrapolation from cognate theory. It would seem plausible that educational inequality might affect societal cohesion through a number of different routes. Unequal education systems are likely to contribute towards greater social and economic inequality in society at large (as well as being the product of it) and in as much as this leads to social conflict we may say that education is in this way acting detrimentally to social cohesion. The effect may occur independently of income inequality in so far as unequal education may exacerbate status and cultural disparities between groups, which can also be a source of conflict. To take a more culturalist explanation, we may say that even where educational inequality leads to greater social differentiation without increased conflict it may nevertheless increase the cultural distance between individuals and groups of individuals in ways which make communication, cooperation and trust more difficult. Another, more social-psychological form of explanation, might be that educational inequalities, and the income and status inequalities they help to produce, generate status anxieties and competition stress for individuals and that stress and anxiety can become barriers to trust and cooperation.

Wilkinson (1996) has argued that most of the variation in levels of public health between countries can be explained by income inequality, rather than average wealth, and that inequality affects health through the stress levels it produces which are known contributors to disease and accidents. A similar argument could plausibly be applied to social cohesion (not least since trust and physical well-being seem to be related).

Our research strongly suggests that educational inequality is related to social cohesion outcomes. However, more research needs to be done before we can say exactly how this occurs. Three areas in particular need to be explored. Firstly, there needs to be a more exhaustive investigation than we have been able to conduct here of the role of various contextual variables which may be influencing both educational equality and social cohesion. These may represent third causes which would qualify our hypothesis regarding inequality and also add to our understanding of necessary consitions. Cross-sectional correlational analysis is particularly prone to finding correlations between variables which are in fact the result of other causes, and more time-series analysis, where the data can be found, is necessarily to rule this out. Secondly, since the direction of causality in relationships between our variables is still unclear, other statistical techniques, such as time-lag analysis, need to be applied using time-series analysis. Thirdly, there needs to be a fuller examination of the processes and mechanisms which may account for the relationships we find between educational equality and social cohesion. Qualitative analysis, including through interviews with students during their studies and in later life, may be conducted to investigate the ways in which learners internalize the meaning of inequality and their own positions within the spectrum of educational achievement and social hierarchies. Such studies would help us to understand how the experience of inequality in different contexts – in education and at subsequent points in life careers – impacts on values and identities which are pertinent for social cohesion. More statistical modelling can also be conducted, not least in relation to plausible mediating variables. Data exist for a range of countries on levels of stress, based on psychological tests, and on other indicators of well-being. This could be analysed alongside other variables.

Education and socialization

According to our initial hypothesis, the other main route by which education could impact on social cohesion is through the socialization process which includes both values and identity formation. It is our values and identities which ultimately condition how we regard and interact with other individuals and groups, determining with whom we associate, how we co-operate and whom we decide to trust. Identity is, in a sense, the most crucial since our received and adopted identities determine the affective and ideological boundaries of our worlds and thus the locus and ambit of our trust and co-operation. Educational sociology has, since its inception, and before identity theory was even invented, regarded socialization as one of the key functions of education, and has continued to maintain this, even in societies where schooling competes more with other socializing agencies. Empirical research on educational socialization has, arguably, rested more on the study of the intentions of educational actors, than on the observation of student value formation, and this may be a weakness, but the assumption in theory remains that education does impact on values.

Our chapters 3 and 4 have sought to analyse various aspects of this process in relation to the question of social cohesion. Given the relative paucity of data and the complexity of the issues, the findings are inevitably provisional, as elsewhere in the book. Tolerance appears as a multifaceted and highly situational variable at the country level and subject to rapid changes over time. We find little evidence that educational inequality impacts on levels of tolerance, although plausible theoretical arguments suggest that it might, but there is evidence for a number of countries, particularly from the studies of education and racism, that levels of education can affect attitudes and behaviours to do with tolerance. However, the effects, as observed in the individual-level data, are highly context-bound, varying in strength and mechanisms from country to country and between social groups. Relations between aggregate levels of education and tolerance across countries are far from clear, probably because tolerance is strongly affected by other country contexts, including levels and types of immigration, and the dominant political discourses surrounding these.

Our findings on the impacts of different types of education on values and identities are equally complex and also highly region-specific. In the cross-national analysis of aggregate data from the IEA study we found that in countries where students reported receiving effective education on pluralism, internationalism, patriotism and elections they also reported having higher levels of tolerance, but there was no relationship to levels of trust. Analysis of the individual-level data, however, showed that relationships between educational experiences and attitudinal outcomes varied substantially by region. Effective teaching about patriotic values was associated with higher levels of ethnic tolerance in southern European countries, for instance, but with lower levels of ethnic tolerance in north-western Europe.

One conclusion from this is that there is little conceptual equivalence in the meaning of some of the terms in different countries. Patriotism may have different signification in southern and central and eastern European compared to north-west European states, so that any associations between this and other variables become difficult to interpret. One way out of this problem is to use, where possible, more objective measures for variables. To date little work has been done on the impact of different education system characteristics on attitudes, other than using the crude measures of time spent in civic education. We would propose that future work may explore this further, particularly in terms of the effects of ethnic mixing in school intakes on the formation of attitudes. Policy makers in various countries are currently making important policy decisions about whether to integrate schools or increase the diversity of schools for different religions and language groups, often based on quite unsubstantiated claims about the benefits of either to community relations. It is time we were able to supply the evidence for more informed policy decisions in these areas.

Education systems and inequality

Our study has focused strongly on the distributional effects of education since for many of our social outcomes it seems to matter more how education is distributed than how much education a population, on average, has. We have therefore gone to some lengths to understand what characteristics of education systems are implicated in increasing or reducing educational equality. Our work here benefits from an exceptional improvement in the quality and coverage of data on educational inequality, made possible by the IALS and PISA studies, and the quality of existing analyses on these data. Our findings, based on logical comparative analysis of systems and outcomes, using qualitative data and descriptive statistics, support those of the OECD and others who have used more analytical statistical methods to analyse relationships across countries and within countries.

Whereas earlier research was unable to determine with any certainty the effects of school organization on degrees of educational equality across countries, our analysis, benefitting from improved data on the distribution of outcomes, provides very strong evidence of system effects on equality. On whichever measure of equality we choose, we find that countries cluster very consistently according to regional and cultural patterns which, for the most part, coincide with types of educational organization. Put at its simplest, those countries with the most developed forms of non-selective or comprehensive schooling tend also to be the countries which achieve most equal educational outcomes – both as measured for 15-year-olds and among adults – and the countries where social background has the least impact on attainment. On the contrary, the countries with most intake selection, school choice, tracking and curricula differentiation, tend to be the most unequal in terms of both outcomes and social inheritance. It may be objected, of course, that other national characteristics may be responsible for these cross-country correlations, and we would not rule out the possibility that differerent national welfare systems may play a significant part. However, the evidence for education system effects would seem to remain very strong.

There will be more data on educational outcomes from repeated surveys of PISA and other programmes in the years to come and this will provide us with the time series data which will allow more robust tests of causal effects between education systems and skills distribution. For the moment, however, there is still plenty more work that can be done to investigate these system effects across countries. More quantitative indicators of system characteristics can be developed which capture the degree of selection and differentiation in school systems and give further insights into the crucial mechanisms which promote educational inequality. There is also much to be gained from comparative studies across regions within countries, such as Switzerland and Germany, where different regions have different forms of educational organization. In allowing us to hold certain state-level factors constant, comparison across sub-national regions can provide exceptionally favourable conditions for analysing system effects.

Policy implications

The findings from this study, if correct, clearly have important implications for education policy. Policy makers in most countries are increasingly concerned with issues of social cohesion and the roles that education may play in promoting this. Three issues dominate policy debates about ways of making education more effective in this area. Firstly, many countries, particularly those with multilingual and multi-faith populations, are concerned with the faith and language of instruction policies to adopt in schools and whether there should be unitary national systems or systems of schools differentiated by language and religion. The trend in Europe and Asia in the 1960s and 1970s was generally towards more unitary systems with secular or multi-faith schools and monolingual or partially bilingual instruction. It would seem that this trend currently is in reverse, not just in the new nation-states of eastern and southern Europe, but also in western countries like England which is increasing its faith schools at a pace. Secondly, many countries are implementing new policies of citizenship education or else changing whole curricula in ways intended to reinforce chosen values and identities. Thirdly, many countries are seeking to increase levels of skills in general and particularly skills deemed relevant to active citizenship.

Our research findings have no direct implications for policies on the organization of schools in terms of language or religion. We find generally that differentiation in schools, in terms of social and educational composition of intakes, is not conducive to social cohesion, and one might, by analogy, extend this argument to religious and linguistic differentiation. However, we lack direct evidence on the effects of this on attitudes. In terms of values education, our research does suggest that schools have effects and that socialization remains an important function of schools. However, precisely what effects result in different contexts from the particular values and identities fostered in schools remains highly obscure to researchers and seems to vary from region to region. Certainly any general presumptions that more patriotic kinds of education are likely to foster greater cohesion seem misplaced, given our evidence, although more focus on learning for pluralism and internationalism does seem to be a positive for the promotion of tolerance.

The major policy implications of our research relate to questions of educational equality. Policy makers in many countries are currently much more focused on raising the average national levels of achievement of their school leavers and adults than on questions of distribution and equality. This is a trend that has gathered pace over the past 25 years, encouraged by the international and national cultures of targets, league tables and country rankings and by the national obsessions with raising skills levels for economic competitiveness. By contrast, questions of equality have been dropping down the agenda in many countries, not least because of completely unsubstantiated but widely held claims that excellence and equality are incompatible. The PISA studies have finally laid this ghost to rest since they show quite clearly that many of the countries with the highest overall levels of achievement are also countries with relatively equal outcomes. The climate of the times may, therefore, be propitious for a reconsideration of issues which have become undeservedly marginalized.

The principal message from this research is that educational equality matters. It probably matters more than is generally acknowledged for economic competitiveness, as we suggest in chapter 6. It most certainly matters for social cohesion. In fact, it seems likely that educational impacts on social cohesion have much more to do with how education is distributed than with how much a nation has overall. And educational equality is – very substantially – amenable to policy interventions. Countries which achieve more equal education and which, on our evidence, benefit therefrom in social cohesion, are countries which believe in the virtues of equality and which design their education systems to enhance it.

Appendix: Datasets Used in This Book

In our data analysis we use a wide variety of international data from many different sources. Where possible we take data from as few datasets as possible in our analysis (making the judgement that this aids the internal consistency of the analysis) and on occasion this may mean that slightly different statistics are used between analyses. For example, data on gini coefficients in chapter 2 comes from the ACLP dataset for the analysis of 'political' indicators and from World Bank data in the analysis of crime indicators (as the crime dataset does not include a measure of income inequality). Where we have created new data sources by merging datasets or extracting data we give the full dataset. In other cases we provide a reference where a full dataset could be obtained.

Chapter 1

As no one dataset could satisfy the types of international comparisons required, a combined dataset was constructed using data from the World Values Survey (WVS), International Adult Learning Survey (IALS), World Bank, Interpol statistics and the International Crime Victim Survey (ICVS). All data used were from the years 1990–2000 Fifteen countries were included in the core dataset: Australia, Belgium, Britain, Canada, Denmark, Finland, Ireland, Netherlands, Norway, Poland, Portugal, Sweden, Switzerland, USA and Germany.

Social cohesion measures were obtained from the most recent country sweep available of the WVS. In most cases, data used were from the 1995–1997 sweep, although when data for these years were not available, data from the 1990 sweep were substituted.

General Trust (GENERAL TRUST) was measured by the percentage of individuals sampled in each country who agreed that most people could be trusted when asked:

'Generally speaking, would you say that most people can be trusted or that you can't be too careful in dealing with people?' (WVS question V27)

Associational memberships (MEMBERSHIPS) was measured by the mean number of associational memberships for sampled individuals in each country, not including memberships of sporting associations (WVS questions V28 and V30–V36).

Trust in government (DEMTR) was measured by the percentage of individuals sampled in each country who agreed or strongly agreed that they had confidence in their parliament (WVS question V144).

Civic co-operation measures cheating on public transport fares (TRANSC) and cheating on taxes (TAX CHEATING) were measured by the percentage of individuals in each country who stated that such actions were never justifiable (WVS questions V193 and V194).

The measure of educational inequality (SKILL INEQUALITY) was obtained from IALS secondary data by dividing the mean prose score of those individuals who had completed tertiary education by the mean prose score of those who had completed upper secondary education only. To compute these scores, we utilized the most recent sweep of IALS data (IALS, 2000). Country statistics for this indicator are detailed in chapter 1.

Measures of income inequality (GINI) and GNP per capita (GNPCAPIT) were taken from the most recently available World Bank Statistics (World Bank 2001, pp. 282–3).

The measure of crime (CRIME) was obtained from Interpol statistics for 1996 (International Criminal Police Organisation 1996). The measure of crime used being the sum of homicides, robberies and violent thefts per 10,000 inhabitants.

The measure of tolerance (TOLERANCE) was obtained from question V57 of the WVS and measures the percentage of respondents in each country who would not mind having an immigrant as a neighbour.

The measure of perceived risk of crime (COMMUNITY SAFETY) was obtained from the mid-1990s, or most recent possible, sweep of the ICVS (International Crime Victims Survey) and measures the mean score for each country from respondents feelings of safety when walking alone after dark in the area (very safe = 1, very unsafe = 4). Figures were not available for Germany and Norway and so these countries were not included in analysis involving this variable.

Social capital/cohesion aggregates for 15 countries

	Abbreviation	General trust	Memberships	Democratic trust	Tax cheating	Transport cheat	Crime	Tolerance	Community safety
Norway	NW	64.80	.61	69.50	47.50	70.20	31.26	81.75	N/A
Denmark	DEN	57.70	.18	42.00	57.30	74.50	47.69	88.95	1.67
Sweden	SW	56.60	.52	44.60	49.30	47.00	85.38	95.34	1.68
Netherlands	NL	55.80	.36	51.60	42.90	55.80	121.46	88.64	1.83
Canada	CAN	50.70	.47	37.90	59.20	61.90	109.21	94.30	1.78
Finland	FIN	46.90	.32	32.40	57.40	62.60	45.42	85.44	1.77
Ireland	IRL	46.80	.23	50.30	48.80	57.50	96.88	93.78	1.99
Germany	D	41.80	.54	29.40	40.10	38.60	86.92	95.60	N/A
Australia	AU	39.90	1.06	30.60	62.10	62.80	37.38	95.42	2.25
Switzerland	SZ	37.80	.68	43.90	53.70	59.30	34.40	89.99	1.87
USA	US	35.00	1.63	30.30	73.60	66.50	209.85	90.31	1.95
Poland	PO	34.50	.03	34.50	55.20	68.10	71.04	75.89	2.29
Belgium	B	30.60	.28	42.80	33.90	57.70	29.84	82.28	1.89
Britain	UK	29.10	.20	46.10	53.90	59.40	144.83	88.30	2.10
Portugal	POR	20.70	.19	33.50	39.90	53.40	62.57	90.53	2.18

Sources: World Values Survey, Interpol, ICVS.

In addition to our main dataset, we also made use of an expanded dataset of 38 countries broadly corresponding to Knack and Keefer's (1997) set of market economies. Data were pooled from WVS sweeps of 1990 and 1995 to arrive at figures for general trust (GENERAL TRUST) and civic participation (MEMBERSHIPS) using the methods described above. Corresponding measures of income inequality (GINI) were obtained from World Bank statistics, but note that for five countries (Argentina, East Germany, Iceland, Taiwan and Ukraine) reliable gini coefficients were not available. Data for countries in the expanded dataset is provided in the table below.

Social capital/cohesion aggregates for 38 countries (expanded dataset)

Country	Abbreviation	General trust	Memberships	Gini
Argentina	ARG	17.1	0.43	N/A
Australia	AU	39.9	1.06	35.2
Austria	A	28.4	0.21	23.1
Belgium	B	30.6	0.28	25
Brazil	BRZ	2.8	0.91	60
Britain	UK	29.1	0.2	36.1
Bulgaria	BUL	23.7	0.11	28.3
Canada	CAN	50.7	0.47	31.5
Chile	CHI	21.9	0.68	56.5
Denmark	DEN	57.7	0.18	24.7
East Germany	EGe	24.9	0.4	N/A
Finland	FIN	46.9	0.32	25.6
France	FR	22.8	0.23	32.7
Hungary	HUN	23.8	0.15	30.8
Iceland	ICE	41.7	0.3	N/A
India	IND	33	0.53	37.8
Ireland	IRL	46.8	0.23	35.9
Italy	I	33.8	0.22	27.3
Japan	J	43.4	0.27	24.9
Mexico	MX	26.4	1.1	53.7
Netherlands	NL	55.8	0.36	32.6
Norway	NW	64.8	0.61	25.8
Peru	PER	4.9	0.58	46.2
Phillipines	PHI	5.5	0.42	46.2
Poland	PO	34.5	0.03	32.9
Portugal	POR	20.7	0.19	35.6
Russia	RUS	23.4	0.14	48.7
South Africa	SA	17.6	1.15	59.3
South Korea	SK	30.3	0.45	31.6
Spain	E	28.7	0.41	32.5
Sweden	SW	56.6	0.52	25
Switzerland	SZ	37.8	0.68	33.1
Taiwan	TAI	40.2	0.36	N/A
Ukraine	UKR	28.8	0.09	N/A
USA	US	35	1.63	40.8
West Germany	D	41.8	0.54	30
Nigeria	NI	19.47	0.59	50.6
Turkey	TU	5.49	0.22	41.5

Source: World Values Survey.

Chapter 2

Political outcomes

Country	Year	edgini	gini	civlib	pollib	unrest	gdp
Australia	1960	0.18				1	19261
Australia	1965	0.20				0	21246
Australia	1970	0.20	32.34			5	25218
Australia	1975	0.21	33.99	7	7	0	25988
Australia	1980	0.20	39.64	7	7	0	27276
Australia	1985	0.20	37.58	7	7	0	28960
Australia	1990	0.21	41.72	7	7	0	30312
Belgium	1960	0.26				6	14310
Belgium	1965	0.25				1	17790
Belgium	1970	0.20				0	22247
Belgium	1975	0.26		7	7	0	24859
Belgium	1980	0.28	27.90	7	7	0	27739
Belgium	1985	0.29	26.22	7	7	1	27325
Belgium	1990	0.29		7	7	0	31730
Bulgaria	1985	0.28	23.42	1	1	0	9662
Bulgaria	1990	0.21	24.53	4	5	12	12817
Canada	1960	0.22	31.11			0	19484
Canada	1965	0.24	31.61			1	22245
Canada	1970	0.25	32.27			3	24906
Canada	1975	0.24	31.62	7	7	1	27350
Canada	1980	0.22	31.40	7	7	0	28725
Canada	1985	0.17	32.81	7	7	0	31147
Canada	1990	0.16	27.56	7	7	5	34380
Denmark	1960	0.28				0	14807
Denmark	1965	0.28				1	17955
Denmark	1970	0.28				0	20021
Denmark	1975	0.28		7	7	0	20250
Denmark	1980	0.27	31.00	7	7	0	21481
Denmark	1985	0.27	32.41	7	7	1	23861
Denmark	1990	0.26		7	7	0	24971
Finland	1960	0.24				0	11577
Finland	1965	0.26				0	13938
Finland	1970	0.27	27.90			0	16980
Finland	1975	0.29	29.26	6	6	0	19698
Finland	1980	0.28	30.86	6	6	0	21788
Finland	1985	0.29	29.20	6	6	0	23700
Finland	1990	0.27		7	7	0	27350
France	1960	0.24	49.00			9	13478
France	1965	0.27	47.00			0	17027
France	1970	0.28	44.00			10	21598
France	1975	0.31	43.00	6	7	7	23818
France	1980	0.36	34.86	6	7	0	26810
France	1985	0.35		6	7	1	27064

Continued

192

Political outcomes (continued)

Country	Year	edgini	gini	civlib	pollib	unrest	gdp
France	1990	0.35		6	7	3	30357
Greece	1960	0.37				0	5151
Greece	1965	0.37				5	7721
Greece	1970	0.37				0	10888
Greece	1975	0.36	34.84	6	6	1	13532
Greece	1980	0.32	33.54	6	6	1	15511
Greece	1985	0.32	34.37	6	6	4	16270
Greece	1990	0.27	35.13	6	7	8	17717
Hungary	1975	0.19	22.04	2	2	0	8803
Hungary	1980	0.16	21.20	3	2	0	10241
Hungary	1985	0.19	22.83	3	3	0	10827
Hungary	1990	0.21		6	6	0	10822
Japan	1960	0.29				20	4998
Japan	1965	0.26	34.80			1	7333
Japan	1970	0.28	35.50			3	11526
Japan	1975	0.28	34.40	7	6	2	13381
Japan	1980	0.26	33.40	7	7	1	16284
Japan	1985	0.26	35.90	7	7	0	18820
Japan	1990	0.25	35.00	7	7	1	22624
Netherlands	1960	0.24				0	17117
Netherlands	1965	0.26				0	20628
Netherlands	1970	0.24				2	25413
Netherlands	1975	0.24	28.60	7	7	0	27421
Netherlands	1980	0.25	27.39	7	7	1	29233
Netherlands	1985	0.25	29.10	7	7	0	28563
Netherlands	1990	0.25		7	7	0	31242
New Zealand	1960	0.21				0	21285
New Zealand	1965	0.21				0	23658
New Zealand	1970	0.23				2	24112
New Zealand	1975	0.18	30.04	7	7	0	25970
New Zealand	1980	0.16	34.79	7	7	0	24614
New Zealand	1985	0.17	35.82	7	7	0	26039
New Zealand	1990	0.25	40.21	7	7	0	25413
Poland	1975	0.22		2	2	0	8642
Poland	1980	0.16	24.87	4	2	0	8491
Poland	1985	0.19	25.27	3	2	0	8079
Poland	1990	0.14	26.24	6	6	2	7467
Portugal	1960	0.58				0	4853

Continued

Political outcomes (continued)

Country	Year	edgini	gini	civlib	pollib	unrest	gdp
Portugal	1965	0.51				2	6189
Portugal	1970	0.50				1	8423
Portugal	1975	0.51	32.28	5	3	17	10354
Portugal	1980	0.42	36.80	6	6	0	11321
Portugal	1985	0.43	36.80	6	7	0	11343
Portugal	1990	0.43	36.76	6	7	0	16637
Romania	1965	0.35				0	1065
Romania	1970	0.35				0	1493
Romania	1975	0.31		2	1	0	2369
Romania	1980	0.31		2	1	0	2861
Romania	1985	0.30		1	1	0	4021
Spain	1960	0.38				0	8186
Spain	1965	0.40	25.39			0	12451
Spain	1970	0.28	28.48			14	16557
Spain	1975	0.35	29.40	3	3	17	20722
Spain	1980	0.39	26.79	5	6	2	21449
Spain	1985	0.37	25.19	6	7	1	21169
Spain	1990	0.36		7	7	0	26364
Switzerland	1960	0.31				0	20149
Switzerland	1965	0.31				0	23660
Switzerland	1970	0.34				0	27218
Switzerland	1975	0.35		7	7	0	27074
Switzerland	1980	0.23		7	7	1	29548
Switzerland	1985	0.25		7	7	0	29848
Switzerland	1990	0.26		7	7	0	32812
Turkey	1960	0.68				10	3194
Turkey	1965	0.66				0	3765
Turkey	1970	0.64	53.94			5	4841
Turkey	1975	0.63	49.95	5	6	9	6416
Turkey	1980	0.59	47.41	3	3	6	6692
Turkey	1985	0.58	45.00	3	5	0	7091
Turkey	1990	0.56		4	6	0	8632
West Germany	1960	0.31				0	13919
West Germany	1965	0.32	29.84			1	17282
West Germany	1970	0.32	32.81			2	21251
West Germany	1975	0.33	31.19	7	7	0	23342
West Germany	1980	0.34	31.07	6	7	2	27273
West Germany	1985	0.35		6	7	3	27252

Continued

Political outcomes (continued)

Country	Year	edgini	gini	civlib	pollib	unrest	gdp
West Germany	1990	0.37		6	7	0	29509
Yugoslavia	1965	0.50	31.34			0	5320
Yugoslavia	1970	0.48	31.74			0	7319
Yugoslavia	1975	0.51	33.07	2	2	0	9704
Yugoslavia	1980	0.47	33.54	3	2	0	12463
Yugoslavia	1985	0.47	32.40	3	2	0	11417
Yugoslavia	1990	0.47	31.88	4	3	11	10007

Source: ACLP / TWF.

Crime

Country	Code	Year	edgini	gini	Murder	Homicde	Rape
Australia	AUS	1970	0.20	32.02	0.01	0.03	0.03
Canada	CAN	1960	0.22	32.04	0.01	0.00	0.00
Canada	CAN	1965	0.24	31.21	0.01	0.00	0.00
Canada	CAN	1970	0.25	31.86	0.02	0.00	0.00
Canada	CAN	1975	0.24	31.62	0.02	0.00	0.00
Chile	CHL	1970	0.33	45.64	0.00	0.07	0.00
Chile	CHL	1975	0.33	46.00	0.00	0.07	0.00
Egypt	EGY	1960		42.00	0.10	0.00	0.01
Egypt	EGY	1965		40.00	0.24	0.20	0.20
Finland	FIN	1970	0.27	31.80	0.20	0.20	0.26
France	FRA	1960	0.24	49.00	0.00	0.00	0.01
France	FRA	1965	0.27	48.00	0.00	0.00	0.01
France	FRA	1970	0.28	44.00	0.00	0.00	0.01
France	FRA	1975	0.31	43.00	0.00	0.00	0.00
Hong Kong	HKG	1975	0.42	40.35	0.00	0.03	0.01
Hungary	HUN	1965	0.21	25.93	0.04	0.00	0.04
Hungary	HUN	1970	0.16	22.91	0.04	0.00	0.05
Hungary	HUN	1975	0.19	22.80	0.04	0.00	0.06
India	IND	1960	0.79	34.64	0.03	0.00	0.00
India	IND	1965	0.77	31.72	0.02	0.00	0.00
India	IND	1970	0.76	31.06	0.03	0.00	0.00
India	IND	1975	0.74	30.51	0.03	0.00	0.00
Indonesia	IDN	1965	0.73	33.30	0.02	0.00	0.00
Indonesia	IDN	1970	0.59	31.70	0.02	0.00	0.00
Jamaica	JAM	1960	0.35	54.31	0.07	0.00	0.16
Japan	JPN	1965	0.26	35.88	0.00	0.03	0.00
Japan	JPN	1970	0.28	35.30	0.00	0.02	0.00
Mexico	MEX	1960	0.56	55.10	0.20	0.34	0.24

Continued

Crime (continued)

Country	Code	Year	edgini	gini	Murder	Homicde	Rape
Mexico	MEX	1965	0.57	55.50	0.00	0.15	0.05
Mexico	MEX	1970	0.51	57.70	0.00	0.13	0.04
Mexico	MEX	1975	0.50	57.90	0.00	0.11	0.04
Netherlands	NLD	1975	0.24	28.60	0.00	0.01	0.01
New Zealand	NZL	1975	0.18	30.05	0.00	0.00	0.00
Pakistan	PAK	1970	0.85	30.24	0.07	0.00	0.02
Panama	PAN	1970	0.47	57.00	0.00	0.11	0.09
Singapore	SGP	1975	0.47	41.00	0.03	0.00	0.03
Spain	ESP	1965	0.40	31.99	0.00	0.01	0.00
Sri Lanka	LKA	1965	0.44	47.00	0.00	0.06	0.01
Sri Lanka	LKA	1970	0.38	37.71	0.00	0.06	0.01
Sri Lanka	LKA	1975	0.37	35.30	0.00	0.08	0.03
Sudan	SDN	1970	0.87	38.72	0.69	0.67	0.68
Thailand	THA	1965	0.48	41.28	0.16	0.00	0.00
Thailand	THA	1970	0.42	42.63	0.19	0.00	0.00
Thailand	THA	1975	0.43	41.74	0.17	0.00	0.00
Trinidad	TTO	1960	0.36	46.02	0.06	0.08	0.07
Trinidad	TTO	1975	0.34	51.00	0.05	0.08	0.13
Tunisia	TUN	1965	0.89	42.30	0.01	0.00	0.26
Turkey	TUR	1970	0.64	56.00	0.00	0.10	0.00
Turkey	TUR	1975	0.63	51.00	0.00	0.07	0.00

Source: AG / TWF.

Chapter 3

See Appendix chapter 1 table for social capital/cohesion aggregates for 15 countries for data used in figures 3.1 and 3.2

Dataset for figures 3.3 and 3.4

Country	Abbreviation	Trust	Tolerance	Solidarity
Australia	AUS	10.3	10	3.16
Belgium	BEL	9.9	10	3.15
Bulgaria	BUL	9.2	9.7	3.08
China	CHI	10	10.4	3.26
Colombia	COL	9.9	10.8	3.18
Cyprus	CYP	10.5	10.9	3.34
Czech	CZE	9.7	10	3.08
Denmark	DEN	11.4	9.6	3.24
England	ENG	10	9.7	3.2
Estonia	EST	9.7	9.7	3.05
Finland	FIN	10.1	9.8	3.1
Germany	GER	10	9.2	3.03

Continued

Dataset for figures 3.3 and 3.4 (continued)

Country	Abbreviation	Trust	Tolerance	Solidarity
Greece	GREE	10.4	10.6	3.27
Hong Kong	HK	10.2	10.5	3.08
Hungary	HUN	10.1	9.5	3.1
Italy	ITA	10.1	9.8	3.17
Latvia	LAT	9.5	9.5	3.03
Lithuania	LITH	9.5	9.6	3.13
Norway	NOR	10.8	10.3	3.11
Poland	POL	9.9	10.6	3.3
Portugal	POR	9.6	10.3	3.41
Romania	ROM	10	10.2	3.26
Russia	RUS	9.4	9.8	2.99
Slovakia	SLO	8.6	9.4	
Slovenia	SLRE	10.3	9.8	3.17
Sweden	SWE	10.2	10.7	3.13
Switzerland	SWI	10.7	9.4	3.07
United States	US	10.4	10.3	3.19

Source: IEA Citizenship Survey.

4A Student perceptions

	Percentage of students who 'Agree' or 'Strongly Agree' with ...			
	In school I have learned to be a patriotic and loyal citizen of my country (patriotism)	*In school I have learned to understand people who have different ideas (pluralism)*	*In school I have learned to be concerned about what happens in other countries (internationalism)*	*In school I have learned about the importance of voting in national and local elections (elections)*
Northern and Western Europe				
Belgium French	47 (1.2)	80 (1.8)	71	49 (2.5)
Denmark	44 (1.1)	72 (0.9)	68 (1.1)	39 (1.3)
England	54 (1.3)	90 (1.0)	74	41 (1.2)
Finland	55 (1.5)	83	67 (1.2)	34 (1.4)
Germany	48 (1.3)	77 (1.0)	74 (0.9)	39 (1.3)
Norway	55 (1.0)	79 (1.1)	76 (1.0)	48 (1.3)
Sweden	42 (2.0)	84	76 (1.6)	57
Switzerland	48 (1.7)	83	77 (1.1)	44 (1.8)

Continued

Student perceptions (continued)

	Percentage of students who 'Agree' or 'Strongly Agree' with ...			
	In school I have learned to be a patriotic and loyal citizen of my country (patriotism)	In school I have learned to understand people who have different ideas (pluralism)	In school I have learned to be concerned about what happens in other countries (internationalism)	In school I have learned about the importance of voting in national and local elections (elections)
Former communist states				
Bulgaria	63	77 (1.7)	60 (1.5)	42 (2.2)
Czech Republic	58 (1.1)	74 (1.2)	57 (1.5)	42 (1.6)
Estonia	48 (1.3)	84	71	43 (1.5)
Hungary	69 (1.3)	71 (1.0)	57 (1.2)	52 (1.2)
Latvia	52 (1.6)	81 (1.1)	72	48 (1.6)
Lithuania	57 (1.2)	79 (1.0)	74	43 (1.3)
Poland	81 (1.1)	79 (1.5)	74	70 (1.4)
Romania	88 (1.0)	89 (0.8)	69 (1.2)	78 (1.2)
Russian Federation	66	87 (0.8)	78 (1.2)	64 (1.8)
Slovak Republic	79 (1.1)	87 (0.8)	76 (1.0)	68 (1.2)
Slovenia	64	80 (1.0)	57 (1.0)	35 (1.2)
Southern Europe				
Cyprus	91 (0.7)	88 (0.7)	81 (0.9)	72 (1.1)
Greece	79 (1.1)	87 (0.9)	68 (1.0)	72 (1.1)
Italy	61 (1.3)	87 (0.9)	79 (1.1)	54
Portugal	84 (0.8)	95 (0.5)	76 (0.9)	48 (1.1)
Other countries				
Australia	60 (1.0)	88 (1.0)	70	55
Chile	87 (0.6)	94 (0.4)	77 (0.9)	76 (1.1)
Colombia	90 (0.9)	93 (0.6)	78 (1.0)	89 (0.9)
Hong Kong	57 (1.1)	85	72	71 (1.0)
United States	68 (1.3)	89 (1.1)	75 (1.1)	73 (1.4)
International mean	64	84	72	55

Notes:
( ) Standard errors appear in parentheses. These are listed if the country mean is either significantly above or below the international mean ($\alpha < 0.01$).

Sources: Torney-Purta *et al.* (2001, p. 136, Table 7.1). Appendix 4A is a reorganized version of Table 7.1.

Country mean scores of institutional trust, national pride, tolerance and political participation

	Institutional trust	National pride	Tolerance	Political participation
Northern and Western Europe				
Belgium French	9.9	8.4 (0.08)	10.0	9.7 (0.07)
Denmark	11.4 (0.04)	9.8 (0.04)	9.6 (0.05)	9.5 (0.04)
England	10.0	9.4 (0.05)	9.7 (0.07)	9.7 (0.05)
Finland	10.1	10.5 (0.05)	9.8	9.7 (0.05)
Germany	10.0	9.0 (0.06)	9.2 (0.07)	9.6 (0.04)
Norway	10.8 (0.04)	9.9	10.3 (0.07)	9.7 (0.04)
Sweden	10.2	9.3 (0.08)	10.7 (0.08)	9.8 (0.04)
Switzerland	10.7 (0.04)	9.2 (0.06)	9.4 (0.07)	9.7 (0.05)
Former communist states				
Bulgaria	9.2 (0.07)	9.9	9.7 (0.10)	10.0
Czech Republic	9.7 (0.05)	10.2 (0.04)	10.0	9.4 (0.04)
Estonia	9.7 (0.04)	9.5 (0.04)	9.7 (0.04)	9.9
Hungary	10.1	10.1	9.5 (0.05)	9.9 (0.04)
Latvia	9.5 (0.06)	9.5 (0.06)	9.5 (0.05)	10.5 (0.07)
Lithuania	9.5 (0.05)	10.0	9.6 (0.03)	9.6 (0.05)
Poland	9.9	11.1 (0.08)	10.6 (0.06)	10.5 (0.06)
Romania	10.0	10.1	10.2	10.5 (0.05)
Russian Federation	9.4 (0.06)	10.0	9.8	10.0
Slovak Republic	10.3 (0.05)	10.5 (0.07)	9.8 (0.05)	9.8 (0.05)
Slovenia	8.6 (0.05)	9.9	9.4 (0.05)	10.0
Southern Europe				
Cyprus	10.5 (0.04)	11.3 (0.03)	10.9 (0.03)	10.4 (0.04)
Greece	10.4 (0.05)	11.4 (0.05)	10.6 (0.05)	9.9
Italy	10.1	9.5 (0.04)	9.8 (0.05)	9.8 (0.05)
Portugal	9.6 (0.05)	10.7 (0.04)	10.3 (0.03)	10.4 (0.04)
Other countries				
Australia	10.3 (0.06)	10.0	10.0	9.8 (0.05)
Chile	10.0	11.1 (0.04)	10.4 (0.03)	10.2 (0.05)
Colombia	9.9	10.9 (0.06)	10.8 (0.04)	11.1 (0.06)
Hong Kong	10.2	8.9 (0.03)	10.5 (0.05)	10.5 (0.05)
United States	10.4 (0.07)	9.9	10.3 (0.06)	10.5 (0.05)
International mean	10	10	10	10

Notes:
( ) Standard errors appear in parentheses. These are listed if the country mean is either significantly above or below the international mean ($\alpha < 0.01$).

Sources: Torney-Purta et al. (2001, pp. 96, 101, 105, 122; Tables 5.1, 5.2, 5.3 and 6.1). Appendix 4B is a reorganized and integrated version of the original tables. The values in these tables, which have been copied in the current table, are the product of Rasch scaling of the items composing each of the four scales.

Chapter 6

Figure 6.1 Components of GDP per Capita

Data provided by Tom May at Qualifications and Curriculum Authority (QCA) UK. Available on request from authors.

Figure 6.2 WEF Economic Competitiveness Rankings

Data from World Economic Forum (2004).

Figure 6.3 Changes in Multi-Factor Productivity Growth and R and D

Data from OECD (2001) *The New Economy: Beyond the Hype*. Paris: OECD, figure 111.2, p. 43.

Figures 6.4 and 6.5 Public Social Expenditure by Country and Year

Total public social expenditure In percentage of GDP

	1980	1985	1990	1995	2000	2001
Austria	22.5	24.1	24.1	26.6	26.0	26.0
Belgium	24.1	26.9	26.9	28.1	26.7	27.2
Denmark	29.1	27.9	29.3	32.4	28.9	29.2
Finland	18.5	23.0	24.8	31.1	24.5	24.8
France	21.1	26.6	26.6	29.2	28.3	28.5
Germany	23.0	23.6	22.8	27.5	27.2	27.4
Greece	11.5	17.9	20.9	21.4	23.6	24.3
Ireland	17.0	22.1	18.6	19.4	13.6	13.8
Italy	18.4	21.3	23.3	23.0	24.1	24.4
Luxembourg	23.5	23.0	21.9	23.8	20.0	20.8
Netherlands	26.9	27.3	27.6	25.6	21.8	21.8
Norway	17.9	19.1	24.7	26.0	23.0	23.9
Portugal	10.9	11.1	13.9	18.0	20.5	21.1
Spain	15.9	18.2	19.5	21.4	19.9	19.6
Sweden	28.8	30.0	30.8	33.0	28.6	28.9
Switzerland	14.2	15.1	17.9	23.9	25.4	26.4
United Kingdom	17.9	21.1	19.5	23.0	21.7	21.8
United States	13.3	13.0	13.4	15.5	14.2	14.8
Scandinavia	24	25	27	31	26.2	26.7
Southern Europe	15	16	19	21	22.0	22.4
Anglo-Saxon	16	19	17	19	16.5	16.8
Core Europe	22	23	24	26	25.1	25.4
OECD-30*	m	m	m	m	23.2	23.6
EU-15	20.6	22.9	23.4	25.6	23.7	24.0

Source: OECD (2004), Social Expenditure Database (SOCX, www.oecd.org/els/social/expenditure).

Figure 6.5   Income Inequality by Country

Income inequality

Country	Gini coefficient
Austria 1997	30
Denmark 1997	24.7
Finland 2000	26.9
France 1995	32.7
Germany 2000	28.3
Greece 1998	35.4
Italy 2000	36
Norway 2000	25.8
Portugal 1997	38.5
Spain 1990	32.5
Sweden 2000	25
Switzerland 1992	33.1
UK 1999	36
US 2000	40.8
Scandinavia	25.6
Core Europe	31.025
Southern Europe	35.6
Anglo-Saxon countries	38.4

Source: World Bank World Development Report 2005.

Figure 6.6   Social Cohesion and Inequality – see data for chapter 1

Source: Green, Preston and Sabates (2003).

Figure 6.7   Modes of Regulation

Source: Green, Hodgson and Sakamoto (2000).

Figure 6.8   Proportion of Workers in High Skilled Jobs by Country and Region

Country	Workers in high skilled jobs (%)
Sweden	55.7
Netherlands	51.7
Finland	46.6
Switzerland	44.7
Norway	44.3
Denmark	41.7
Czech Republic	40.5
Canada	39.4
United Kingdom	36.9
United States	35.8
Hungary	35.3
Germany	34.4
New Zealand	33.9
Austria	33.9
Ireland	31.5
Slovenia	29.4
Poland	28.7
Portugal	25.6
Chile	16.5
Scandinavia	47.1
Core Europe	41.1
Anglo-Saxon countries	35.5

Source: OECD, Learning and the Information Age (2000).

Figure 6.9   Mean Literacy Scores by Country and Country Group from IALS

	Prose mean	Document mean	Quantitative mean
Nordic	288.3	296.4	296.8
Core Europe	270.5	277.5	282.7
English Speaking	273.7	269.3	271.7
UK, USA, Ireland	268.7	264.8	269
USA, UK	270.2	267.5	271.2

Figure 6.10   Dispersion of Skills in IALS by Country and Country Group

	Prose SD	Document SD	Quantitative SD	Combined SD
Nordic	17.9	16.5	16.8	17.1
Core Europe	19.2	20.2	20.8	20.1
English-Speaking	19	18.9	19.6	19.7
UK, USA, Ireland	19.8	22.6	22.6	20.8
USA, UK	19.8	23.6	23.6	22.1

Figure 6.11   Dispersal of Scores for Reading, Maths and Science by Country Group

Adult Literacy Survey Scores

Country	Prose mean	Prose SD	Document mean	Document SD	Quantitative mean	Quantitative SD	Combined SD
Canada	278.8	10	279.3	11.7	281	7.8	9.8
Germany	275.9	11.2	285.1	17.8	293.3	9	12.6
Ireland	265.7	19.8	259.3	14	264.6	20.5	18.1
							29.7
Netherlands	282.7	30	286.9	29.3	287.7	30	
Sweden	301.3	11.9	305.6	11.6	305.9	8.9	10.8
Switzerland (FR)	264.8	12.3	274.1	10.6	280.1	15.8	12.9
Switzerland (G)	263.3	10.5	269.7	7.8	278.9	9.9	9.4
USA	273.7	10.4	267.5	15.8	275.2	17.2	14.4
Australia	274.2	25.5	273.3	26.6	275.9	28.7	26.9
Belgium (FL)	271.8	30	278.2	30	282	30	30
New Zealand	275.2	19.1	269.1	15.7	270.7	22.3	19.0
UK	266.7	29.2	267.5	30	267.2	30	29.7
Denmark	275	14.9	293.8	19.5	298.4	19.3	17.9
Finland	288.6	27.9	289.2	19.7	286.1	21.78	23.12
Norway	288.5	16.9	296.9	15.1	296.8	17.4	16.4
Portugal	222.6	18.9	220.4	23.5	231.4	22.5	21.6
Switzerland (It)	264.3	21.3	271	25.6	274.4	30	25.6
Nordic	288.35	17.9	296.375	16.475	296.8	16.845	17.0
Core Europe	270.4	19.2	277.5	20.1	282.7	20.7	20.1
English-speaking	273.72	19	269.3	18.9	271.7	19.5	19.6
UK, USA, Ireland	268.7	19.8	264.7	19.9	269	22.5	20.7
USA, UK	270.2	19.8	267.5	22.9	271.2	23.6	22.1

Figure 6.12   Proportion of Adults Participating in Adult Education

	Total participation rate	Mean hours/adult
Finland	56.8	121.2
Denmark	55.7	122.2
Sweden	52.5	
Norway	47.9	114.9
New Zealand	47.5	135
UK	43.9	93.5
Switzerland	39.7	58.6
US	39.7	67.4
Canada	37.7	115.1
Netherlands	37.4	90.6
Slovenia	31.9	67.3
Czech Republic	25.5	42.7
Ireland	24.3	115.1
Belgium (FL)	21.2	27.4
Hungary	19.3	36.1
Chile	18.9	49.2
Portugal	14.2	
Poland	13.9	20.8
Nordic	53.2	119.4
Core Europe	32.8	58.9
Anglo-Saxon	38.6	105.3

Notes and References

1 Education and Social Cohesion: Re-Centring the Debate

1. National values for distributions of educational outcomes are calculated from the International Adult Literacy Survey data since these provide direct measures of skills which are deemed better indicators of education that the years of schooling measures commonly used by human capital theorists. Social attitude measures for a sample of countries are taken from the World Values Surveys of 1990 and 1995 and from national crime statistics (from Interpol). Gini coefficients for income inequality in different countries come from World Bank Statistics. Appendix 1 explains how our charts were derived for the main and expanded datasets.
2. Estimates were computed using the SPSS computer package.
3. The test for significance is $p < 0.05$ for a two-tailed test.
4. This conflicts with Knack and Keefer's (1997) findings from WVS that aggregate national levels of civic co-operation co-vary with social trust scores.
5. Eurobarometer surveys in 1976 and 1986 asked respondents in nine European countries how far they trusted people in other named countries. The rank ordering on countries' perceived trustworthiness was the same in both years with the Swiss, the Danes and the Dutch being most trusted and the Irish, Italians and Russians being least trusted. America, Britain and France lay in the middle (Inglehart 1990, p. 399).

3 Education, Tolerance and Social Cohesion

1. The recent row about the publication of Danish cartoons depicting Mohammed in a fashion abusive to Muslims could be taken as an example of the unease sometimes experienced within Danish culture in relating to foreign cultures and religions. The fact that these very inflammatory cartoons were published in the first place and the ineptitude of the government responses when outrage predictably ensued across the world suggests considerable naïvety, not to say insensitivity, amongst those concerned.

4 Ethno-Linguistic Diversity, Civic Attitudes and Citizenship Education

1. The ELF is calculated with a Herfindahl concentration formula from data compiled in a global survey of ethnic groups published in the *Atlas Narodov Mira* (1964) (see Posner 2004).

    The Herfindahl concentration formula is: $ELF = 1 - \sum_{i=1}^{n} s_i^2$ where s_i^2 is the share of group i ($i = 1, \dots, n$).

To illustrate the use of this formula, we calculated the ELF for three hypothetical cases. In case A the population is divided in two ethnic groups, one making up 75% and the other 25% of the population. In case B there are two ethnic groups both comprising 50% of the population. In case C the population is divided in three ethnic groups, one numbering 50% and the other two each 25% of the population.

Case A (75/25):   ELF = 1 − (0.56 + 0.06) = 0.38
Case B (50/50):   ELF = 1 − (0.25 + 0.25) = 0.5
Case C (50/25/25): ELF = 1 − (0.25 + 0.06 + 0.06) = 0.63

2. Knack and Keefer's civic co-operation construct is a composite variable composed of five items which in addition to the two the current study uses (tax and transport) include 'claiming government benefits you are not entitled to', 'keeping money that you have found' and 'failing to report damage you've done accidentally to a parked vehicle'.
3. The results of this analysis can be obtained from the author.
4. In this regression analysis GNI per capita has a standardized coefficient of −.17, a t-statistic of −.734 and a significance of .473. Heterogeneity has a standardized coefficient of −.19, a t-statistic of −.834 and a significance of .415. The adjusted R^2 is −.04 (i.e. only 4% of the variance is explained). The N (European countries) is 20.
5. The analysis for the 1995 wave produced a GNP per capita with a standardized coefficient of .65 and a significance of .000 and an ELF with a standardized coefficient of −.09 and a significance of .45. The 1990 analysis produced a GNP per capita with a standardized coefficient of .58 and a significance of .000; an ELF with a standardized coefficient of −.13 and a significance of .896. The 1981 analysis produced a GNP per capita with a standardized coefficient of .55 and a significance of .016 and an ELF with a standardized coefficient of −.04 and a significance of .86. The 1995 analysis was conducted on a sample of 42 countries, the 1990 analysis on a sample of 39 countries, the 1981 analysis on a sample of 20 countries.
6. Miller's view that education should foster patriotism has, as could be expected, met with substantial criticism. Brighouse (2003), for instance, argues that patriotic education forces feelings of state loyalty onto the child, leaving it no choice to freely explore his/her ties of belonging. By doing so it violates the freedom of choice principle, which should be the only permissible educational guideline in a liberal democratic state. He further contends that patriotic education may actually be detrimental to social justice as it competes with loyalties and attachments that are in a better position to promote social justice.
7. An independent samples t-test revealed that the differences between the regions' mean scores on the four civic education items were all significant at a 0.01 level.
8. The results of this analysis can be obtained from the author.

5 Comprehensive Schooling and Educational Inequality

1. The evidence from the recent Third International Maths and Science Study (TIMSS) is less clear-cut but awaits full analysis.

2. This analysis is substantially drawn from the PhD thesis by Susan Wiborg: S. Wiborg (2004) *Uddannelse og social samhørighed: Udviklingen af enhedsskoler i Skandinavien, Tyskland og England. En komparativ analyse.* PhD dissertation, Copenhagen, DPU/Forlag.
3. Marsden and Ryan (1995) also argue that larger German firms offer better prospects of promotion for skilled workers than UK firms, although this may now be changing (see Brown 1997).
4. We owe this insight to Hilary Steedman at the LSE.
5. Although Greece is currently introducing new forms of integrated upper secondary schools.

6   Models of Lifelong Learning and the 'Knowledge Society': Education for Competitiveness and Social Cohesion

1. World Economic Forum (2004) *Global Competitiveness Report*, 2003–4, p. 39.

Bibliography

Abizadeh, A. (2004) 'Historical Truth, National Myths and Liberal Democracy: On the Coherence of Liberal Nationalism', *The Journal of Political Philosophy*, 12(3), 291–313.

Abramson, P. and Inglehart, R. (1994) 'Education, Security and Postmaterialism: A Comment on Dutch and Taylor's "Postmaterialism and the Economic Condition,"' *American Journal of Political Science*, 38(3), 797–814.

Albert, M. (1993) *Capitalism against Capitalism*. London: Whurr Publishers.

Anderson, P. (1994) *Lineages of the Absolutist State*. London: Verso.

Apple, M. (2001) *Educating the "Right" Way: Markets, Standards, God and Inequality*. London: Routledge.

Archer, G. and Gartner, R. (1984) *Violence and Crime in Cross-National Perspective*. Michigan: Yale University Press.

Ashton, D. and Green, F. (1996) *Education, Training and the Global Economy*. London: Edward Elgar.

Atkin, C.K. (1981) 'Communication and Political Socialization', in D. Nimmo and K. Sanders (eds), *Handbook of Political Communication*. Beverly Hills, CA: Sage, pp. 299–328.

Atlas Narodov Mira (1964) Miklukho-Maklai Ethnological Institute at the Department of Geodesy and Cartography of the State Geological Committee of the Soviet Union, Moscow.

Axelrod, R. (1986) 'An Evolutionary Approach to Norms', *American Political Science Review*, 80, 1095–1111.

Baert, P. (1998) *Social Theory in the Twentieth Century*. Cambridge: Polity Press.

Ball, S. (2003) *Class Strategies and the Education Market: The Middle Classes and Social Advantage*. London: Routledge Falmer.

Banfield, E. (1958) *The Moral Basis of a Backward Society*. New York: Free Press.

Beck, U. (2000) *What is Globalization?* Cambridge: Polity Press.

Benn, M. and Chitty, C. (2004) *A Tribute to Caroline Benn: Education and Democracy*. London: Continuum.

Blanden, J., Gregg, P. and Machin, S. (2005) *Intergenerational Mobility in Europe and North America*. London: Sutton Trust.

Blau, F. and Kahn, L. (1996) 'International Differences in Male Wage Inequality: Institutions Versus Market Forces', *Journal of Political Economy*, 194(4), 791–837.

Blum, A., Goldstein, H. and Guérein-Pace, F. (2001) 'International Adult Literacy Survey: An Analysis of International Comparisons of Adult Literacy', *Assessment in Education*, 8(2), 225–46.

Boli, J. (1989) *New Citizens for a New Society: The Institutional Origins of Mass Schooling in Sweden*. Oxford: Pergamon Press.

Bothenius, A., Lohman, J.M. and Pescher, J.L. (1983) 'Comparing Educational and Occupational Attainment in Hungary and the Netherlands: A LISERAL Approach', *Bulletin Vakgroep Methoden en Techhnieken*, 53. Groningen: Sociolingisch Instituut.

Boucher, L. (1982) *Tradition and Change in Swedish Education*. Oxford: Pergamon Press.

Boudon, R. (1974) *Education, Opportunity and Social Inequality*. London: Wiley-Interscience.

Bourdieu, P. (1980) 'Le Capital Social: Notes Provisoires', *Actes de La Recherche en Sciences Sociales*, 31, 2–3.

Bourdieu, P. (1986) 'The Forms of Capital', in J. Richardson (ed.), *Handbook of Theory and Research for the Sociology of Education*. Westport, CT: Greenwood Press.

Bourdieu, P. and Passeron, J.-C. (1979) *The Inheritors: French Students and their Relation to Culture*, trans. Richard Nice. Chicago: University of Chicago Press.

Braithwaite, J. and Braithwaite, V. (1980) 'The Effect on Income Inequality and Social Democracy on Homicide', *British Journal of Criminology*, 20(1), 45–53.

Brehm. J. and Rahn, W. (1997) 'Individual-Level Evidence for the Causes and Consequences of Social Capital', *American Journal of Political Science*, 41(3), 999–1023.

Brighouse, H. (2003) 'Should We Teach Patriotic History?', in K. McDonough and W. Feinberg (eds), *Education and Citizenship in Liberal-Democratic Societies: Teaching for Cosmopolitan Values and Collective Identities*. Oxford: Oxford University Press.

Brown, A. (1997) 'Becoming Skilled during a Time of Transition: Observations from Europe,' Monograph, Department of Educational Studies, University of Surrey, Guildford.

Brown, G., Micklewright, J. and Waldmann, R. (2000) 'In Which Countries is Learning Achievement Most Unequal?', Unpublished paper to CEE seminar, June, UNICEF, Florence.

Brown, P. and Lauder, H. (2000) 'Human Capital, Social Capital, and Collective Intelligence', in S. Baron, J. Field and T. Schuller (eds), *Social Capital: Critical Perspectives*. Oxford: Oxford University Press, pp. 226–42.

Brown. P., Green, A. and Lauder, H. (2001) *High Skills: Globalization, Competitiveness and Skills Formation*. Oxford: Oxford University Press.

Brubaker, R. (1992) *Citizenship and Nationhood in France and Germany*. Cambridge, MA: Harvard University Press.

Bynner, J. and Ashford, S. (1994) 'Politics and Participation: Some Antecedents of Young People's Attitudes to Political System and Political Activity', *European Journal of Social Psychology*, 24, 223–36.

Canovan. M. (1996) *Nationhood and Political Theory*. Cheltenham: Edward Elgar.

Carnoy, M. (1993) 'School Improvement: Is Privatization the Answer', in J. Hannaway and M. Carnoy (eds), *Decentralization and School Improvement*, San Francisco, CA: Jossey-Bass.

Castells, M. (1997) *The Information Age: Economy, Society and Culture, Vol. II: The Power of Identity*. Oxford: Blackwell.

CEDEFOP (1987) *The Role of the Social Partners in Vocational Training and Further Training in the Federal Republic of Germany*. Berlin: CEDEFOP.

Checchi, D. (2001) *Education, Inequality and Income Inequality*, DARP Discussion Paper No. 52, DARP. London: London School of Economics.

Coffield, F. (2000) 'Introduction', in F. Coffield (ed.), *Differing Visions of the Learning Society*, Vol. 1. Cambridge: The Policy Press.

Coleman, J. (1988) 'Social Capital and the Creation of Human Capital', *American Journal of Sociology*, 94, Supplement, S95–S120.

Collier, P. (1998) 'The Political Economy of Ethnicity,' Paper for the Annual World Bank Conference on Development Economics, Washington DC, 20–21 April.

Coomber, L. and Reeves, J. (1973) *Science Education in Nineteen Countries: An Empirical Study.* New York: Wiley.

Cox, O. (1970) *Class, Caste and Race.* New York: Monthly Review Press.

Crouch, C., Finegold, D. and Sato, M. (1999) *Are Skills the Answer? The Political Economy of Skill Creation in Advanced Industrial Countries.* Oxford: Oxford University Press.

Cummings, W.K. (1980) *Education and Equality in Japan.* Princeton, NJ: Princeton University Press.

De Mooij, R. and Tang, P (2003) *Four Futures of Europe.* The Hague: Centraal Planbureau.

De Tocqueville, A. (1955) *The Old Regime and the French Revolution,* trans S. Gilbert. Garden City, NY: Doubleday.

De Tocqueville, A. (1966) *Democracy in America,* edited by J.P. Mayer and translated by G. Lawrence. New York: Harper Row.

De Witte, H. (1999) 'Everyday' Racism in Belgium: An Overview of the Research and an Interpretation of Its Link with Education' in L. Hagendoorn and S. Nekuee (eds), *Education and Racism: A Cross-National Inventory of Positive Effects on Education and Racial Tolerance.* Aldershot: Ashgate, pp. 47–74.

Department for Education (Scottish Office) (1992) *Teaching and Learning in Japanese Elementary Schools.* London: HMSO.

Deutsch, K.W. (1966) *Nationalism and Social Communication: An Inquiry into the Foundations of Nationalism.* Cambridge, MA: The Massachusetts Institute of Technology.

DiPasquale, D. and Gleaser, E. (1999) 'Incentives and Social Capital: Do Homeowners Make Better Citizens?', *Journal of Urban Economics,* 45, 354–84.

Dokka, H.J. (1967) *Fra Allmueskole til Folkeskole.* Bergen: Universitetsforlaget.

Dore, R. (1982) *Education in Tokugawa Japan.* London: Athlone.

Dore, R. (1997) *The Diploma Disease: Education, Qualification and Development,* 2nd edition. London: Institute of Education.

Dore, R. (2000) *Stock Market Capitalism: Welfare Capitalism, Japan and Germany Versus the Anglo-Saxons.* Oxford: Oxford University Press.

Dore, R. and Sako, M. (1989) *How the Japanese Learn to Work.* London: Routledge.

Durkheim, E. (1947) *The Division of Labour in Society.* New York: The Free Press.

Durkheim, E. (1992) *Education et Sociologie.* Paris: Presses Universitaites de France.

Duru-Bellat, M. and Mingat, A. (1999) 'How Do Junior Secondary Schools Operate? Academic Achievement, Graching and Streaming of Students', in A. Leschinsky and K. Mayer (eds), *The Comprehensive School Experiment Revisited: Evidence from Western Europe.* Berlin: Peter Lang.

Duru-Bellat, M. and Suchaut, B. (2004) 'Organisation and Context, Efficiency and Equity of Educational Systems: What PISA Tells Us' Unpublished paper. University of Bourgogne, Dijon.

Easterly, W. and Levine, R. (1997) 'Africa's Growth Tragedy: Policies and Ethnic Divisions', *The Quarterly Journal of Economics,* CXII, 1203–50.

Edwards, B. and Foley, M. (1998) 'Civil Society and Social Capital Beyond Putnam,' *American Behavioural Scientist,* 42(1), 124–139.

Emler, N. and Frazer, E. (1999) 'Politics: the Education Effect', *Oxford Review of Education,* 25(1 and 2), 271–2.

Esping-Andersen, G. (1985) *Politics against Markets*. Princeton, NJ: Princeton University Press.

Esping-Andersen, G. (1990) *The Three Worlds of Welfare Capitalism*. Cambridge: Polity.

Esping-Andersen, G. (2003) 'Unequal Opportunities and Social Inheritance', in M. Corak (ed.), *The Dynamics of Intergenerational Income Mobility*. Cambridge: Cambridge University Press.

European Commission (EC) (1999) *Continuing Training in Enterprises: Facts and Figures*. European Training and Youth. Brussels: European Commission.

European Commission (2000) *A Memorandum on Lifelong Learning* at Website: http://europa.eu.int/comm/education/life/memoen.pfd.

European Commission (2002) *Continuing Vocational Training Survey 2*. Luxembourg: Office for Official Publications of the European Communities.

Featherman, D.L. and Hauser, R.M. (1978) 'Design for a Replicate Study of Social Mobility in the United States', in K. Land and S. Spilerman (eds), *Social Indicator Models*. New York: Russell Sage Foundation.

Fine, B. (2001) *Social Capital Versus Social Theory: Political Economy and Social Science at the Turn of the Millennium*. London: Routledge.

Fine, B. and Green, F. (2000) 'Economics, Social Capital, and the Colonization of the Social Sciences', in S. Baron, J. Field and T. Schuller (eds), *Social Capital: Critical Perspectives*. Oxford: Oxford University Press.

Finegold, D. and Soskice, S. (1988) 'The Failure of Training in Britain: Analysis and Prescription', *Oxford Review of Economic Policy*, 4(3), 21–53.

Foley, M. and Edwards, B. (1998) 'Beyond de Tocqueville: Civil Society and Social Capital in Comparative Perspective', *American Behavioural Scientist*, 42(1), 5–20.

Fox, A. (1994) *Work, Power and Trust Relations*. London: Faber and Faber.

Fukuyama, F. (1999) *The Great Disruption: Human Nature and the Reconstruction of Social Order*. London: Profile Books.

Fuller, B. and Robinson, R. (eds) (1992) *The Political Construction of Education*. New York: Praeger.

Garnier, M. and Raffalovich, L.E. (1984) 'The Evolution of Equality of Educational Opportunity in France,' *Sociology of Education*, 57(1), 1–11.

Gavaert, A. (1993) 'Ethnocentrisme bij Scholieren. Een Onderzoek naar de Geslachtverschillen Inzake de Houding Ten Opzichte van Migranten.' Unpublished report of Psychology Department, Leuven (cited) in L. Hagendoorn and S. Nekuee (eds), *Education and Racism: A Cross-National Inventory of Positive Effects on Education and Racial Tolerance*. Aldershot: Ashgate.

Gellner, E. (1983) *Nations and Nationalism*. Oxford: Blackwell Publishing.

Gillborn, D. (1995) *Racism and Antiracism in Real Schools: Theory, Policy, Practice*. Buckingham: Open University Press.

Gillborn, D. and Youdell, D. (2000) *Rationing Education: Policy, Practice, Reform and Equity*. Buckingham: Open University Press.

Gopinathan, S. (1994) *Educational Development in a Strong-Developmentalist State: The Singapore Experience*. Paper presented at the Australian Association for Research in Education Annual Conference.

Gough, I. (1999) 'Social Welfare Competitiveness: Social Versus System Integration', in I. Gough and G. Olofsson, *Capitalism and Social Cohesion: Essays on Exclusion and Integration*. Basingstoke: Macmillan – now Palgrave Macmillan.

Gough, I. and Olofsson, G. (1999) 'Introduction: New Thinking on Exclusion and Integration' in I. Gough and G. Olofsson (1999) *Capitalism and Social*

Cohesion: Essays on Exclusion and Integration. Basingstoke: Macmillan – now Palgrave Macmillan.

Gowricharn, R. (2002) 'Integration and Social Cohesion: the Case of the Netherlands', *Journal of Ethnic and Migration Studies*, 28(2), 259–73.

Gradstein, M. and Justman, M. (2001) *Education, Social Cohesion and Economic Growth*, CEPR Discussion Paper 2773. London: CEPR.

Gramsci, A. (2001) *Selections from the Prison Notebooks*, edited and translated by Q. Hoare and G. Nowell Smith. London: Electric Book Company.

Granovetter, M. (1978) 'The Strength of Weak Ties', *American Journal of Sociology*, 78(6), 1360–80.

Green, A. (1990) *Education and State Formation: The Rise of Education Systems in England, France and the USA.* London: Macmillan.

Green, A. (1997) *Education, Globalisation and the Nation State.* Basingstoke: Macmillan – now Palgrave Macmillan.

Green, A. (1998) 'Core Skills, Key Skills and General Culture: In Search of the Common Foundation in Vocational Education', *Evaluation and Research in Education*, 12(1), 23–44.

Green, A. (1999) 'East Asian Skills Formation Systems and the Challenge of Globalization', *Journal of Education and Work*, 21(3), 253–79.

Green, A. (2000) 'Converging Paths or Ships Passing in the Night? An "English" Critique Japanese School Reform', *Journal of Comparative Education*, 36(4), 417–35.

Green, A. (2003) 'The Many Faces of Lifelong Learning: Recent Education Policy Trends in Europe', *Journal of Education Policy*, 17(4) 611–26.

Green, A., Hodgson, A. and Sakamoto, A. (2000) 'Financing Vocational Education and Training', in P. Descry and M. Tessaring (eds), *Training in Europe. Second Report on Vocational Training Research in Europe 2000*, Volume 1. Cedefop Reference series. Luxembourg: Office for Official Publications of the European Communities.

Green, A. and Preston, J. (2001a) 'Education and Social Cohesion: Re-centering the Debate', *Peabody Journal of Education*, 76(3 and 4) 247–84.

Green, A. and Preston, J. (2001b) 'Finding the Glue that Can Fix the Cracks in our Society,*THES*, 22 June.

Green, A., Preston, J. and Sabates, R. (2003a) 'Education, Equality and Social Cohesion: a Distributional Approach', *Compare*, 33(4), 453–70.

Green, A., Preston, J. and Sabates, R. (2003b) *Education, Equity and Social Cohesion: A Distributional Approach*, Wider Benefits of Learning Centre Report 7. London: Institute of Education.

Green, A. and Wiborg, S. (2004) 'Comprehensive Schooling and Educational Inequality: An International Perspective' in C. Chitty (ed.), *A Tribute to Caroline Benn: Education and Democracy.* London: Continuum.

Green, A., Wolf, A. and Leney, T. (1999) *Convergences and Divergences in European Education and Training Systems.* London: Bedford Way Papers, Institute of Education.

Haegel, F. (1999) 'The Effect of Education on the Expression of Negative Views Towards Immigrants in France: the Influence of the Republican Model put to the Test', in L. Hagendoorn and S. Nekuee (eds), *Education and Racism: a Cross-National Inventory of Positive Effects on Education and Racial Tolerance.* Aldershot: Ashgate, pp. 33–46.

Hagendoorn, L. (1999) 'Introduction: a Model of the Effects of Education on Prejudice and Racism', in L. Hagendoorn and S. Nekuee (eds), *Education and*

Racism: A Cross-National Inventory of Positive Effects on Education and Racial Tolerance. Aldershot: Ashgate, pp. 1–20.

Hahn, C. (1998) *Becoming Political: Comparative Perspectives on Citizenship Education*. Albany, NY: State University of New York Press.

Hall, P. (1999) 'Social Capital in Britain', *British Journal of Politics*, 29, 417–61.

Hall, S. and du Guy, P. (eds) (1996) *Questions of Cultural Identity*. London: Sage.

Halman, L. (1994) 'Variations in Tolerance Levels in Europe: Evidence from the Eurobarometer and European Values Study', *European Journal on Criminal Policy and Research*, 2–3, 15–38.

Halsey, A.H., Heath, A. and Ridge, J.M. (1980) *Origins and Destinations*. Oxford: Clarendon Press.

Handl, J. (1986) 'Sex and Class Specific Inequalities in Educational Opportunity in Western Germany, 1950–1982', unpublished manuscript.

Hannan, M. (1979) 'The Dynamics of Ethnic Boundaries in Modern States', in M. Hannan and J. Meyer (eds), *National Development and the World System: Educational Economic and Political Change, 1950–1970*. Chicago: University of Chicago Press, pp. 253–75.

Her Majesty's Inspectorate (HMI) (1991) *Aspects of Upper Secondary and Higher Education in Japan*. London: HMSO.

Hildebrand, B. and Sting, S. (1995) (eds) *Erziehung und Kulturelle Identität*. New York: Waxman.

Hill, M. and Lian Kwen Fee (1995) *The Politics of Nation-Building and Citizenship in Singapore*. London: Routledge.

Hillgate Group (1987) *The Reform of British Education*. London: Hillgate.

Hjerm, M. (2004) 'Defending Liberal Nationalism – At What Cost?', *Journal of Ethnic and Migration Studies*, 30(1) 41–57.

Hobsbawm, E.J. (1969) *Industry and Empire*. Harmondsworth: Penguin.

Holloway, S.D. (1988) 'Concepts of Ability and Effort in Japan and the United States,' *Review of Educational Research*, 58(3), 327–45.

Holton, R. and Turner, B. (1986) *Talcott Parsons on Economy and Society*. London: Routledge.

Horsman, M. and Marshall, M. (1994) *After the Nation-State: Citizens, Tribalism and the New World Order*. London: HarperCollins.

Huntington, S. (2004) *Who Are We?: The Challenges to America's National Identity*. New York: Simon and Schuster.

Husen, T. (1998) *International Study of Achievement in Maths: a Comparison of Twelve Countries*, vol. 2. Stockholm: International Association of Evaluation in Educational Achievement.

Hutton, W. (1995) *The State We're In*. London: Jonathan Cape.

Ichikawa, S. (1989) 'Japanese Education in American Eyes: a Response to William K. Cummings,' *Comparative Education*, 25(3), 303–7.

Ignatiev, N. (1995) *How the Irish Became White*. New York: Basic Books.

Inglehart, R. (1990) *Culture Shift in Advanced Industrial Society*. Princeton, NJ: Princeton University Press.

Inkeles, A. and Sirowy, L. (1983) 'Convergent and Divergent Trends in National Education Systems', *Social Forces*, 62(2), 303–33.

International Association of Evaluation of Educational Achievement (IEA) (1988) *Science Achievement in Seventeen Countries*. London: Pergamon Press.

International Criminal Police Organization (Interpol) (1996) *International Crime Statistics, 1996*. Paris: General Secretariat, International Criminal Police Organization.

Isling, Å. (1984) *Kampen för Och Mot en Demokratisk Skola 1*. Stockholm: Sober Förlags AB.

Jasinska-Kania, A. (1999) 'The Impact of Education on Racism in Poland Compared with other European Countries', in L. Hagendoorn and S. Nekuee (eds), *Education and Racism: a Cross-National Inventory of Positive Effects on Education and Racial Tolerance*. Aldershot: Ashgate, pp. 75–92.

Jensen, J. (1998) *Mapping Social Cohesion: The State of Canadian Research*. Ottawa: Canadian Policy Research Networks Inc.

Jonsson, J. (1999) 'Dismantling the Class Society through Education Reform? The Success and Failure of Swedish School Politics', in A. Leschinsky, and K. Mayer (eds), *The Comprehensive School Experiment Revisited: Evidence from Western Europe*. Berlin: Peter Lang.

Kaestle, C.F. (1983) *Pillars of the Republic: Common Schools and American Society, 1780–1860*. Toronto: Hill and Wang.

Keep, E. (1998) *Was Ratner Right?* Economic Report, 12(3), Employment Policy Institute.

Kennedy, B., Kawachi, I. and Brainerd, E. (1998) 'The Role of Social Capital in the Russia Mortality Crisis', *World Development*, 26(11), 2029–43.

Kerr, D. (1999) *Re-Examining Citizenship Education: The Case of England*. Reading: NFER.

King, J. (1992) *A History of Marxian Economics: Vol II, 1929–1990*. Basingstoke: Macmillan – now Palgrave Macmillan,

Knack, S. (2000) *Trust, Associational Life and Economic Performance in the OECD*. Washington, DC: World Bank.

Knack, S. and Keefer, P. (1997) 'Does Social Capital Have an Economic Payoff? A Cross-Country Investigation', *The Quarterly Journal of Economics*, CXII, 1251–88.

Kok Report (2004) *Facing the Challenge: The Lisbon Strategy for Growth and Employment: Report of the High Level Group Chaired by Wim Kok*. Office for Official Publications of the European Communities, Luxembourg.

Kymilicka, W. (1995) *Multicultural Citizenship: A Liberal Theory of Minority Rights*. Oxford: Oxford University Press.

Kymlicka, W. and Straehle, C. (1999) 'Cosmopolitanism, Nation-States, and Minority Nationalism: A Critical Review of Recent Literature', *European Journal of Philosophy*, 7, 65–88.

LaPorta, R., Lopez de Silanes, F., Shleifer, A. and Vishny, R. (1997) 'Trust in Large Organizations', *American Economic Review*, 87, 333–8.

Lauder, H., Hughes, D. and Waston, S. (1999) *Trading in Futures – Why Markets in Education Don't Work*. Milton Keynes: Open University Press.

Lauglo, J. (1995) 'Forms of Decentralisation and the Implications for Education', *Comparative Education*, 21(1), 5–30.

Lauglo, J. and McLean, M. (1995) *The Control of Education*. London: Kogan Page.

Leschinsky, A. and Mayer, K. (eds) (1999) *The Comprehensive School Movement Revisited: Evidence From Western Europe*. Berlin: Peter hang.

Lloyd, C. and Payne, J. (2004) *'Idle Fancy' or 'Concrete Will?' Defining and Realising a High Skills Vision for the UK*. SKOPE Research Paper No. 47. Warwick: SKOPE, University of Warwick.

Lockwood, D. (1964) 'Social Integration and System Integration', in G.K. Zollschan and W. Hirsch (eds), *Explorations in Social Change*. London: Routledge, pp. 244–57.

Lockwood, D. (1992) *Solidarity and Schisms: The Problem of Disorder in Durkheimian and Marxist Sociology*. Oxford: Clarendon Press.

Lockwood, D. (1999) 'Civic Integration and Social Cohesion', in I. Gough and G. Olofsson, *Capitalism and Social Cohesion: Essays on Exclusion and Integration*. Basingstoke: Macmillan – now Palgrave Macmillan, pp. 63–84.

Lisbon European Council (2000) Declaration of the European Council's Lisbon Goal Can be Found at: http://europa.eu.int/comm/empolyment_social/employment_strategy/index_en.ht

Lukes, S. (1973) *Emile Durkheim. His Life and Work: A Historical and Critical Study*. Penguin, Harmondsworth.

Lundvall, B.-A. (2005) *The Economics of Knowledge and Learning*, unpublished paper presented to GENIE seminar July 2005, Aalborg University, Aalborg.

Mann, M. (1987) 'Ruling Class Strategies and Citizenship', *Sociology*, 21, 339–54.

Marinetto, M. (2003) 'Who Wants to be an Active Citizen? The Politics and Practice of Community Involvement', *Sociology*, 37(1), 103–20.

Marsden, D. and Ryan P. (1985) 'Work, Labour Markets and Vocational Preparation: Anglo-German Comparisons of Training in Intermediate Skills,' in L. Bash and A. Green (eds), *World Yearbook of Education: Youth, Education and Work*. London: Kogan Page, pp. 67–79.

Marx, K. and Engels, F. (1976) *Theses on Feuerbach*. Peking: Foreign Languages Press.

Marx, K. and Engels, F. (1968) Manifesto of the Communist Party, in *Selected Works*. London: Lawrence and Wishart.

Masters, W.A. and McMillan, M.S. (1999) 'Ethnolinguistic Diversity, Government and Growth,' Unpublished paper.

Maxwell, J. (1996) *Social Dimensions of Economic Growth: Eric J. Hansen Memorial Lecture*, 25 January, University of Alberta.

McGlynn, C., Niens, U., Cairns, E. and Hewstone, M. (2004) 'Moving Out of Conflict: The Contribution of Integrated Schools in Northern Ireland to Identity, Attitudes, Forgiveness and Reconciliation', *Journal of Peace Education*, 1, 147–63.

McLean, M. (1990) *Britain and a Single Market Europe: Prospects for a Common School Curriculum*. London: Kogan Page.

McMahon, W. (1999) *Education and Development*. Oxford: Oxford University Press.

Messner, S.F. (1982) 'Poverty, Inequality and the Urban Homicide Rate,' *Crimionlogy*, 20, 113–14.

Michalski, W., Miller, R. and Stevens, B. (1997) 'Economic Flexibility and Societal Cohesion in the Twenty-First Century: An Overview of Issues and Key Points of Discussion,' in OECD, *Societal Cohesion and the Globalizing Economy: What Does the Future Hold?* Paris: OECD.

Miller, D. (1989) *Market, State and Community: Theoretical Foundations of Market Socialism*. Oxford: Oxford University Press.

Miller, D. (1995) *On Nationality*. Oxford: Clarendon Press.

Moore, M. (2001) 'Normative Justifications for Liberal Nationalism: Justice, Democracy and National Identity', *Nations and Nationalism*, 7, pp. 1–20.

Mortensen, N. (1999) 'Mapping System Integration and Social Integration,' in I. Gough and G. Olofsson (eds), *Capitalism and Social Cohesion: Essays on Exclusion and Integration*. Basingstoke: Macmillan – now Palgrave Macmillan, pp. 13–37.

Newton, K. (1999) 'Social and Political Trust in Established Democracies,' in P. Norris (ed.), *Critical Citizens*. Oxford University Press.

Newton, K. and Norris, P. (2000) 'Confidence in Public Institutions: Faith, Culture or Performance?,' in Susan J. Pharr and Robert D. Putnam (eds), *Disaffected Democracies: What's Troubling the Trilateral Countries?* Princeton, NJ: Princeton University Press.

Nickell, S. and Layard, R. (1998) *Institutions and Economic Performance*. Discussion Paper. London: London School of Economics.

Nie, N., Junn, J. and Barry, K. (1996) *Education and Democratic Citizenship in America*. Chicago: University of Chicago Press.

Nielsen, F. (1985) 'Toward a Theory of Ethnic Solidarity in Modern Societies', *American Sociological Review*, XLII, 479–90.

Niemi, R.G. and Junn, J. (1998) *Civic Education: What Makes Students Learn?* New Haven: Yale University Press.

Norris, P. (2002) *Making Democracies Work: Social Capital and Civic Engagement in 47 Societies*. KSG Faculty Working Group Paper. Boston, MA: Harvard University.

OECD (1994) *School: A Matter of Choice*. Paris: OECD.

OECD (1996) *Lifelong Learning for All*. Paris: OECD.

OECD 1997) *Societal Cohesion and the Globalizing Economy: What Does the Future Mold?* Paris: OECD.

OECD (2000) *Literacy in the Information Age*. Paris: OECD.

OECD (2001a) *Knowledge and Skills for Life: First Results from PISA 2000*. Paris: OECD.

OECD (2001b) *The New Economy: Beyond the Hype*. Paris: OECD.

OECD (2002) *Reading for a Change: Performance and Engagement Across Countries. Results from PISA 2000*. Paris: OECD.

OECD (2003) *Beyond the Rhetoric: Adult Learning Practices and Policies*. Paris: OECD.

Olson, M. (1971) *The Logic of Collective Action*. Cambridge, MA: Harvard University Press.

OSA (1994) *Structures of Vocational Education and Training and the Match Between Education and Work; An International Comparison*. Synthesis Report by J. Gordon, J.-P. Lallarde and D. Parkes. Paris: European Institute of Education and Social Policy.

Osler, A. and Starkey, H. (2000) 'Citizenship Education and National Identities in France and England: Inclusive or Inclusive?,' *Oxford Review of Education*, 27(2), 287–306.

Parsons, T. (1975) 'Some Theoretical Considerations on the Nature and Trends of Change of Ethnicity,' in N. Glazer and D. Moynihan (eds), *Ethnicity: Theory and Experience*. Boston, MA: Harvard University Press.

Parsons, T. (1991) *The Social System*. London: Routledge.

Passim, H. (1965) *Society and Education in Japan*. New York: Teachers' College Press.

Patten, A. (1999) 'The Autonomy Argument for Liberal Nationalism', *Nations and Nationalism*, 5, pp. 1–17.

Payne, J. (2005) *What Progress are We Making with Lifelong Learning? A Study of Norwegian Competence Reform*. SKOPE, University of Warwick.

Pearce, N. (2000) 'The Ecological Fallacy Strikes Back', *Journal of Epidemiology and Community Health*, 54, 326–7.

Peri, P. (1999) 'Education and Prejudice against Immigrants', in L. Hagendoorn and S. Nekuee (eds), *Education and Racism: A Cross-National Inventory of Positive Effects on Education and Racial Tolerance*. Aldershot: Ashgate.

Perkin, H. (1996) *The Third Revolution: Professional Ethics in the Modern World*. London: Routledge.

Pettigrew, T. and Meertens, R. (1995) 'Subtle and Blatant Prejudice in Western Europe', *European Journal of Social Psychology*, 25, 57–75.

Posner, D. (2004) 'Measuring Ethnic Fractionalization in Africa', *American Journal of Political Science*, 48(4), 849–63.

Preston, J. (2004) 'Lifelong Learning and Civic Participation: Inclusion, Exclusion and Community' in T. Schuller, J. Preston, C. Hammond, A. Brassett-Grundy and J. Bynner (eds), *The Benefits of Leaning: The Impact of Education on Health, Family Life and Social Capital*. London: Routledge Falmer, pp. 137–58.

Preston, J. and Feinstein, L. (2004) *Adult Education and Attitude Change*, Centre for Research on the Wider Benefits of Learning Research Report Number 11, Centre for Research on the Wider Benefits of Learning, Institute of Education, London.

Preston, J. and Green, A. (2001) *Education and Political Engagement: Results from the British Social Attitudes Survey 1986–1998*, Paper presented at BERA Conference on 14 September.

Pritchard, R. (1999) *Reconstructing Education: East German Schools and Universities after Unification*. Oxford: Berghahn Books.

Przeworski, A., Alvarez, M., Cheibub, J. and Limongi, F. (2000) *Democracy and Development: Political Institutions and Well-Being in the World, 1950–1990*. Cambridge: Cambridge University Press.

Putnam, R. (1993) *Making Democracy Work: Civic Traditions in Modern Italy*. Princeton, NJ: Princeton University Press.

Putnam, R. (1995a) 'Tuning In, Tuning Out: The Strange Disappearance of Social Capital in America (the 1995 Ithiel de Sola Pool Lecture)', *Political Science and Politics*, December, 664–83.

Putnam, R. (1995b) 'Bowling Alone: America's Declining Social Capital', *Journal of Democracy*, 6(1), 61–78.

Putnam, R. (2000) *Bowling Alone: The Collapse and Revival of American Community*. New York: Simon and Schuster.

Raajmakers, Q. (1993) 'Opvattingen over Politek en Maatschappij,' in W. Meeus and H. Hart (eds), *Jongeren in Nederland. Een Nationaal Survey naar Ontwikkeling in de Adolescentie en naar Intergenerationele Overdracht*. Amersfoort: Academische Uitgeverij, pp. 106–31.

Ragin, C. (1981) 'Comparative Sociology and the Comparative Method', *International Journal of Comparative Sociology*, 22 (1–2), 102–17.

Ramirez, F. and Boli, J. (1987) 'The Political Construction of Mass Schooling: European Origins and Worldwide Institutionalisation', *Sociology of Education*, 60, pp. 2–17.

Reich, R. (2001) *The Future of Success*. New York: Alfred A. Knopf.

Roeder, P.G. (2005) 'Ethnolinguistic Fractionalization (ELF) Indices, 1961 and 1985'. Website: http//:weber.ucsd.edu\~proeder\elf.htm (16 February 2001) (consulted 25 January 2005.

Roediger, D. (1991) *The Wages of Whiteness: Race and the Making of the American Working Class*. London: Verso.

Rubenson, K. (2002) *The Nordic Model of Adult Education.* Centre for Higher Education Research, University of British Columbia, Vancouver.

Said, E. (1978) *Orientalism.* New York: Vintage.

Schuller, T., Baron, S. and Field, J. (2000) 'Social Capital: A Review and Critique' in S. Baron, J. Field and T. Schuller (eds), *Social Capital: Critical Perspectives.* Oxford: Oxford University Press, pp. 226–42.

Schwartz, S. (1994) 'The Fallacy of the Ecological Fallacy: The Potential Misuse of a Concept and the Consequences', *American Journal of Public Health,* 84(5), 819–24.

Shavit, Y. and Blossfeld, H.-P. (1983) *Persistent Inequality: Changing Educational Attainment in Thirteen Countries.* Boulder, CO: Westview Press.

Simon, B. (1981) *The Two Nations and the Educational Structure, 1780–1870.* London: Lawrence and Wishart.

Sjöstrand, W. (1965) *Pedagogikens Historia 3:2.* Lund: CWK Gleerups Förlag.

Skowronek, S. (1982) *Building a New American Nation: The Expansion of National Administrative Capacities, 1877–1920.* Cambridge: Cambridge University Press.

Skocpol, T. (1996) 'Unravelling from Above', *The American Prospect,* 25, 20–5.

Skovgaard-Petersen, V. (1976) *Dannelse og Demokratic.* Copenhagen: Gyldendals Paedagogiske bibliotek.

Smelser, N. (1976) *Comparative Methods in the Social Sciences.* Prentice Hall, Englewood Cliffs, NJ.

Smith, A.D. (1995) *Nations and Nationalism in the Global Era.* Cambridge: Polity Press.

Sniderman, P. and Gould, E. (1999) 'Dynamics of Political Values: Education and Issues of Tolerance,' in L. Hagendoorn and S. Nekuee (eds), *Education and Racism: a Cross-National Inventory of Positive Effects on Education and Racial Tolerance.* Aldershot: Ashgate, pp. 137–58.

Stolle, D. and Rochen, T. (1998) 'Are All Associations Alike?', *American Behavioural Scientist,* 42(1), 47–65.

Streeck, W (1989) 'Skills and the Limits of Neo-Liberalism: The Enterprise of the Future as a Place of Learning', *Work, Employment and Society,* 3(1), 89–104.

Streeck, W. (1997) 'German Capitalism: Does it Exist? Can it Survive?', *New Political Economy,* 2(2), 237–56.

Takeuchi, T. (1991) 'Myth and Reality in the Japanese Educational Selection System', *Comparative Education,* 27(1), 101–112.

Tamir, Y. (1993) *Liberal Nationalism.* Princeton, NJ: Princeton University Press.

Teichler, U. (1993) 'Structures of Higher Education Systems in Europe', in C. Gellert (ed.), *Higher Education in Europe.* London: Jessica Kingsley, pp. 23–36.

Thomas, V., Wang, Y. and Fan, X. (2000) *Measuring Education Inequality: Gini Coefficients of Education,* World Bank Working Paper. Washington, DC: World Bank.

Tönnies, F. (2001) *Community and Civil Society,* edited and translated by J. Harris. New York: Cambridge University Press.

Torney-Purta, J. (2002) 'Patterns in the Civic Knowledge, Engagement, and Attitudes of European Adolescents: The IEA Civic Education Study', *European Journal of Education,* 37, 129–41.

Torney-Purta, J., Lehmann R., Oswald, H. and Schulz, W. (2001) *Citizenship Education in Twenty-eight Countries: Civic Knowledge and Engagement at Age Fourteen.* Amsterdam: The International Association for the Evaluation of Educational Achievement.

Touraine, A. (2002) *Can We Live Together?* Cambridge: Polity.

UNDP (2002) *Human Development Report 2002: Deepening Democracy in a Fragmented World*. Oxford: Oxford University Press.

UNESCO (1996) *Learning – The Treasure Within: Report of the International Commission on Education for the 21st Century*. Paris: OECD.

Van Kesteren, J., Mayhew, P. and Nieuwbeerta, P. (2000) *Criminal Victimisation in Seventeen Industrialised Countries: Key-findings from the 2000 International Crime Victims Survey*. The Hague: Ministry of Justice.

Verbeck, G. and Scheepers, P. (1999) 'Education, Attitudes towards Ethnic Minorities and Opposition to Affirmative Action,' in L. Hagendoorn and S. Nekuee (eds), (1999) *Education and Racism: a Cross-National Inventory of Positive Effects on Education and Racial Tolerance*. Aldershot: Ashgate, pp. 163–202.

Warde, A., Tampubolon, G., Tomlinson, M., Roy, K., Longhurst, B. and Savage, M. (2001) 'Tendencies of Social Capital: Dynamics of Associational Membership', BSA Annual Conference, Manchester, April.

Weber, E. (1979) *Peasants into Frenchmen: The Modernization of Rural France, 1870–1914*. London: Chatto.

White, M. (1987) *The Japanese Educational Challenge*. London: Macmillan.

Whitty, G., Power, S., and Halpin, G. (1998) *Devolution and Choice in Education: The School, the State and the Market*. Buckingham: Open University Press.

Wiborg, S. (2004a) 'Education and Social Integration: a Comparative Study of the Comprehensive School Systems in Scandinavia', *London Review of Education*, 2(2), 87–93.

Wiborg, S. (2004b) *Uddannelse og Social Samhørighed: Udviklingen af Enhedsskoler i Skandinavien, Tyskland og England. En Komparativ Analyse*, PhD dissertation. DPU/Forlag, Copenhagen.

Wilkinson, R. (1996) *Unhealthy Societies: The Afflictions of Inequality*. London: Routledge.

Williams, R. (1958) *Culture and Society, 1780–1950*. Harmondsworth: Penguin.

Winkler, D. (1993) 'Fiscal Decentralization and Accountability: Experience in Four Countries,' in J. Hannaway and M. Carnoy (eds), *Decentralization and School Improvement*. San Francisco, CA: Jossey-Bass.

Winkler, J. (1999) 'Explaining Individual Racial Prejudice in Contemporary Germany', in L. Hagendoorn and S. Nekuee (eds), *Education and Racism: A Cross-National Inventory of Positive Effects on Education and Racial Tolerance*. Aldershot: Ashgate, pp. 93–136.

Woolcock, M. (2000) *Using Social Capital: Getting the Social Relations Right in the Theory and Practise of Economic Development*. Princeton, NJ: Princeton University Press.

World Bank (2001) *World Development Report: Attacking Poverty*. Oxford: Oxford University Press.

World Economic Forum (2004) *The Global Competitiveness Report 2003–2004* edited by Porter, M.E., Schwab, K., Sala-i-Martin, X. and Lopez-Carlos, A. Geneva: World Economic Forum.

Author Index

Abizadeh, A.   92
Abramson, P.   84
Albert, M.   142
Anderson, P.   136
Archer, G.   60, 67
Atkin, C.K.   112
Atlas Narodov Mira   206
Axelrod, R.   31

Ball, S.   56, 76, 173
Banfield, E.   30
Beck, U.   2, 24
Becker, G.   25
Benn, M.   137, 173
Blandon, J.   164
Blau, F.   42
Boli, J.   22, 130
Bothenius, A.   119
Boucher, L.   8, 23, 172
Boudon, R.   138–9, 173
Bourdieu, P.   25, 120, 138, 173
Braithwaite, J.   50
Brehm, J.   29
Brighouse, H.   207
Brown, A.   208
Brown, G.   44
Brown, P.   26, 44, 128, 134, 142, 159, 169, 170
Brubaker, R.   133
Bynner, J.   53

Canovan, M.   90
Carnoy, M.   136
Castells, M.   1–2, 24
CEDEFOP   134
Checchi, D.   36, 59, 61, 145, 173
Coffield, F.   24
Coleman, J.   19–27
Collier, P.   93
Comte, A.   6–7
Coomber, L.   126
Cox, O.C.   88

Crouch, C.   142, 159
Cummings, W.K.   125

De Mooij, R.   144–6, 165
De Tocqueville, A.   6–7, 25, 27, 28, 52, 176,
De Witte, H.   86
Department for Education   125
Deutsch, K.W.   99
DiPasquale, D.   26
Dokka, H.J.   130
Dore, R.   125–7, 142
Durkheim, E.   7–9, 21–3, 77, 177
Duru-Bellat, M.   135, 139

Easterly, W.   93
Edwards, B.   25, 33–4
Emler, N.   19, 53, 61, 72, 83
Engels, F.   6
Esping-Anderson, G.   120, 130–1, 152, 171
European Commission   24, 141

Featherman, D.L.   119
Fine, B.   26, 31, 33
Finegold, D.   142, 159
Foley, M.   25, 33–4
Foucault, F.   8
Fox, A.   42
Fukuyama, F.   31–2, 177
Fuller, B.   23, 181

Garnier, M.   119
Gavaert, A.   86
Gellner, E.   99
Gillborn, D.   89
Gopinathan, S.   23
Gough, I.   6, 8–9, 77
Gowricharn, R.   79
Gradstein, M.   57
Gramsci, A.   31
Granovetter, M.   30–1

Subject Index